THE PARIS GUN

THE GUN AND CARRIAGE IN POSITION AND READY FOR ACTION

THE PARIS GUN

THE BOMBARDMENT OF PARIS BY
THE GERMAN LONG-RANGE GUNS
AND THE GREAT GERMAN
OFFENSIVES OF 1918

BY

HENRY W. MILLER
LIEUTENANT-COLONEL U.S. ORDNANCE

GEORGE G. HARRAP & CO. LTD.
LONDON   BOMBAY   SYDNEY

First published 1930
by GEORGE G. HARRAP & CO. LTD.
39-41 Parker Street, Kingsway, London, W.C.2

AN EXPLANATION

THE plans of the German campaign of 1918 were perfected in the autumn and early winter of 1917, when the collapse of Imperial Russia made it safe to transfer most of the divisions which had been fighting on that front to France. In these plans the activities for the year were divided into three distinct but vitally related and interdependent parts. The field armies, greatly augmented by the transfers from the Russian front, were to deliver smashing surprise blows on the French and British fronts alternately, so that they might exhaust and finally divide the Allied armies. The German fleet was definitely bottled up by mine fields and the Allied fleet, so the submarines were assigned the task of preventing American supplies and troops from reaching France. And various agencies were to concentrate on the destruction of the fighting morale of the non-combatants, both near and far from the front lines. In short, war was to be made so effective and so terrible that the reserves and supplies of the Allies would be exhausted and their will-to-fight broken. Success in at least two of these divisions was vital to a successful ending of the War in 1918. Success in all three would greatly hasten it.

The first two offensives of the field campaign were carried out with success beyond expectation. In fact, it will probably always be a question as to how the entire campaign of the year might have ended had the second offensive not been quite so successful. The disastrous third and last offensive, which was not in the year's plans, but was a direct result of the over-success of the second, resembled the efforts, and the fate as well, of Napoleon and his armies in their frantic attempt to win through to a decision at Waterloo on June 18, 1815, before the preponderance of power and the tide of progress could turn.

The morale-breaking phase of the campaign began on the night of January 30–31, with a raid on Paris by thirty 'planes which dropped 144 bombs containing 7400 pounds of high explosive. This was the most formidable raid of the entire war. It was in the nature of a violent preparatory bombardment. Eighty-two bombs were dropped on Paris on the night of March 8–9, and eighty-eight on the night of March 11–12. All of this preceded any activity of the field armies. Paris was a deliberate point of concentration, because it was assumed that that city would advertise fully the campaign of terror to all of France, England, and America. The bombardment of Paris by long-range cannon was deliberately delayed until the field armies should begin their first offensive. It would then have its greatest effect.

The bombardment of Paris in its more significant aspects may be classed with two other bombardments of history, which, because of their short duration and simplicity of operation, have seemed to warrant only brief discussion. The city of Constantinople (which had been regarded as impregnable for nearly ten centuries) fell a rather easy prey to the Turks in 1453, principally, we believe, because of the first employment against its walls of several of the huge cannon of the time, termed 'bombards.' Three or four times a day these hurled large balls of granite, weighing several hundred pounds, against the walls, slowly hammering and shaking down the carefully laid masonry. The period of impregnability of masonry fortifications had passed.

Between August 5 and 9, 1914, some new and previously unheard-of German guns destroyed the supposedly impregnable turret fortifications about Liége with astonishing ease and rapidity. These cannon were 17-inch mobile

AN EXPLANATION

mortars, capable of firing 1700-pound projectiles containing 560 pounds of explosive and operated at elevations as high as 65 degrees. At such elevations the projectiles ascended to a height greater than their range, and dropped with great accuracy and irresistible force on to their targets. The date of August 9, 1914, spelled the end for all time of masonry and steel fortifications.

The bombardment of Paris as the third of the spectacular bombardments, in two of which formal fortifications were first rendered pregnable and secondly obsolete, represents the victory over what was considered to be safe distance. The German Army was seventy miles from Paris at its nearest point, and no one dreamed of an artillery bombardment until the German Army was within less than twenty-five miles.

HENRY W. MILLER

CONTENTS

		PAGE
I.	THE FIRST OFFENSIVE	13
II.	THE BOMBARDMENT CONTINUES	40
III.	THE LONG-RANGE GUNS	70
IV.	THE SECOND BOMBARDMENT	124
V.	THE BEAUMONT BATTERY	181
VI.	THE THIRD AND LAST GREAT OFFENSIVE	211
VII.	THE GREAT RETREAT	265
	BIBLIOGRAPHY	275

ILLUSTRATIONS

	PAGE
The Gun in Position and Ready for Action	*Frontispiece*
Early Shells of the First Bombardment	19
Map and Air Photograph of the Mont-de-Joie and Crépy Station	30
The Topographical and Official Centres of Paris	37
The Zero Point of Paris	37
The Church of Saint-Gervais and Notre-Dame	37
Montmartre	44
The Heart of Paris	44
Damage done in the Church of Saint-Gervais	67
Damage done by Shells	69
Position No. 1, and the Branch Railway leading to it	78
Front Page of Firing-list for one of the 8·26-inch Guns at Crépy	92
Range-table from Firing-list for one of the 8·26-inch Guns	94
The Evolution of the Paris Shell	106
305-mm. and 340-mm. Rifles	128
Destruction at the Madeleine	147
Diagrams showing where Certain Shells dropped	163
Refugees going South toward the Marne	174
Shell Destruction at the Place de la République and the Rue de Courtry	174
Supposed and Actual Positions of the Paris Gun	183
The Railway Gun-carriage	186
Gantry Crane used in installing the Steel Caisson and Base for the Gun-carriage	186
Positions B and C	188

THE PARIS GUN

	PAGE
THE ROTATING STEEL BASE FOR THE GUN-CARRIAGE	190
PLAN OF THE EMPLACEMENT	190
FRONT PAGE OF FIRING-LIST FOR THE 9·13-INCH GUN IN THE BOIS DE CORBIE	196
RANGE-TABLE FROM FIRING-LIST FOR THE 9·13-INCH GUN	198
POSITION NO. 2	208
TREE LADDER AT POSITION NO. 3	208
RELATIVE SIZES OF THE SHELL AND POWDER CHARGE	208
THE PARIS GUN	259
GENERAL DISTRIBUTION OF THE SHELLS OF THE FOUR BOMBARDMENTS	270

MAPS

PARIS AND ITS ENVIRONS	15
THE GERMAN FRONT ON MARCH 20, 1918	38
THE GERMAN LINES BEFORE AND AFTER THE SOMME RETREAT	77
THE THREE GUN POSITIONS AT CRÉPY	80
DIAGRAM OF EMPLACEMENT NO. 2	81
THE NEW WESTERN FRONT, 1918	119
THE FRONT ON THE EVENING OF MAY 30, 1918	149
THE GERMAN GAINS FROM MAY 27 TO JUNE 13, 1918	179
THE HAM-NOYEN-CRÉPY REGION	184
PLAN OF THE BEAUMONT GUN EMPLACEMENT	192
THE MARNE FRONT ON JUNE 12, 1918	213
ATTACK DIRECTIONS PROPOSED BY THE FIRST ARMY	218
ATTACK DIRECTIONS SUGGESTED BY THE SEVENTH ARMY	220
THE NEW POSITION OF THE PARIS GUN	230
THE MARNE SALIENT AND ATTACK FRONT ON JULY 14, 1918	237
THE OPPOSING FORCES ON THE MARNE IN 1918	239
GERMAN GAINS IN THE OFFENSIVE OF JULY 15, 1918	247
THE WESTERN FRONT IN FRANCE AND BELGIUM	273

THE PARIS GUN

I

THE FIRST OFFENSIVE

PARIS UNDER SHELL-FIRE

March 23, 1918

SATURDAY, the 23rd, began to dawn in Paris as one of those rarely beautiful early spring mornings for which France is famous. A persistent dull rumble, as of an approaching storm, came out of the north from the savage offensive begun two days before, in the early morning hours of March 21, by the German armies of Von Hutier, Marwitz, and Below against the British Fifth Army under General Gough before Amiens and Byng's Third Army to the north. But neither the sinister significance of the offensive, going worse than badly for the British armies, nor the hour and a half of suspense of the night before, between the terrifying warning by siren horns of the approach of German bombing 'planes and the ringing of bells and the sounding of the 'retreat' by bugles to announce their return across the lines and the end of danger, could diminish the delight of the early risers with the beautiful morning. Slowly the mists last to rise over the Seine floated away, and by seven o'clock all Paris was a-sparkle with bright spring sunshine.

All over the great city men and women were preparing to leave for their early morning appointments, offices, factories, and shops. By 7.15 the streets began to fill, Métro lines were working up to their 8.15 heaviest morning load; the whole great city of Paris was tuning up for another of its busy days, withal an anxious one, as was evident from the intent faces in the streets and in the Métro cars, eagerly examining the early papers to learn of yesterday's happenings on the Front.

Time's pendulum and Fate's plans worked on inexorably to 7.20, when the few people about on the Quai de Seine, in the north-eastern section of the fortified portion of Paris, were violently startled by the crash of something that exploded on the stone pavements in front of house No. 6 along the Quai. Fragments and missiles hissed through the air, spattering the stone buildings and breaking windows. Apparently no one was hurt. The immediate question in every one's mind was, What was it? To soldiers it sounded like the explosion of a 77-mm. high-explosive shell; to civilians it resembled the crash of a 22-pound air bomb, the sound of which was becoming familiar to people in Paris. Examination of the exact spot of the explosion failed to answer the question. As always, a few hurried to the scene, curiosity overcoming caution. Fragments of metal were found, some of them too hot to hold. These were shown to the gendarmes of the vicinity, who had been instructed to hurry to the scenes of explosions of air bombs, the only kind Paris had known so far, and for three years only at night. To some of those more distant who had heard the explosion it meant the enemy; to others something less serious; most of the people of the city had not heard it at all. So by itself this one explosion meant but little.

Some days before the great hand-grenade factory at La Courneuve, a short distance to the north-east of Paris, had been destroyed in a series of explosions that eclipsed even the noise of the 660-pound air bombs dropped on Paris in the night raid of January 30–31. The people of Paris and its suburbs were at once notified by posters that some unexploded grenades would be destroyed, and that they should not be alarmed if several more explosions occurred during the following days. So to some of those not so near this

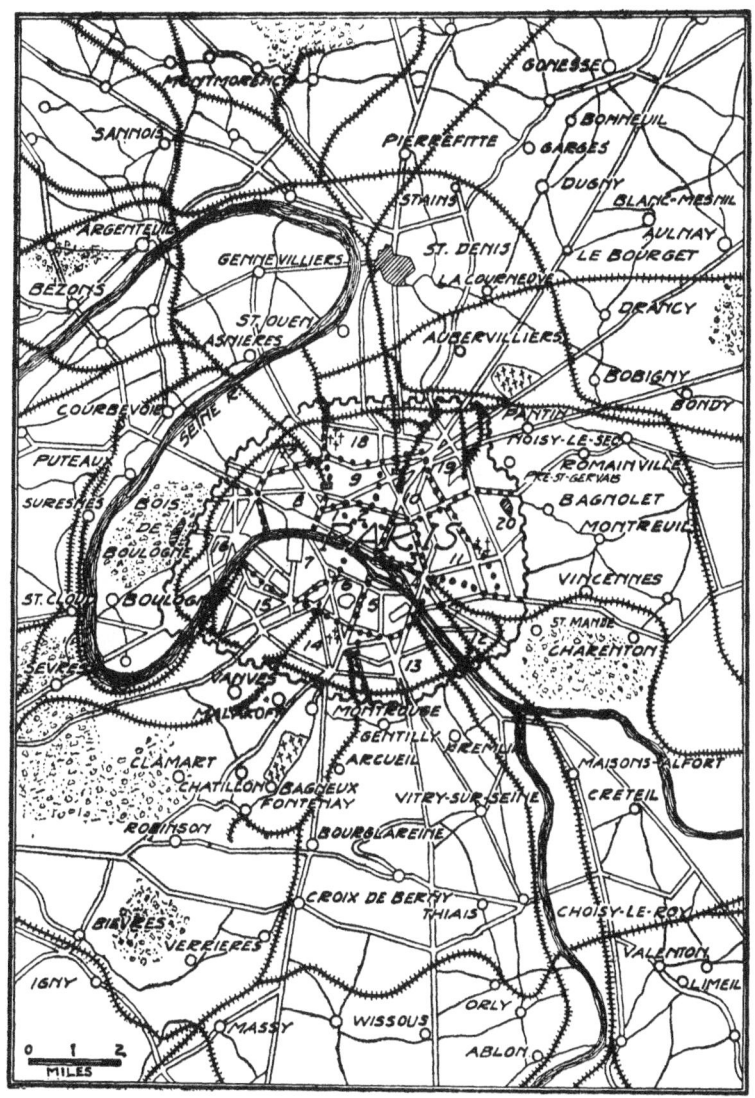

PARIS AND ITS ENVIRONS

was merely one of those explosions. To others it was just another of the multitude of unusual things happening during the War, to be alarmed over or to be dismissed with a resigned shrug and the familiar " C'est la guerre." In most of the city things went on as usual; streets were becoming filled with motor-cars, wagons, and hand-carts; people hurried along the pavements, and business at the newspaper-stands was brisk. The new offensive was alarming, and newspapers were greatly in demand.

For twenty minutes nothing further happened; no screeching of sirens, no sounds but the growing hum of a great city starting the busiest day of the week. The more timid near the scene of the explosion ventured out to see what had happened; the crowd grew rapidly; gendarmes questioned people and jotted down notes in their pocket-books. Speculation was rife as to the nature of the bomb and its source. Those about examined the damage, studied the fragments of metal, searched the sky for 'planes, and hazarded guesses with their neighbours. " Air bombs," was the common verdict. But what curious bombs!

At 7.40 a second explosion occurred, not so loud to those at the scene of the first, because it was a mile and a half away. But the sound and shock were terrific to the hundreds about the Gare de l'Est, where it occurred. The pavements here were crowded, even so early. In front of the railway-station there is an entrance to the three Métro lines which have a junction at this point. The bomb struck on the cobbles of the Boulevard de Strasbourg, not a hundred feet from one entrance to the Métro lines, and exploded entirely above the surface of the street. For an instant the hundreds of people were stunned; the cobbles were torn up for several yards, and fragments of metal and stone spattered the walls of houses and wounded the people; the concussion broke windows all about, and turned over and demolished a news-stand and some carts. The natural instinct of the crowd was to flee in any direction from the

THE FIRST OFFENSIVE

point of the explosion. Eight of those who lay about on the streets and pavements were dead. Thirteen others were more or less seriously hurt. When the first effect of the shock had passed, some of the crowd and proprietors of shops hurried to the dead and wounded and carried them into the shops or assisted them on their way. If those who launched that bomb could have seen the effect, they probably would have felt that they had made a very effective beginning. Only the second bomb, and it landed in the centre of one of the busiest streets, near one of the busiest Métro stations, at nearly the busiest hour of the day; hardly to be bettered for the greatest effect on morale.

But tragedy is so relative and so local. To those only a quarter the distance across the city this sound was merely that of another explosion of grenades at La Courneuve. Most of the people in the city had not heard it, or only so faintly as not to notice it. As the people about the scene became assured that the danger was past, they gathered about the spot in the street as if expecting to find there the answer to the question. Fragments of metal were found, thick, heavy, ragged; some of them were grooved, some threaded, some machined smooth and cylindrical, as on a lathe. Some one picked up a piece of copper with grooves in it. The larger fragments were too hot to hold; one of them bore the designation 8•. "Air bomb" was still the verdict. But why no anti-aircraft barrage firing on the edge of the city, no sirens sounding on the larger buildings and on the fire-engines driven through the streets on such occasions? Intense concern and curiosity prevailed about the scenes of the two explosions. But in most of the city, and to most of the people, nothing had happened. Two unusual sounds had been heard, but such sounds mean so much less in the daytime than at night, and particularly at the time when one is concerned with starting one's day's work.

The second explosion set the wheels of officialdom grinding. Anything that happens in so public a place, killing

THE PARIS GUN

eight and wounding thirteen of a crowd that is hurrying by three separate Métro lines to all parts of the city, quickly receives every variety of attention. The gendarmes immediately telephoned to headquarters the nature and extent of the calamity in so far as their hasty examination permitted them to explain. Newspaper offices learned from police headquarters the causes of the sounds and where the explosions had occurred. Reporters hurried to the scenes. Those who had been near by when the second explosion occurred met acquaintances in the Métro trains and told the story, probably without loss of dramatic details. Many changed cars and told others. The three Métro lines from the Gare de l'Est became multiple and amplifying telephones reporting the happening in all directions within the hour.

President Poincaré, M. Clemenceau, and General Herr's Artillery office were called from police headquarters and told such details as were known. Officers of the Army technical offices were already inquiring about the sounds: why and where? They took nothing for granted. Artillery and air-service officers and experts on explosives departed at once to investigate. There was intense activity at the aerodromes on the northern edge of the city, and airmen were climbing into the sky to find the supposed 'planes that were dropping the bombs. The observers at the anti-aircraft batteries were searching the sky with glasses and sound-detectors; it was a perfectly clear day, and one should be able to find easily the large, slow bombing 'planes, however high.

Officers of the Service for the Defence of Paris were more than active; they had learned from the Police Department what the sounds meant, and were calling the front-line observers through French Army Headquarters at Provins to learn why they had not been informed as usual of the passing of the 'planes over the lines. Always when 'planes were detected crossing the line at night the Service for the

SECOND SHELL: IN THE BOULEVARD DE STRASBOURG, ENTRANCE TO THE MÉTRO STATION

SECOND SHELL: IN THE BOULEVARD DE STRASBOURG, NEAR THE GARE DE L'EST

RECONSTRUCTED SHELL

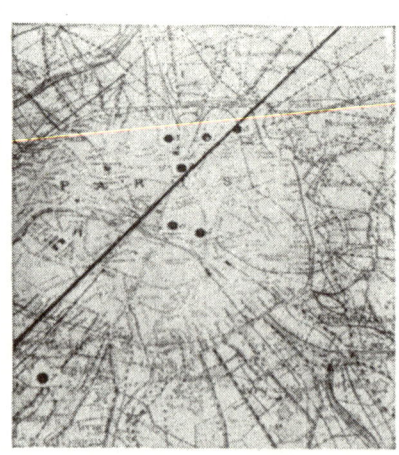

THE FIRST SEVEN SHELLS

THE FIRST OFFENSIVE

Defence of Paris was called over a direct line through Provins, and the sirens on buildings and fire-engines began their screeching, airmen climbed into the sky, anti-aircraft gunners went on watch, searchlights pierced the darkness with their shafts of light. But the observers at the Front insisted that no 'planes had crossed; there must be some mistake.

Twenty-five minutes more passed; plenty of time for any small alarm to be dispelled and for those at a distance to forget the sound. And most of the people of the city had not heard either explosion. In this time some newspaper reporters had visited one or the other of the scenes, gathered some details, taken a picture or two, and were hurrying back to their offices to make up an 'extra.' Representatives of the Municipal Laboratory and Army offices visited the scenes. To both of these the gendarmes gave fragments of metal which they had found or had taken from others. M. Poincaré, M. Clemenceau, and Colonel Battisti also visited the scene of the second explosion.

At 8.5 there was a third explosion, in the Rue de Château-Landon. Except to those in the immediate vicinity, the sound was more muffled than the previous two; the shell had burst within a building. But it had an alarming significance to those living near the scene of the first explosion, only a quarter of a mile to the north-east. The Rue de Château-Landon was a short street, only a few blocks east of the Gare du Nord. The building struck was a relatively new, reinforced concrete factory and storage building on the west side of the street. The bomb struck the front wall just above the steel girder over some double doors or windows on the street side of the second floor. It was travelling with such velocity that it passed through the concrete above and behind the steel beam before it exploded, probably in mid-air. All of the windows, frames and glass alike, were blown out, and the concrete sills and sides of the doorway shattered. But on the floor below the small panes of glass were not broken; nor above. Apparently the full force of the explosion was spent in the space of the second floor and in partially demolishing the concrete walls. Fragments of the bomb were strewn all about the second floor, which fortunately was unoccupied. A few people hurried in the direction of the sound from the scenes of the other two explosions.

Still the business of the city grew with no noticeable interruption. The Métro trains were now carrying their heaviest loads. Children were at school or on their way. Shops and offices were open or were opening. Rumours were spreading rapidly; but Paris is a great city, and it is not easy either to accelerate or to reduce appreciably the activity of such a machine in the daytime, particularly at such a time of the day. Officers of the Paris Defence Service were debating what to do. Artillery officers and Municipal Laboratory men were studying the bomb fragments and the effects. At 8.17, after an interval of twelve minutes, only half the previous, and too short to permit one to forget the last sound, a bomb passed through a north-east top-floor window at No. 15 Rue Charles-Cinq, and exploded as it was passing through the floor into the story below. This house, which was three stories high and of the older type of construction, with walls of rubble masonry, light-hewn beams in the roofs and floors, and thin-tile roof, was two and a half miles from the scene of the first explosion, two miles from the second, and two and a quarter miles from the third. The Rue Charles-Cinq was another short street only two blocks long, running north-west and south-east, parallel to the Seine, and only two blocks from it at the Ile de Saint-Louis.

The explosion at 8.17 was the least extensively heard of the four; quite muffled, since it was entirely within walls. But tragedy accompanied it; one person was killed, the ninth in an hour, for it was now just an hour since the bombs had begun to fall. The average interval in this

THE FIRST OFFENSIVE

hour had been fifteen minutes. This, though but an average, was to fix itself on the public mind for a long time. Firemen hurried to the scene lest the destruction be of such a character as to start a serious fire; fortunately no fire was started.

The machinery of the Parish Defence Service office, the Police Department, the Municipal Laboratory, and the Artillery offices was grinding furiously. Air observers had climbed two miles and more into the sky and searched in vain for the bombing 'planes or Zeppelins. The telephones in all technical service offices were jangling or were busy with conferences about the nature of the bombardment and the curious fragments of metal. It was already clear to the air-bomb and artillery-projectile experts that the bombs were not air bombs. No air-bomb case was ever made of steel over two inches thick; nor was any such case ever supplied with copper bands. And some of the fragments of this thing had grooves in them, cut in the steel itself.

At the offices of the Paris Defence Service the more vitally serious question was, What shall be done about it? Provision had been made for day-time air raids. But no such raids had occurred since May 11, 1915. Much had happened since. The people of Paris had undergone great hardships; perhaps they could be thrown into a serious panic if the wrong steps were taken. Nothing serious happened when alarms were given at night; people were at home; shops, offices, factories were closed. But what would happen now, at such a time of the day, and all through the day, the busiest day of the week, with the people already greatly worried over the most serious of all offensives so far waged on the Western Front since 1914 or at Verdun in 1916. The decision to sound a general alarm was not to be made hastily nor lightly. Another explosion occurred at 8.35, after an eighteen-minute interval, at No. 24 Rue des Ardennes. This was far up in the north-east corner of the walled sections of the city. The

THE PARIS GUN

street, three blocks long, ran almost north and south, and No. 24 was on the east side of the centre block. It was two and a half miles from the scene of the last explosion in the Rue Charles-Cinq and three-quarters of a mile from the first. The sixth bomb struck at 8.50 in the courtyard at the rear of the Hôtel Beauvais at No. 68 Rue François-Miron, less than half a mile from the previous. The material damage was not as great as was the shock and alarm to the people of the hotel. They had heard plainly the previous two explosions and faintly the second at 7.40. In spite of all that had happened, however, the bombardment with its six bombs in ninety minutes had not seriously alarmed 1 per cent. of the people of the city. Many had been hearing the sounds, and rumours were travelling rapidly. But this was one of the world's largest cities; that portion within the walls was nearly eight miles east and west by five north and south, and this was not much more than half of all of Paris. The sounds were beginning to travel about with much greater leaps than in the beginning. By half- and quarter-mile leaps at first, now by two- and two-and-a-half-mile leaps. There was really no following them. The locations of bursts seemed to be along a fairly well defined north-east and south-west path, but apparently there was no objective. So far air-bombers had been trying to drop their bombs at definite points, on definite and important objectives; the gas-works, electric power plants, munition factories, and the Ministry of Armament. Apparently these bombs were not aimed at anything; if they were, the marksmanship was exceedingly poor, or the choice of targets was beyond comprehension. The Quai de Seine was of little importance, and three bombs had been dropped in this vicinity. The second bomb had a real effect, but on people instead of on any important buildings. The other two were hardly to be considered.

The seventh bomb upset any calculations which real or so-called experts may have attempted. It struck in the

THE FIRST OFFENSIVE

suburb town of Châtillon, south-west of Paris proper, and the point of the explosion, in front of the cemetery, at No. 30 Rue de Saint-Cloud, was four and a half miles from the last and a quarter from the first. This was at 9.4, an interval of fourteen minutes since the last. Most of the people in Paris proper did not hear this, and those who were beginning to be alarmed had an interval of nearly half an hour since the explosion at 8.50 to become reassured before anything further happened.

In most quarters and in some offices the belief still prevailed that Paris was being subjected to an air raid; a new and peculiar variety that was being staged in conjunction with the great offensive. In other offices there was doubt growing to a certainty that it was not an air raid; the bombs were not bombs, but *projectiles*. But those to whom the fragments of metal meant projectiles knew that even to say projectiles implied an absurdity. One must have a gun to shoot a projectile. Frenchmen could not be shooting upon their own city. The last issue of bonds was not selling any too rapidly, it was true, and if Parisians could be made to believe that they were under enemy gun-fire they might contribute more rapidly even what little they had left. But this thought was absurd. Propagandists had not hesitated to exaggerate any and all isolated atrocities into general practices to stir people to greater energies, to a more deadly fighting temper. But the deliberate shelling of one's own capital, the treasure of the whole nation. . . . Inconceivable! Though a few people insisted upon this explanation, those in the technical offices dismissed it. Men of the Municipal Laboratory and the Artillery headquarters, General Herr's office, had come to the conclusion that the 'bombs' were projectiles, which can be fired only from guns, and Germans certainly were firing them. But from where? That could not be answered.

The question confronting the Paris Defence Service could no longer be evaded. The bombs had been dropping for nearly two hours; nine people had been killed, seventeen wounded, houses demolished, and alarming rumours were spreading; even that the German Army was within field-gun range of Paris. The business of the city was going on with little noticeable interruption or derangement, but gradually the rumours were affecting it. It made little difference to the Defence Service officers whether the bombs were bombs from aeroplanes or projectiles from guns. The effect was the same. A new emergency had arisen. The observers at the Front insisted that no bombing squadrons had passed over, not even isolated bombing 'planes, and certainly not Zeppelins. The airmen in the sky over Paris could find nothing, the battery observers could see nothing. Seemingly there was nothing.

Between 9.4 and 9.15 information was received of the seventh explosion, in Châtillon. A momentous decision was then made, and at 9.15 the order was given and at once carried out to sound the sirens. The significance of this decision was appreciated by those responsible; it was not easy to make it, and, once executed, it could not be recalled. At 9.15, with the offices and shops all over the city functioning almost as usual, underground trains, buses, and tram-cars running normally, children at school, men and women at work, many entirely ignorant of the disturbances, the sirens on all large buildings and on fire-engines passing through the streets began that screeching which for three years had been a dread sound to all Parisians. The effect was electrical. No wonder! They had come to expect it at night. Only the night before the sirens had sounded a raid, and for an hour and a half people waited in their homes or in the underground shelters for the crashing explosions. Instead, the bells and bugles sounded " All's well " without any bombs having been dropped. People had forgotten day raids, so the effect was all the more pronounced. Those giving the order for the alarm knew it would be, and had delayed as long as they could. At 9.14

THE FIRST OFFENSIVE

all or nearly all was going well in most of the city. At 9.15 millions of people were suddenly being told to seek shelter and at once. They had no idea why, no knowledge of the nature of the danger, but they had learned that when the sirens sounded it was time to act without any delay. So men, women, and children everywhere dropped what they were doing, and a goodly proportion of them sought shelter; three millions of people at their day-time occupations.

No one could escape the sounds of those sirens. They were either very well or very poorly designed for their purpose. The very sound of them was terrifying and never to be forgotten. For over three years Parisians had been hearing them and always at night, when whatever is apt to produce a feeling of terror is doubly effective. The city had had 384 bombs of all sizes dropped on it in twelve raids. On many nights two, three, and even four alarms had been sounded, some of them false. 'Planes had been detected crossing the line, and the observers had no choice but to notify Paris at once. The sirens were sounded immediately, and one knew that he had about twenty minutes to seek shelter. The entire city had been dark at night. The globes of the gas-lamps had been painted a dark blue and the gas turned so low that there was not sufficient light to see even the pavements. In three years a hundred thousand people had left the city for less nerve-racking places. Those remaining experienced a reaction to the sounds of the sirens that was out of proportion to the probabilities of personal danger. A few paid no attention to them. The business of the girls, soliciting along the Boulevards de Capucines and des Italiens, continued with but little change, a pitiful sign of desperate straits or of peculiar disregard of real danger. But most of the people were more prudent.

On the night of January 30–31, not two months before, the worst raid of the entire War had taken place. On that night 144 bombs were dropped on the city, two of them weighing 660 pounds each. That night would never be forgotten; in thinking of it one remembered sirens, and, beginning twenty minutes later, the crashing explosions of bombs, sometimes two almost together. On the night of March 8–9 eighty-two bombs were dropped. And only twelve days since, on the night of March 11–12, another raid had been made in which seventy 'planes came over and dropped eighty-eight bombs. The alarm for that raid was sounded at 9.30. It was a beautiful starlight night; perfect for a raid. The streets as usual were almost without light. The lamps merely defined the edges of the pavements. When the sirens began their din the performances in theatres stopped at once, hotel doors were closed, some people in the streets ran, others sought refuge more leisurely at the doors to underground shelters marked with the tiny blue lamps. That night the sirens sounded no false alarm, for twenty minutes after their first alarm people began to hear above the city the buzz characteristic of the German 'planes; also the hum of the French 'planes. The captive balloons that one saw anchored in the Tuileries Gardens and elsewhere about the city were let up with their streamers of steel wires to entangle unwary bombers; the anti-aircraft guns crackled all about the city, and shrapnel shells burst in rapid succession all about the sky; a gorgeous spectacle. Then as one watched and listened something struck with a sharp rattle on a tiled roof, or with a soft plunk in the earth near by; shrapnel balls sprinkled over the city. And after a few minutes one saw the brilliant glare of an exploding bomb off to the north-east, and heard at once the roar and rattle of it. The Germans may have been staging a reception for Mr Newton Baker, the American Secretary of War, that night. He had arrived in Paris during the day on his first trip of inspection. And they did a thorough job, seeking out the Ministry of War, the gas-works, and other important places. The damage wrought was not cleared up in a day, and people had ample

THE FIRST OFFENSIVE

opportunity to see what the bomb explosions, heralded by the sirens, meant.

On the night of March 8-9 one bomb crashed through the six-story building at No. 5 Rue Geoffroy-Marie, completely demolishing it. The fire which was started was extinguished with difficulty. The tenants of that building escaped only through their prudence in seeking deep cellars when the sirens sounded. Pedestrians comprehended all this at a glance as they saw those familiar sights of destruction.

Even in the ordinary, uneventful day the Parisian was not permitted to forget that he lived in a besieged city. Plate-glass windows everywhere were criss-crossed and decorated in the most fantastic designs with strips of gummed paper to prevent the concussions of near-by explosions from breaking them. Glass thus reinforced stands great abuse before it will break. And all about the city works of art, statues, ornate gates, were piled over with bags of sand. All about the Louvre, the Tuileries Gardens, and in the Place de la Concorde bags of sand were conspicuously in evidence.

So the effect of the alarm sounded by the sirens at 9.15 was truly electrical. Those who gave the order knew it would be. Bus- and taxi-drivers pulled up to the kerbs and hurried into the nearest *cafés*, cellars, or other shelters. The passengers were left to dispose of themselves as they saw fit. They too sought shelter. Tram-cars were stopped, and the drivers and passengers remained in the cars or alighted, as they chose. Workers in many offices, shops, factories, left for other shelters, or sought the most protected places in their buildings. Shops, *cafés*, restaurants were closed. Pedestrians hurried down the steps into Métro stations if any were near. In a few places there was dangerous crowding, and some were hurt. Ticket-offices in the railway-stations were closed, and some trains were cancelled. The city just stopped, and it did not require long. From the usual Saturday morning activity at 9.15 it was reduced in a comparatively few minutes almost to midnight inactivity; the silence became painful, and for the next hour the explosions of the bombs landing even miles away could be heard.

Fortunately there were no signs of panic in this rapid transformation; no hysterical behaviour. Either as his native characteristic or as a war acquisition, the average Frenchman looked annoyed or worried under such circumstances; the peculiar pucker of his face on this occasion may have indicated fear, but not panic. He was extremely annoyed, and intensely concerned to know the reason for the alarm. Had it anything to do with the offensive? Had there been a break-through up on the Front? The War had developed in the people of France a peculiar resignation to the unusual, an acceptance of the inevitableness of tragedy. Most families had lost at least one member, but women did not weep. Each new tragedy, reverse, loss, seemed only to add to that concentrated cold fury that boded none the less ill to the enemy because it was usually hidden under a serene exterior. So the millions of Parisians sought shelter promptly, with obvious signs of great concern, some fear, but with no signs of panic. The hoped-for answer to the vital question in the Defence Service office actually was, that people cannot participate in such a war for three and a half years and retain much, if any, capacity to be panicky. School-children were marched as in fire drill to underground shelters, and when later in the morning M. Poincaré and M. Clemenceau visited a girls' school of about six hundred pupils they found them singing the *Marseillaise*. The courts had just started, and they continued to dispose of the cases of those prisoners at hand; orders were given that no others be brought from the prisons.

The alarm had been given, obeyed. It remained then to be seen to what good or bad ends. Meanwhile other

THE FIRST OFFENSIVE

wheels were grinding. Even before the alarm was sounded it had been determined in the Artillery office that the 'bombs' were projectiles; of peculiar design, but nevertheless projectiles. Projectiles always imply guns, absurd and impossible as that might seem in this case. So far the Service for the Defence of Paris had not had to deal with guns. Since it became some one's duty to find, and, if possible, silence the guns, the Army Artillery Service automatically became a part of the Paris Defence Service. Among the fragments brought into the Artillery office were grooved pieces of copper and steel which showed that the gun had approximately sixty-four rifling grooves. The existence of grooves in fragments of steel was significant. Another fragment showed signs of screw-threads midway in the shell cavity where a plate with a fuse might have been screwed in. There was evidence of a fuse in the base. The shell probably had two fuses. An 8-inch shell, one or two narrow copper bands, the steel of the shell grooved, two fuses, and an abnormally thick side-wall, over 2 inches, at the base.

'Extra' papers quickly appeared on the streets. The newsboys were besieged, and many papers were sold before the police could seize them. The people detained in shelters were naturally more than eager for news. In the main the extras had not been censored. The orders against 'too much' news, however accurate, were severe. The managers of some of the papers, mostly the socialistic variety, saw fit to be explosively irritated over this interference with their business.

By 9.30 the Artillery officers were beginning to admit to themselves that the projectiles might be coming from within the German lines. The grooves in the steel and the enormously heavy side-walls and base of the projectile indicated an extremely high-power pressure, hence probably a correspondingly high initial velocity of the shell. It was true that the nearest point of the German line was sixty-seven miles away. The gun would certainly be at least six and possibly as much as ten miles behind the lines for even moderate safety. This made at least seventy-three and perhaps seventy-seven miles. No such range as this had ever been heard of. Artillerists knew of a 6-inch gun of unusual length, 80 calibres, that had been made and tested in England some thirty years before by Sir Andrew Noble, with which an unprecedented velocity of the projectile, 3200 feet per second, had been attained. Similar velocities had been attained in more recent tests, but with resultant ranges never in excess of thirty miles. In these days of spectacular developments, however, especially in the field of science, one was willing to believe almost anything possible. So with nothing very definite to confirm it, the conclusion was reached, particularly in the Artillery office, that the bombardment was being conducted from within the German lines. Much more information than was then available would be necessary to determine anything further, particularly the exact location of the gun or guns. More definite information on the locations of explosions and effects was being received. This enabled a plotting of the first seven bursts on the city map. A line through bursts 5 and 7 passed almost due north-east, through the centre of the city. Bursts 1 and 2 were almost on this line, and 3 and 6 at almost equal distances from it, but on opposite sides. The points of impact with the buildings which had been struck were on the north and east sides. So the projectiles were coming from the north-east.

Maps of the Army fronts were consulted for clues as to position. A line running due north-east through the centre of Paris passed through the centre of the pronounced 'corner' of the German line created the year before, when they retired on the Somme. The city of Laon was in this corner, or pocket, and the point of this corner was, or had been two days before, the nearest point of the German line to Paris. Some officers remembered, and by reference at once confirmed, that during the previous September formidable

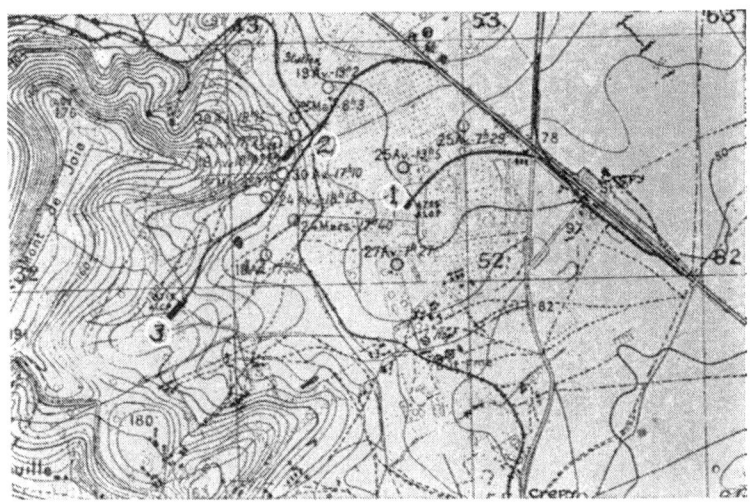
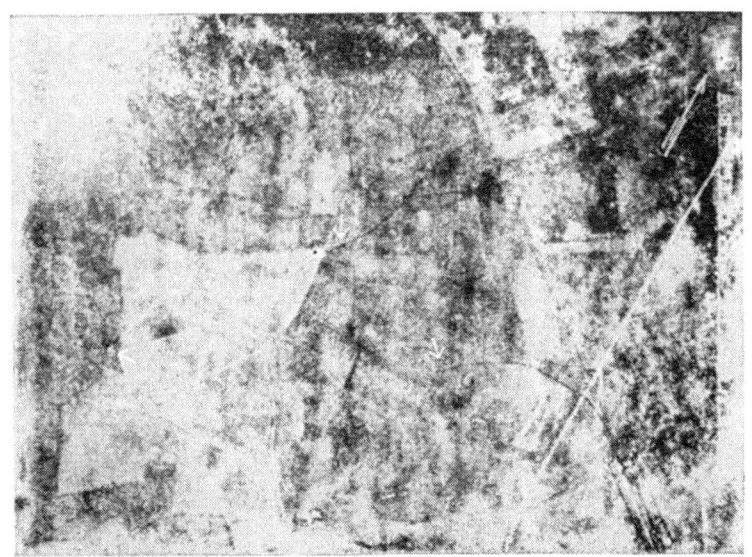

Map and Air Photograph taken March 6 of the Mont-de-Joie and Crépy Station

THE FIRST OFFENSIVE

excavating, possibly for large-gun emplacements, had been noticed in this salient. And an air photograph taken in merely general reconnaissance over this region on March 6 revealed two new railway curves of the kind commonly used in the French Army for railway artillery, leading off to the south-west from the Laon-Amiens railway line near the little village of Crépy. The railway lines were very distinct on the photograph, but whatever was at their ends, if anything, where the excavating had been seen in progress, had been so well camouflaged as to defy detection. In such an emergency one is sorely tempted to accept seemingly reasonable conclusions. Perhaps it was not surprising, then, that certain Artillery officers came to the conclusion as early as 9.30 that Paris was being bombarded by a new long-range gun of about 8-inch calibre, probably located in the region of Laon, and more than likely on one of those two new railway curves at Crépy, about 120 kilometres, or 75 miles, from the centre of Paris. They telephoned this information to the French General Headquarters at Provins, and from there the information was relayed to General Bourgeois, who was in command of the sound-ranging division of the French armies, composed of thirty-two units distributed along their front. The same information was given to various other technical offices in Paris, and before eleven o'clock it was telephoned to the American technical headquarters in Tours.

A *communiqué* was made up at ten o'clock in some office in Paris, one of those from which information was given to the Press, and sent to the newspaper offices. This was displayed on bulletin boards and read as follows:

> At 8.20 some German 'planes which were flying at a very great altitude succeeded in crossing the lines and in attacking Paris. They were at once pursued, both by the Paris Defence aeroplanes and those of the Front. Several of the points of fall of bombs have been registered. There are a few victims. A later *communiqué* will specify the results and the details of the raid.

Projectiles continued to fall at more or less regular intervals, but at ever increasing distances from each other. At 9.20, five minutes after the alarm was sounded, one fell far up in the north-east corner of the city, seven miles from the last in Châtillon, but not quite a quarter of a mile from the fifth at 8.35, in the Rue des Ardennes. No one was killed or wounded. The next, fifteen minutes later, at 9.35, fell in a garden, just south of the Luxembourg Gardens, on the south side of the Seine, and four miles from the last shot. Again no one was killed and no one hurt. Practically every one had by this time sought shelter.

At 9.45, after a ten-minute interval, another projectile struck, in the eighteenth *arrondissement*, only a mile from the one at 9.20. Again no one was killed or wounded. Only five minutes later, a record short interval for the day, a shell struck the roof or back wall of a five-story apartment building in the Rue Manin, completely demolishing the roof and back walls of two rooms. The people of this apartment were absent. Another good demonstration was provided of the destruction wrought upon houses of the older type of construction.

It was now thirty-five minutes since the alarm had been sounded, and the city was so silent, if one may say that so great a city is ever silent, that the people who had sought shelter everywhere, in cellars, shops, or Métro, and were listening for any sounds that would tell them the reason for the alarm, could hear almost every explosion. Only a few people were in the streets. Some impatient and reckless ones had not sought shelter. Others had emerged quickly to learn the nature of the danger or to continue on some urgent mission. Had the bombardment been started in the night people would have sought shelter promptly and would have remained there. But in the day, in the morning, on Saturday, a beautiful, bright spring day, it was different. One imagines so much when one cannot see. Sunshine seems to mock even real danger. By eleven

THE FIRST OFFENSIVE

o'clock more people were out. They had been hearing the explosions, north, south, but had seen nothing; they received no direct information; the explosions did not seem so severe, so the streets slowly became more active. Lunch-time was not far distant, many housewives had not provided for it, nor for the evening meal; and provisions had to be secured for Sunday. Shops were offering the usual Saturday supplies of food. Paris housewives did their own shopping. Danger or no danger, sirens or not, there were many things that had to be done. And the younger people, boys and girls who worked in offices, shops, small factories, had escaped from their work for the day, and soon thousands of them were in the streets, searching the skies for the supposed 'planes, or trudging toward their homes. The transportation of the city had died at 9.15 and remained dead for six hours; in some cases for the remainder of the day. Many of the people who had been on the Métro trains that drew into stations at 9.15 and stopped had decided to walk underground, and people were found walking the Métro tracks in both directions all over the city. This had never been done before and might never be done again. The emergency was unique. Many people remained for hours in the first places which they could reach when the alarm was sounded. The long silence following the projectile of 11.20 was reassuring, however, so greater numbers of people left shelter and went about their business.

At noon the streets were almost crowded with people seeking food. Most shops, *cafés*, and restaurants had been closed. Some proprietors had merely closed their doors and shutters, and people might come in. A few shops which were open on the street had been kept open all the time, and here women might be seen with their baskets, bargaining for what they wished, obviously nervous, glancing apprehensively toward the sky. Elsewhere a customer and the merchant were so absorbed in the bargain as to be unaware for the time of any danger. It was noticeable that many people hugged the walls of the houses as they hurried along the pavements. The silence, from 11.20, still unbroken at 12.30, was reassuring.

Various newspapers continued to publish 'extras' or to put into their regular noon issues some of the facts of the bombardment, the places, effects, and casualties. The police had orders to suppress at once all such issues, however, and some of the publishers were arrested for their disregard of censorship. The people wanted news; any papers containing even a pretence of news therefore sold rapidly, and some managers were highly incensed over the suppression of their papers. Either they did not comprehend what the general publishing of all information would do or they did not care. M. Clemenceau spoke the truth when he said some time before in the Senate that he was " fighting foes within and without."

The first projectile of the afternoon struck at exactly one o'clock in the Tuileries Gardens near the edge of the Seine, spattering the boats with fragments of metal but injuring no one. At 1.15 another struck the cobbles on the north side of the pavement about the great statue in the centre of the Place de la République. People were all about again, and, though the heavy iron lamp-post not ten feet away was not demolished, two people were killed and nine wounded on the pavement on the other side of the tramlines. The Place was soon crowded with people eager to see the damage. At about the same time a wedding procession was in progress down in the Rue Saint-Antoine, only a block from the place where the fourth projectile burst at 8.17 in the morning. The bride, dressed in white, her train borne by two young girls, and leaning on the arm of a proud *poilu*, decorated with the Croix de Guerre, descended the steps of the church near the corner of the Rue Saint-Paul, and the procession passed down the street as though nothing more unusual than their wedding was

THE FIRST OFFENSIVE

taking place in the city. The nineteenth projectile fell in the Rue Riquet at 1.35. It struck a low building, roofed with tile and glass. The force of the explosion destroyed all the glass and a large part of the tile, but did little damage to the steel roof framework. The next, ten minutes later, fell within a stone boundary wall and high board fence along the Avenue Jean-Jaurès. It spent most of its energy in blasting out a hole about six feet in diameter and three feet deep in the soft earth. A shed near by was demolished, and the baskets and boxes in it were strewn all about. No one was hurt.

There was an interval of an hour before the last projectile burst north of the city in Pantin, on the railway track about a quarter of a mile from the railway-station. Within this hour the bells and bugles had sounded the "All's well," indicating the probable end of danger. The noises of the city had been gradually increasing, and the streets were busy again, so relatively few people heard the last explosion.

From 7.20 until 2.45 twenty-five projectiles had struck in and about Paris, killing sixteen people and wounding twenty-nine. A number of buildings had been demolished, and the business of one of the world's greatest cities had been brought to a standstill for an hour or two and demoralized for the remainder of the day.

Life must go on even in the shadow of such menace, however; so the city appeared to be functioning normally by evening. But the minds of the people were not. So long as a city remains far enough from the lines or the enemy to be free of bombardment by cannon its inhabitants retain a feeling of comparative security. But once it comes under the guns, a feeling akin to despair is apt to replace that of security. The exodus of people from the city, quietly encouraged by the police during the past few months, was certain to be greatly hastened.

A second *communiqué* was sent to the newspapers at four

o'clock. This was displayed on their boards and set for the night and morning papers. It said:

> The enemy fired on Paris with a long-range gun starting at 8 A.M. At intervals of a quarter of an hour shells of 240-mm. calibre fell on the capital and its suburbs. There are about a dozen dead and about fifteen wounded. Measures are being taken to counter-shell the gun.

At 4.30, two hours after the bells and bugles had announced the end of the bombardment, the gendarmes found it necessary to force many people, who had remained in the Métro stations for five or six hours, to leave. The effects of the emergency were many and differed greatly. Some people never sought shelter; many again took to the streets within an hour or so of the alarm. Some people ran to shelter in terror, and many of them remained in the shelter all day. A few had to be compelled to leave. All transportation ceased, and much of it was not resumed. A few shops did not close at all. Most shops remained closed till late afternoon. Midinettes were seen tripping along the streets, delivering parcels at midday, and weddings took place at times and places previously arranged, while houses were being demolished, people killed and wounded. Some factories released their employees and sent them home, afoot, of course. And in the late afternoon of an almost perfect spring day millions of Parisians finally shook themselves free of the memory of the previous night's raid alarm and the menace of the first day of the most spectacular bombardment of history, and hurried to their belated shopping and delayed tasks. They were fairly certain that in less than six hours they would be treated to another air raid, if not a night bombardment. And they were not disappointed, for at 8.50 the sirens on the buildings and on fire-engines rumbling through the streets sounded another alarm. 'Planes had been heard passing over the lines at the Front. Towns and places of military importance nearer

THE TOPOGRAPHICAL AND OFFICIAL
CENTRES OF PARIS

THE ZERO POINT
OF PARIS

THE CHURCH OF SAINT-GERVAIS AND NOTRE-DAME

THE FIRST OFFENSIVE

the Front were bombed instead of Paris, however, and at 10.10 the bugles and bells sounded the " All's well " again. All in all, a lovely day indeed!

A plotting on the maps in the Artillery office of the places where projectiles had burst during the day showed many interesting things. This plotting had been in progress all day, and men of the Municipal Laboratory and the Artillery office had been busy gathering shell fragments and studying the scenes of destruction. Their reports were all in by evening. But little of this information would be given out, and most of the people of the city would remain in ignorance of the places where the projectiles fell, the number, the extent of the damage, the casualties, and the more vital details. But in the technical offices, particularly the Artillery office, work went on feverishly, and the most painstaking studies were made. It was seen from the map as it had been plotted by late afternoon that twelve of the twenty-two or twenty-five shots (there was some uncertainty about this) had fallen in the general region of the Quai de Seine, in the north-eastern section of the city. Three fell close to the Seine on the north side, two more on the south side of the Seine within the walls, two entirely over the city, one of them in Châtillon and the other in Vanves, and one short of the city in Pantin. The distance from the shot in Pantin to that in Châtillon was more than eight miles. The twelve near the Quai de Seine were within a circle two miles in diameter. All of the shots were certainly distributed along a north-east line passing through the centre of the city.

Shortly after nine in the morning, when it seemed certain to the artillerists that the bombardment was by artillery, guns or a gun, and the guess was hazarded that this gun was located in the Laon Corner, possibly near Crépy, this information was telephoned to General Headquarters at Provins and to General Bourgeois, who was in command of the sound-ranging division of the French armies. He

THE PARIS GUN

was instructed to set some of his thirty-two units along the Front at the work of locating the gun firing on Paris. They had no success during the morning, their instruments registering only a confusion of sounds. But they reported noticeably increased volumes of sound at somewhat the same intervals as those between explosions in Paris, and

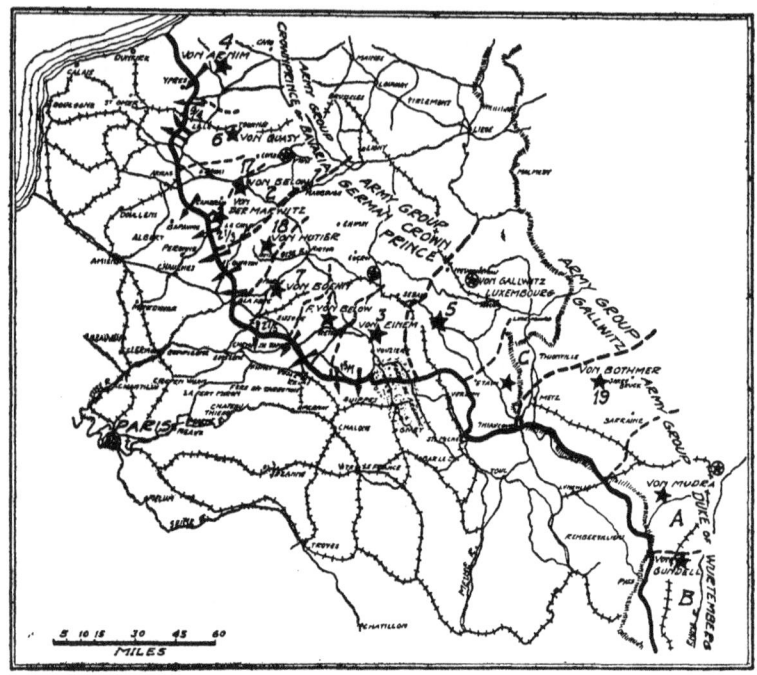

THE GERMAN FRONT ON MARCH 20, 1918

these sounds came from the suspected region of Crépy. Many guns were firing at rather irregular intervals from the Laon Corner.

The air reconnaissance service had also been busy, and late in the day some observers returned with the report that all the area in the Laon Corner was covered with a haze of smoke, surely from smoke-pots, and that though they could not see anything clearly, it seemed that there were guns firing from some railway lines near Crépy. They, too,

THE FIRST OFFENSIVE

reported increased volumes of sound at somewhat similar intervals to those recorded in Paris, though the area under suspicion was so well protected with anti-aircraft guns as to necessitate hasty work.

When all of this information had been assembled in the Artillery office late in the day the officers there thought themselves justified, particularly in view of the extremity of the emergency, in concluding that the two curved tracks at Crépy photographed on March 6 housed the gun or guns. Something had to be done to stop the bombardment, and at once. Orders were therefore telephoned late in the evening to Group Commander Stapfer at Mont-Notre-Dame to detach a battery of his 305-mm., or 12-inch, rifles on Batignolles railway-carriages and start them at once for Vailly, on the Soissons-Rheims railway. They were to be emplaced as quickly as possible on any available siding near Vailly, and would begin firing at the earliest possible moment on the map point whose co-ordinates were 47 . 23. This was at the end of the shorter railway curve on the air photo of March 6.

II
THE BOMBARDMENT CONTINUES

IN Paris Sunday the 24th began as beautiful a day as the never-to-be-forgotten Saturday. It was cool, and early pedestrians walked briskly. Eighty miles north the offensive continued relentlessly. General Gough's Fifth British Army was having a desperate time maintaining anything resembling a continuous line to hold back the advancing columns of grey-clad soldiers slowly approaching Amiens. The blow struck on the 21st had caught the British armies holding 125 miles of front with practically the same forces with which they had held only eighty miles a few months before. On the continued insistence of the French Government, the British had agreed in January to take over forty miles more, and Gough's Fifth Army replaced the French troops on the front where now his inadequate forces were being so mercilessly mauled and belaboured. Allied artillery rumbled and roared continuously to tear up the roads over which the Germans would have to advance their artillery and transports to support their infantry. Trucks and railway trains had been hurrying ceaselessly for two days from the south, west, and north, with French and British reinforcements to assist the almost demolished Fifth Army. These reserves had been billeted in villages everywhere behind the lines.

The first pages of the morning papers were devoted to the situation on the Front and to the Saturday bombardment of Paris. There was little in them that was reassuring. Facts were presented in the most favourable light, but people had been fed so much ill-supported optimism that

THE BOMBARDMENT CONTINUES

they no longer accepted what they read as facts. They simply scanned each issue eagerly and diligently, and awaited confirmation.

In the river-valleys up on the Front a cold fog blanketed everything. It shielded the guns from air observers and bombers, troop concentrations from airmen who would rake them with machine-guns, and from air observers who would report them to the batteries in the rear. Advancing grey figures wearing gas-masks appeared out of this fog to weary Allied machine-gunners, as unhuman things walking mechanically over the shell-ploughed earth. This same fog shielded completely that region where the gun or guns that bombarded Paris the day before were supposed to be. Air observers were prepared to go over at daylight to attempt again to locate them. The blanket of mist was a great boon to the crews of those guns. It did not hinder their operations in the least, for the whole country was covered with a similar fog on Saturday. Indeed, it seemed that the bombardment had been stopped when a fresh wind came up in the afternoon and swept away the mist and flattened the smoke-screen to the ground. That may have been only a coincidence, but both the sound-spotters and air observers on the Front had noticed it.

The people of Paris retired on Saturday night after the " All's well " at 10.10 with the full expectation of a continuation of the bombardment on the morrow. Many who could had decided during the day to leave the city. Others who were compelled to remain accepted the bombardment as just another of the War's emergencies, to be lived through as best one could. Perhaps the Sunday papers would furnish sufficient enlightenment to enable all to comprehend the situation better and plan for it. Few there were at the end of Saturday who did not know in some way that the bombs were projectiles fired from guns rather than bombs dropped from 'planes. The public so readily accepted certain seeming impossibilities, giving

THE PARIS GUN

the engineer and the scientist full credit for the power to perform miracles.

No one was surprised, therefore, when a dull boom announced at 6.50 on Sunday morning that a second day's bombardment had begun. The projectile struck the corner of the rubble masonry wall at the back of a house in the Rue de Meaux. The Rue de Meaux was almost parallel to the Quai de Seine beside which the first projectile burst on Saturday morning at 7.20, and near which half of that day's projectiles fell. The first place struck on Sunday was not more than half a mile from No. 6 Quai de Seine. The projectile missed the corner of the next house by only a few inches. There was a recess between the two. It burst instantly on striking the wall just beside a second-floor window and wrought heavy damage within and without. One person was killed and fourteen wounded. This information would probably have been welcome to the gunners who had heard the shell depart a few minutes before. In all of Saturday's bombardment of twenty-five shots, on a busy day, with people abroad everywhere during most of the day despite the alarm and the hour or hours spent by many under shelter, only forty-five people were among the casualties. The first shell of Sunday morning took a toll of fifteen, one-third of that of the previous twenty-five.

Within a few minutes the screeching of sirens warned the people all over the city that another raid or bombardment had begun, and that they should seek shelter. Many did so promptly. Tram-cars, buses, Métro trains were stopped again, as on the day before. There had not yet been sufficient time to decide what to do in the transportation service in this new emergency. It behoved none to trifle during a real air raid; transportation was rightly stopped then. It would be necessary to arrange otherwise, however, for the bombardment; certain risks would have to be taken. Some special measures for the new emergency were already

THE BOMBARDMENT CONTINUES

being announced in the morning's papers, *Le Matin* in particular, which some had received by this time and even before the first projectile burst at 6.50.

Almost at once a second projectile struck, the interval only nine minutes. The explosions of both were heard distinctly throughout most of the city because of the Sunday silence. This projectile struck in the Rue Julien-Lacroix, a mile and a quarter from the first. The havoc it wrought was more than serious. It burst almost in front of the church Notre-Dame-de-la-Croix. The day was Palm Sunday, and many people were hurrying to early Mass. The shell struck almost at the corner of the Rue Julien-Lacroix and the narrow Rue d'Eupatoria, which passed along the north side of the church. When the people recovered somewhat from the shock and took count of the damage it was found that two had been killed and eighty wounded: more information that would have interested the gunners. Another fact of this brief bombardment was significant: the interval of nine minutes. Although there had been an apparent interval of five minutes on Saturday, it was doubted; the well-authenticated short interval of ten minutes had followed the ninth shot; that was after the gun crew had warmed up to its job. The tremendous toll of wounded from this second projectile was to set a record for the many days to come, not merely for any one projectile, but for any whole day's bombardment, though a later projectile took a greater toll of killed.

The second shell demonstrated something more: the danger to crowds or even small groups of people. On the Front men advancing in a charge, holding trenches, or in reserve behind the lines dared not operate in large groups. Solid formation in a charge might be good for morale, but fatal for casualties. Crowded trenches were deadly places. It was imperative to warn the people at once against useless gathering in crowds.

The next two projectiles, which arrived at intervals of

nine and sixteen minutes, fell outside the city walls, the one at 7.8 far out in Bobigny, and the next at 7.24 in Pantin. The first of these was four miles from the fatal second projectile. To those plotting the locations of the bursts, which was done as rapidly as information could be received from the gendarmes, it was significant that two of the first four projectiles fell short of the city proper, one far short. No one knew yet whether there was a single target at which the guns were aimed, or, in the parlance of the artillerist, on which the guns were laid, or whether there were many targets. The suspicion was that Paris, just Paris, was the target. Every city has somewhere an officially designated point or spot within its limits that represents that city on the maps. This seldom coincides with the geographic centre of the city. It is apt to be in some convenient public place, and is marked by a monument, slab or stone, or metal plate. The 'centre' of Paris was designated by a small slab of granite marked with a cross and set in the cement pavement in the centre of the Place before the great cathedral of Notre-Dame-de-Paris, on the Ile de la Cité. That point was Paris in geography. The artillerists found on Saturday night, after they had finished plotting the bursts for the day, that the probable 'line of arrival' passed close to that point. For the time at least it was assumed that this was the target, that the gun or guns were firing at this point. The only established fact was that Paris was being 'shot up' by a gun, and was not being bombed from 'planes.

Some theories with reference to the bombardment and precautions and provisions for safeguarding the public in the new emergency were announced in the morning papers. *Le Matin* published the *communiqués* which had been given out at 11 A.M. and 4 P.M. on Saturday. The first contained the rather natural announcement that the city was being bombed from 'planes operating at such a height as to render them invisible. But it contained also the statement that

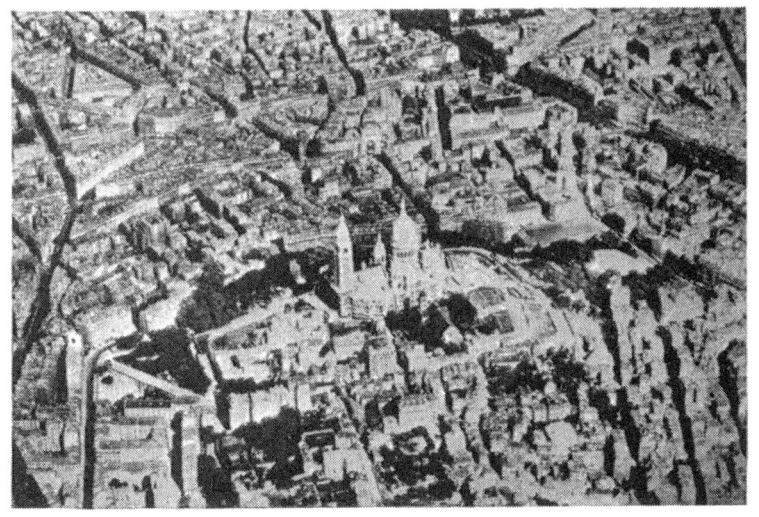

MONTMARTRE

THE HEART OF PARIS

THE BOMBARDMENT CONTINUES

those 'planes were at once pursued both by Paris Defence 'planes and by others on the Front. Those who composed that *communiqué* had been hard pressed for real information. There was general disappointment over the meagre information concerning the damage done by the projectiles, which the second *communiqué* declared them to be. It was assumed correctly that the censors had not permitted the papers to describe the damage to property or to list the places struck. This would be giving valuable information to the enemy. French papers would go to Switzerland at once, and Swiss correspondents had the privilege of transmitting whatever the French papers published. The characteristics of the projectiles, however, were described in great detail. *Le Matin* contained illustrations of two large fragments with the information that the shell was 240 mm. in diameter, that it had two narrow copper bands, and that the body of the shell was enlarged to the outside diameter of the copper bands in advance of each for a distance of about three inches. There were sixty-four grooves in each enlarged section, machined in when the shells were made. The sides of the shell varied in thickness from two and three-quarter inches near the base, an abnormal thickness for so small a calibre, to three-quarters of an inch at the front, where some sort of plug had been screwed in. The explosive charge, for which there was but little space, was divided into two parts by a plate, or diaphragm, screwed into the shell at about its middle. There was a large hole in the centre of this plate, probably for a fuse, and six smaller holes around it. The damage wrought by the projectiles was materially less than that caused by the ordinary 8-inch shell with its 50 per cent. greater space for explosive.

On the front page of *Le Matin*, under a picture showing people in the street looking and pointing toward the sky, was a small map with Paris marked in the lower left corner, and Saint-Gobain and Laon in the upper right. A heavy line was drawn between Paris and Saint-Gobain. In the text of the article one read: "It was soon known [on Saturday] that the gun that was bombarding Paris had just been discovered by air observers in the forest of Saint-Gobain, seventy-five miles from Paris, and measures were taken at once to counter-shell it." " Soon " could certainly not have meant before 11 A.M., else why the *communiqué*? The whole of the forest of Saint-Gobain was obscured from the air by a thin but quite sufficient haze till nearly three o'clock in the afternoon. A heavy blanket of smoke covered almost all of the Laon Corner. Sound-rangers reported that shortly after noon they thought they could distinguish sharper and louder reports over the multitude of miscellaneous gun reports at intervals of from fifteen to twenty minutes in that region. But that the gun had been discovered in the forest of Saint-Gobain, that was conjecture, newspaper licence, in the absence of facts. The Laon Corner was the part of the line closest to Paris, so why not there? And if there, why not in the forest of Saint-Gobain for concealment? At best it could have been nothing more than the seemingly logical deduction made in the Artillery office on Saturday night.

The Theory of the Astronomer Nordmann

There was an interesting discussion in *Le Matin* of the probable characteristics of a gun that the writer believed could shoot a projectile a distance of sixty-two miles or more. This was by a M. Charles Nordmann, an astronomer who had interested himself in and become acquainted with the science of ballistics. From the statement of the second *communiqué*, that Paris was being bombarded by a gun located within the German lines, he deduced that the gun would have to have a range of sixty-two miles or more. He recalled the astonishment over the bombardment of Dunkirk starting on April 28, 1915, by a gun twenty-three and a half miles distant. That had been quickly explained as

THE BOMBARDMENT CONTINUES

the work of one of the newest 15-inch naval guns on a sea-coast carriage with provision for elevating the gun to 45 degrees or higher, so that the maximum range might be secured. Such guns had never been used at their maximum range on ships, for the elevations and ranges were usually limited to correspond to the limits of visibility; the elevations had therefore not exceeded 25 degrees, and the resulting ranges had been little more than half the possible maximum.

M. Nordmann mentioned the fact that in a vacuum the range of a shell at any angle of elevation of the gun depends directly on the initial velocity. Thus if a 3-inch gun could be fired in a vacuum its maximum range would be about eighteen miles. Its range through atmosphere was less than one-third of that. The 15-inch shells left the Dunkirk gun at a velocity of 2624 feet per second. In a vacuum that would give a range of forty miles. The actual range was twenty-three and a half miles. Thus the resistance of the air reduced the theoretical range to one-half or less.

If an initial velocity of 5250 feet per second, or twice the actual velocity, were assumed for the 15-inch gun, the theoretical range of forty miles would be multiplied by four; that is, the range would increase as the square of the velocity, and the range in vacuum would be four times forty miles, or one hundred and sixty miles. Only those who had designed the Paris Gun could answer the question as to whether the actual range would be multiplied by the same factor, four. In considering this one had to remember that the resistance of the air increases greatly with an increase in velocity, while at the same time a projectile travelling to so great a range mounts to heights where the air is very rare and the greater part of its flight is in air so rare as to exert almost a negligible resistance through the greater portion of the flight. It was not known whether the contrary factors cancelled each other or not. If it were assumed that they did, then the actual range of the 15-inch

THE PARIS GUN

naval gun with a muzzle velocity of 5250 feet per second would be ninety-four miles. That was, of course, only what *might* be attained if any such muzzle velocity *were* possible. M. Nordmann said that an initial velocity of about 3900 feet per second was the service velocity for the light, long 2.5-inch naval gun. (This was an error, for no service velocity greater than 3200 feet per second was being realized with any gun in any army or navy at the time, except, perhaps, with the Paris Gun.) Seemingly, then, it would only have been necessary to realize the same velocity of 3900 feet per second with the 9.5-inch gun to make the bombardment of Paris contain but few elements of mystery. The gun would have to be longer, and perhaps of special steel. The rifling of the steel body of the projectile was a new element, for it meant that the copper bands were not depended upon to give the projectile its motion of rotation necessary to stabilize it in its long flight. But at the same time, it would seem that such guns would have but a very short life. And as to the feat of striking an eight-mile target at a distance of sixty-three miles, that was no more difficult than striking a ten-yard target from one hundred yards.

This able discussion seemed to dispose of the gun at once; to rob it of its intriguing elements of mystery. But much was left to conjecture; the astronomer merely pointed out what *ought* to be possible if certain other things *were* possible. He knew that in the realm of high-power artillery the attempt to attain an extra mile of range may be classed with the effort of a runner who can run a hundred yards in ten seconds to do it in nine.

The "New York Times"

The *New York Times* for Sunday devoted a liberal portion of the front page to a discussion of the Saturday bombardment. It said:

THE BOMBARDMENT CONTINUES

Paris is being bombarded by a gun said to be 74½ miles away! French capital is under fire. Ten have been killed and fifteen or more wounded in mysterious bombardment. Paris is 62 miles from the Front. Projectile of 9.5-inch calibre shows rifle marks and evidently came from a gun. Bombardment puzzles Ordnance chiefs. No cannon so far known to Ordnance experts can cover such a range.

It said further:

Early news of the bombardment has been officially confirmed this afternoon [Saturday], and at this time measures for counter-attacking the enemy's cannon are under execution. . . . The city [Paris] received its third warning of an air attack with unshaken nerves at nine o'clock to-night. The people refused to hide in cellars and other underground shelters in the day raid. . . . The subway stations were crowded. . . . The streets always had great crowds watching for an air battle or some other stirring incident. . . . After the aerial battle most of those who had taken refuge in cellars, hearing no sound after half an hour's stay, came out and remained out in the streets and about their doors, wondering at the prolongation of the raid. . . . Paris wore an aspect recalling the early days of 1914.

Turning from the dispatches of its Paris correspondents, the *Times* said:

Officials at Washington doubt the 62-mile shelling: they say no gun could carry that far. The 22-mile bombardment of Dunkirk set a record, and officers of the American, French, and British corps freely concede that they have never dreamed of a gun with a range greater than 30 miles. Some officers frankly doubt that shells from a cannon have fallen in Paris. None are willing to believe that the Germans have invented a gun that can shoot 60 miles. [The ranges vary, 74½, 62, and 60 miles.] Some are inclined to believe that the twenty so-called shells were air bombs. Some even suggest that monster 'planes capable of carrying 9.5-inch guns have been used, though no one has so far conceived of any such combination. It might be possible, however, to use a light-weight 9.5-inch howitzer. [This is the cannon between the mortar and rifle in length.] Another theory is that the shells may

THE PARIS GUN

have been fired from a French or British gun, seized by traitors or mutineers, and turned on the capital from a near point. It is suggested too that perhaps this is the work of a great shell-throwing apparatus operated on the principle of centrifugal force.

This last is an idea which, like 'perpetual motion,' repeatedly returns for discussion.

One American officer, Colonel Dunn by name, regards such a gun as theoretically possible, but he doubts the practicability of one. Another officer says that a gun which could shoot a 9.5-inch projectile 62 miles would have to be from 100 to 150 calibres long, and that such a gun would be of little value because of the impossibility of handling it with any degree of sureness.

Unusual liberties were taken in discussing the lengths of guns. Fifty calibres was the maximum length of service rifles at the time. The doubling of this to 100 calibres was but a dream, so why not 150 calibres as well? Thus the newspaper records and conjectures for the day. And theories even more fanciful and absurd were to be expounded.

New Regulations

It became obvious to officers of the Paris Defence Service and others early on the first day of the bombardment that additional regulations would have to be provided for the new emergency and the all too frequent air raids of the past few weeks. The 'sirens,' by which the alarms for the bombardments had been sounded on both mornings, had been used previously for air raids only. The effect of them was therefore such as to interfere too seriously with the necessary routine business of the city. A new method of warning people of a bombardment had to be adopted. *Le Matin* and other papers published some of the new regulations on Sunday:

1. Signs will be posted at the corners of the busiest streets indicating very clearly the shelters located in the immediate neighbourhood.

THE BOMBARDMENT CONTINUES

2. When the alarm for a bombardment is sounded the doors of buildings may not and shall not be closed, in order that the public may find an immediate refuge in the hallways and vestibules.

3. Public establishments, especially the larger shops, shall keep their emergency doors open, and shall post numerous and clearly seen signs indicating the exits as well as the nearest shelters.

4. To insure in so far as possible the safety of persons taking refuge in cellars, etc., the proprietors of such are ordered to block or protect the ventilators or windows of such cellars by some stationary device, a wall, sandbags, wood, hay covered with earth, etc. Ten days is allowed to carry out this order.

5. It is from now on prohibited to light up at night the newspaper-stands, Morris columns, and in general all devices for publicity with the exception of certain public structures where the lights will be extinguished by the gendarmes on the sounding of an alarm.

Beginning to-morrow, a bombardment by cannon will be announced by the beating of drums and blowing of whistles by the gendarmes. This is to be known as " Alarm No. 3." When this alarm is sounded people are prohibited from gathering in crowds. The " All's clear " for bombardments by cannon will be given as for air raids, by the ringing of bells and blowing of bugles.

Vigorous objection was voiced in *Le Temps* against too many regulations. It was felt that more harm could be done by too many directions than by too few. Particular stress was laid on the necessity for continuing all public activities, all munitions-manufacturing, maintaining all varieties of transportation as usual, and for keeping Métro stations free of people who were merely seeking shelter.

Le Petit Parisien contained a statement concerning a certain alarming rumour that was started the day before that the German Army had broken through the French line and was close enough to Paris to shell it with ordinary guns. This was branded as a vicious lie, probably started by a German sympathizer. Without mentioning the source of their information, they said further that the German gun was seven and a half miles from the French lines, hence

THE PARIS GUN

seventy miles from Paris. *Le Journal* said the gun was of 9.5-inch calibre and had been made in Austria.

The Bombardment goes on

The Palm Sunday bombardment continued without interruption. The fourth projectile, which burst in Pantin at 7.24, was followed in rapid succession by others at irregular intervals. At 7.45 a projectile struck the wall of a factory in the Rue Oberkampf. The explosion destroyed a part of the brick wall, some machinery, and shattered all the windows on the second floor. The shop was deserted, so no one was hurt. Nine minutes later another projectile fell at the Villemain Military Hospital, in the Rue des Récollets. At eight o'clock one fell outside the city along the Route de Bourget, leading up to Senlis and Compiègne. Others followed at intervals of 15, 10, 33, 9, 9, 14, 17, 13, and 9 minutes to 10.9, when one struck the church in the suburb town of Le Blanc-Mesnil, killing four and wounding seven. From then the intervals were 20, 13, 13, 5, 21, 12, and 53 minutes to 12.26, when the bombardment ceased. Perhaps the gun had become over-heated. In the ensuing interval of over five hours some projectiles may have fallen far short of the city, in woods, farms, market gardens. None were discovered.

The " All's well " was sounded at 3.30. But long before, during most of the day, in fact, the streets, boulevards, and parks were filled with people. The bombardment seemed to be losing its element of terror. Very few people had seen any signs of destruction, and the newspapers contained no descriptions of it, and reported the casualties very indefinitely. It was not surprising, therefore, and more than gratifying to those city officials who had been so concerned over the effects of the bombardment, that the public attitude was so fine. An attitude of bravado and recklessness even was noticed among the younger people.

THE BOMBARDMENT CONTINUES

The cessation of the bombardment at 12.26 went relatively unnoticed, except by those who were plotting the locations of the bursts. The gendarmes and a few civilians began to wonder after a time why they no longer heard the dull or sharp crashes of the exploding projectiles as they had been hearing them all the morning. Others merely remembered late in the afternoon that they had heard no explosions since about noon.

Behind the baffling curtain between the people of Paris and detailed knowledge of what was and had been happening there was unceasing vigilance and action. On the French front captive balloons with observers searching for some definite signs of the locations of the gun or guns had been hanging in the sky all day, as all the day before, targets for the German field-guns and the machine-guns of 'planes. Airmen had made frequent trips over the Laon Corner, but again the whole country was obscured by a mist or smoke, or perhaps both. The sound-rangers had been on the alert since nine o'clock Saturday morning, but still with no success. The 12-inch railway battery, ordered up from Mont-Notre-Dame by way of Soissons the night before, reached Vailly at dawn. This was on the Soissons-Rheims railway, five miles from the front lines and fourteen miles from the shorter curved track in the Laon Corner seen on the air photo of March 6. The men had been labouring since early morning to emplace one of the guns for firing at the end of the shorter curved track, though there was still no confirmation that the Paris Gun was there. The 12-inch-gun-mounts which reached Vailly on Sunday morning were more easily emplaced and prepared for action than some $13\frac{1}{2}$-inch railway gun-carriages that were on the way. Half a day usually sufficed if conditions were favourable. The work of the French gunners, as of the Germans operating the Paris guns, would be 'map shooting' at a target that could neither be seen nor observed. The *orienteur* officer and his assistants were busy all the morning in

THE PARIS GUN

working out the firing data so that they might begin as soon as the carriages were emplaced.

One gun was emplaced by noon, and at 12.30 the first shot was fired at the end of the shorter and closer curve. They continued firing most of the afternoon. Reports reached them in mid-afternoon that no projectiles had fallen in Paris since 12.26. The guess that the Paris Gun was at the end of the short curve must have been right. Lucky for them that they had found that chance picture of March 6!

At 5.40 the sound-rangers got their first definite observation. Their instruments clearly recorded a heavy-gun discharge in the Laon Corner. When worked out on the map the point from which the sound came was found to be just midway between the ends of the two curved tracks shown on the air photo of March 6. This information checked with the report from Paris that a projectile had fallen at 5.45. Five minutes seemed too long, however, for a projectile to traverse a range of seventy-five miles. A checking of watches finally reduced the interval to exactly three minutes.

The maps of the city of Paris with the locations of the bursts for Saturday and Sunday separately and combined received the closest study in the Artillery office. They revealed so many interesting facts. If the gun or guns were located in the railway curves in the Laon Corner and the centre of Paris were the target, assumptions which were generally accepted by the end of the second day, then the range from the end of the southern and shorter curve, called No. 1, was exactly 120 kilometres, 74.6 miles. If all projectiles of the two days had been fired from that point the average range for March 23 was 74.2 miles and for March 24 71.8 miles, a material loss in range for the second day. The completed study of all the facts gathered in the two days made it seem that the geographic rather than the official centre was the target. This point was at the eastern

THE BOMBARDMENT CONTINUES

end of the Palais du Louvre in the Rue de Louvre; it was about half a mile from the official centre at the Notre-Dame. This was drawing fine distinctions, and might be unwarranted, but the line of arrival through the geographic centre, which it would seem more logical for the battery to select, passed through the greatest concentration of bursts for each day. If the geographic centre, the range of which was exactly the same as that of the official centre, were the target, the projectiles were striking it quite accurately as to direction, but the gun was consistently 'under-shooting.' There was an excellent concentration on the line of arrival for Saturday, when the gun must have been new. The concentration was less for Sunday, but nevertheless clearly in the same region, between the Quai de Seine and the Gare de l'Est. The dispersion or erratic behaviour of the gun was noticeably increasing. There was considerable speculation as to what had caused two of the projectiles of Saturday to go so far over the target. It was assumed that the gun was aimed always at one point, and its natural dispersion depended upon to scatter the projectiles about more or less evenly. But with such a noticeable concentration, about two miles short of the target, what could have caused two of them to go six miles farther, four miles over the target? Perhaps later events would explain.

Monday, March 25

At one o'clock on Monday morning the sorely harassed Parisians were awakened by the screeching sirens announcing a probable air raid. They had been informed in the Sunday newspapers that thereafter the sirens would announce air raids only. Paris was certainly receiving its full share of war; two bombardments and three air raid alarms in fifty-three hours. It is said that one will become insane, at least temporarily, if he be prevented by one means or another from sleeping. This has frequently been described as one of the medieval forms of torture. Many Parisians, with sundry mutterings about the assiduous attentions of the Germans, climbed out of their beds and repaired to the cellars. Others who were thoroughly disgusted with all the 'straffing,' turned over and tried to go to sleep again, but not without muttering too about what they thought of it all. The " All's well " was sounded by the bells and bugles at 1.45 without any bombs having been dropped. It is not improbable that those who sought shelter would have felt somewhat less annoyed had a bomb or two been dropped. Their trouble would have seemed somewhat less futile.

At 6.50 A.M. the first projectile from the already facetiously named ' telegraph gun ' burst in the Allée-Verte, which ran between the Rue St Sabin and the Boulevard Richard Lenoir in the eleventh *arrondissement*. This was nearly a mile and a half from the point at which the first projectile burst on Saturday. No one was harmed. Ten minutes later the fifty-third projectile of the bombardment struck in the Rue Tandou, killing one person and wounding another. The Rue Tandou was another short street two blocks long, very close to the Quai de la Loire, opposite the Quai de Seine. The shell burst at the back of a house on the north side of the street. The short interval of ten minutes seemed to indicate that, as on Sunday, more than one gun was firing.

Then, as though to prove that the tragic and the ludicrous are constantly jostling each other to lead life's procession, the alarm was given in the manner announced on Sunday. The explosions of the two projectiles had been heard over most of the eastern and northern sections of the city, at least by the gendarmes who had been instructed to listen for them. It had been announced in the Sunday papers that future alarms of bombardments would be sounded by the gendarmes using drums and whistles. The Police Department had not suggested this. It was forced on them. And it was not easy to find enough drums to supply all the

THE BOMBARDMENT CONTINUES

policemen of such a city as Paris. Each policeman had a whistle. The barracks about Paris had been searched for all available drums, and those passed out as far as they would go; to those in the districts most affected first. Those who received them had stored them at convenient places on their routes. Some gendarmes hurried to these places just after 6.50 when the first projectile burst, others after the second at seven o'clock, and proceeded to obey their orders, however distasteful. Paris gendarmes, and for that matter French policemen everywhere, are above all conscientious. So at seven o'clock, when a projectile had just fallen, killing one person and wounding another, Paris was inadvertently treated to one of the most mirth-provoking sights it had witnessed for a long time.

It may seem easy to beat a drum, but it is not. The skill and art of a trained drummer are rightly deserving of praise and admiration. The novice is but a clown at it. The Paris gendarme was a sedate, dignified individual. He represented law and order, and was loved and well regarded by practically all. And here, in the midst of this bombardment, he was projected rudely upon the stage to be a clown. Clowns, or something, were needed to break the tension ; but that the gendarmes should officiate as such was not intended.

Here and there, in all directions, was heard the beating of drums and blowing of whistles. They made relatively little noise as compared with the sirens, but it was ample to attract the attention of pedestrians. The sight was, to put it mildly, funny. French people have a keen appreciation of the ridiculous, the absurd. And by coincidence they were just then in that frame of mind in which every emotion is magnified. Here came a sedate policeman, spick and span in his meticulously neat uniform, sheepishly beating a drum and blowing a whistle. His technique in beating the drum compared favourably with that of the three-year-old who has received a drum at Christmas. Pedestrians and others who came to their doors to see what it meant stared in amazement, and then a goodly number of Parisians simply roared with laughter. It was a rare gendarme who was able to share the humour of his predicament. The jibes, chaffing, and taunts they were compelled to suffer were well-nigh beyond endurance. Here some impertinent young people who had been hurrying to work lined up on either side of a gendarme and beat imaginary drums with him. One pedestrian, seeing the amazing sight, turned to his companion—in the hearing of the gendarme—with, " Ooh, là là! regardez là, c'est Napoléon, le petit caporal." Elsewhere a gendarme was asked what he was advertising, where was the show, how much were potatoes to-day? The gendarme was likened by some to the town-crier of the provincial towns, by others to the ' barker ' of a side-show.

Alarm No. 3, though terribly embarrassing for the gendarmes, was a huge success. It was not repeated. It was not necessary; once was enough. The relief from the shrieking of the sirens and the mirth over the ludicrous substitute broke for many people the tension that had been great and serious since Saturday. Had trained drummers passed through the streets sounding the ' long roll ' employed at military executions the effect would have been different. That impressive 'long roll,' as sounded by a trained drummer, has a dread, ominous portent that one perceives without an explanation. The drum and whistle alarm as carried out, however, was like the experience of the first appearance of the tanks in the British Army on September 15, 1916. How sorely pressed the Allies were at that time! The great offensive against Verdun was still in progress, and morale was low in both French and British armies. And then those queer prehistoric animals, called tanks, crawled through the British lines on their bellies to spit a hail of bullets into the Germans, to flatten their machine-guns, gunners, and barbed wire into the

THE BOMBARDMENT CONTINUES

earth; clumsy, but efficient, the long-hoped-for answer to the problem of the machine-gun. The British Army shook with laughter over the sight of those clumsy, powerful, but, to them, benevolent beasts.

At ten minutes past seven another projectile fell in the Rue des Nonnains-d'Hyères, wounding two persons. This was a short street between the Rue de Rivoli and the Seine at the Ile de Saint-Louis, and two and a half miles from the last projectile. In five minutes another fell out in Pantin, short of the city; a fifth at 7.40 farther out, in Drancy, and the bombardment ceased. This was astonishing, for at this time on each of the previous two days the gun crews seemed to be just warming up to their jobs.

The Monday session of the Municipal Council opened with a speech by its president, M. Adrien Mithouard, commenting on the atrocity of the bombardment and urging all public officials to remain at their posts and perform their tasks efficiently regardless of the new danger. The Council provided for signs and open doors at shelters and public places. A sign, of paper, about twelve by eighteen inches, was ordered, printed, and distributed about the city, to be pasted or fastened at the doors leading to places of shelter, some already in use and others to be selected. Such signs would be conspicuous from a distance of a block. The tiny night-lamps, only six inches on a side, could not be seen easily in the day. The paper signs were to have on them in six-inch letters the word *abri*. Provision was made also for shelter trenches in parks and other open spaces about the city, the trenches to be covered in some manner. Special shelters for school-children were provided for. Further precautions were discussed and advised for the protection of public monuments. The question of organizing colonies of school-children outside Paris was considered. At the Sorbonne posters stated that the authorities were providing special protection for children.

Visits of public officials to the markets disclosed that

THE PARIS GUN

though a few stalls were closed, and in places the management was a bit nervous, business was nearly as brisk as usual. By noon all stalls were open. Stores, shops, *cafés*, restaurants, all were open, and all transportation was maintained without interruption. At the house of correction prisoners were not permitted to walk in the yard during the bombardment. On Sunday all except two special prisoners, Messrs Caillaux and Humbert, accused of treasonable trafficking with the Germans, were kept in their cells. Those two were given permission to walk.

The newspapers of the day contained more interesting comments, reports, and theories. A Swiss paper of Bâle reported a German official *communiqué* of Sunday, the 24th, as saying: " We have bombarded the fortified city of Paris with some long-range guns." The *Strassburger Post* said, commenting on the bombardment: " This bombardment is not only a measure of retaliation; it is also an extremely powerful war measure, psychologically and materially."

Paris papers, *Le Temps*, *Le Matin*, and others, reported more information and theories. General Mochot, head of the Artillery Technical Department, said:

> The existence of a gun with a range of 100 to 120 kilometres did not astonish ballisticians: it was a marvellous invention, but not impossible. Many, most, points of its design were obscure: contrary to expectation, the projectile had neither the weight nor the length that one would expect for such a range. All shells had exploded and were so completely shattered that it had been impossible to reconstruct one, except very crudely. Perhaps soon an unexploded one would be found.

Another expert who was consulted discussed particularly the excessive velocity necessary for such a range. He said that French experimenters had attained velocities of 1000 and 1100 metres per second, but only in what were termed ' polygon ' trial firings; not under normal firing conditions. The favourite ' polygon ' cannon was one with a hexagonal instead of a circular hole through it; the projectile then,

THE BOMBARDMENT CONTINUES

for testing purposes, was a section of a hexagonal steel bar, twisted to fit the spiral hole through the gun. There could be no shearing of copper bands with such a projectile, or 'slug,' as it was called when used for test purposes. It must rotate with the twist of the hexagonal bore of the gun. The idea of such a gun was not new; it had been tried by a Mr Whitworth in England in 1856 while he was experimenting to determine the proper shape of the grooves in a rifled cannon and the proper degree of twist of the rifling. The expert who mentioned the 'polygon' gun thought that the 9.5-inch German gun (as it was still believed) would have to be excessively long, perhaps 100 calibres, making it about 92 feet in length. He thought the accuracy of firing at such a range excellent, the pattern being 6.3 miles long by 1.3 wide. (He was mistaken; it was at least 9.4 miles long by 2.5 wide; but even this was good.)

M. Georges Claude, of liquid air fame, and a member of the Armament Commission, was appealed to, and supported thoroughly all that had been said on Sunday by the astronomer Nordmann. He, like M. Nordmann, felt that the gun merely represented a great stride forward in the development of the conventional cannon. An unusually long cannon capable of withstanding a very high powder pressure, thus insuring a high initial velocity of the projectile, possibly 5200 feet per second, which travelled to so great a range because of the fact that the gun was given an unusual elevation; the projectile then passed quickly through the dense lower air, and the greater part of its path was through air so rare as to offer relatively little resistance in its flight.

The 'rocket,' or self-propelled projectile, was discussed in *Le Temps*. This shell, though projected by a gun, helped itself along by the blast of gases issuing from its base. It was thought that the portion of the interior behind the diaphragm was filled with powder for this purpose. The 'catapult' idea was discussed also. It was recalled that in

THE PARIS GUN

1913 M. Esnault Peterie delivered a paper before the Société de Physique, demonstrating how a device, a wheel approximately 328 feet in diameter, rotating at the speed of forty revolutions per second, could hurl a projectile into space with a velocity of 41,000 feet per second.

The 'shrapnel' theory was mentioned in both the London and the New York *Times*. Some one believed that the gun was of large calibre, perhaps 15 inches, and fired a shell which was in itself another cannon. At some point in its flight this projectile-cannon fired a second shell contained within. This was the one that reached Paris. In support of this it was said that double reports for each projectile were being heard on the Front. (This, however, is inherent in high-velocity firing.) The theories of a pneumatic gun, the gun landed near Paris from a Zeppelin, and others, all were presented for what they were worth. It was recalled in the London *Times* that this gun of a calibre of about 9.5 inches was of practically the same calibre as the gun employed in the Jubilee experiments at Shoeburyness in 1887. Those experiments were for the purpose of testing the ballistic tables and artillery theory of the day. That gun, set at 40 degrees of elevation, had fired a 380-pound projectile to a range of twelve miles. The opinion of an artillery expert was added, to the effect that the powder for the German gun would have to be quite slow burning, the length of the cannon about 100 calibres, the powder pressure about 54,000 pounds per square inch, the shell weight from 300 to 350 pounds, and the life of the gun from 200 to 300 rounds.

The London *Times* correspondent forwarded some interesting information from war correspondents' headquarters. He said:

> Last December we had information from prisoners that the Germans had ready some guns of unusually long range. In January there were said to be at least four, and perhaps seven, of these in existence. They were said to be 15-inch guns lined down

THE BOMBARDMENT CONTINUES

to 8.3 inches. They were 79 feet long with a test range of 47 miles and an expected range of 62.5 miles. The shell was reported to be 59 inches long, to have a very long point, two copper bands, and rifling in front of these. The weight of the shell was 350 pounds. The main shell was two feet long, and the false cap three feet. The copper bands were one inch wide, and the rifling before each three inches wide. The calibre length of the gun was 104, muzzle velocity 4500 to 5000 feet per second, and elevation in firing 55 degrees.

Apparently this unusual information appeared in no other paper.

Le Temps contained a brief discussion of a novel method proposed a year before by a Russian scientist, M. Chilowsky, for increasing the range of artillery. Possibly the Germans were employing it. In this method a portion of the interior of the projectile, the forward portion, was filled with a slow-burning, non-detonating mixture which was ignited, on firing, by a fuse in the point. As the projectile proceeded on its flight the hot gases issuing from an orifice in the point enveloped it in a film, thereby reducing the friction, or resistance of the air. It was said that this suggestion had been approved for trial by the Ministry of Inventions, and trials had shown that the range of the 37-mm. guns could be increased from 55 to 72 per cent. and of large guns to as much as 100 per cent. Tests were still in progress.

The continued silence from 7.40, though not at all understood, led those at the Paris Defence Service office to conclude by eleven o'clock that the bombardment was over for the day, and at 11.40 the "All's well" was sounded by the ringing of bells and sounding of bugles. But 'all' was not 'well' yet, for at 3.48 another projectile fell in the great cemetery of Père Lachaise, playing serious havoc with the prim monuments and vaults. The interval since the shot at 7.40 had been eight hours and eight minutes. There probably were some interesting reasons for this. The next

THE PARIS GUN

and last shell burst two hours and forty-two minutes later, far out in Pantin in a garden along the Rue Benjamin-Delessert. The shell in the cemetery was the farthest off the line of arrival so far, and the last shot the farthest out of the city; the one 2.5 degrees to the left of the target and the other 5.7 miles short of it. Fourteen men, eleven women, and two children had been killed, and one hundred and fifty-two men, women, and children wounded by fifty-eight projectiles in three days.

Three Days' Silence

The guns were silent on Tuesday, Wednesday, and Thursday. No one knew why, but it was appreciated none the less. In this period the bombardment gradually lost its prominent place in the papers in favour of the offensive still furiously in progress to the north. Both French and foreign papers of Tuesday, however, devoted a great deal of space to it. Clearly the bombardment was regarded as one of the major dramatic events of the War. The German papers quoted liberally from French, British, Swiss, and Italian papers. The *Berliner Tageblatt* headed its Tuesday, March 26, article: " The state of mind of the public in Paris and London. . . . Bitter attacks on Clemenceau." It said:

> The socialistic Press of Paris directs a bitter attack on Clemenceau, who alarms the people of Paris more with his contradictory official reports than do the shots of the German long-range gun. . . . On Saturday, the 21st, and on Sunday forenoon, twelve shells fell in Paris. One-fourth of the capital is especially badly damaged. The nearer one approaches to the damaged area the more noticeable is the effect, and within the area itself all is dead. The underground trains of the nineteenth and twentieth *arrondissements* do not run to the end stations. Severe proceedings have been instituted against those who have published lists of the places where shells have exploded. . . French papers show many blanks

THE BOMBARDMENT CONTINUES

attributable to the censors. The rigorous censorship of Paris papers prevents the French people from knowing the truth, the fearful hours which the population of Paris spent in cellars from early Saturday morning till five o'clock in the evening. . . . At two o'clock Saturday afternoon the Paris anti-aircraft guns were still firing a barrage. . . . Military experts feel that two guns were firing on Sunday. The interval of from fifteen to twenty minutes on Saturday was reduced to seven minutes for Sunday.

The Swiss correspondent of the *Tageblatt* said :

The bombardment has disrupted the entire public life of the capital. Most of the Paris newspapers retain the well-known headings, " Cold blood," " heroic calm," etc., which do not mean anything. All rich people are leaving Paris. The railway-stations are filled with those making their escape. Many theatres play in cellars. . . . The city [Paris] has the same aspect as in the days of terror in August 1914. . . . An artillery expert says in the London *Evening News* that the new invention came as a complete surprise to England.

The continued silence of the guns on Wednesday and Thursday seemed a justification for the assertion published in Paris papers that they had been silenced, put out of action by the French counter-battery guns so quickly installed on the Front. The Press, of course, could not say where the French guns were ; that would be giving to the Germans too quickly the information that would permit them to direct some of their guns on to the French batteries.

The artillery service of the Army had not been idle meanwhile. Other French heavy guns were being installed, some 13.5-inch guns of higher power and greater range than the 12-inch guns which began firing at 12.30 noon on Sunday. Air observers reported many huge shell craters from the 12-inch shells all about and between the two railway curves in the Laon Corner, and men and officers of the French batteries were convinced that they had demolished or damaged the guns on those curves and that the bombardment had ceased as a consequence.

THE PARIS GUN

During this period of inactivity it was decided (but not announced) that alarm No. 3, which had proved so amusing on Monday morning, would not be repeated. The much-abused gendarmes made a vigorous protest against the indignity. In anticipation of a continuation of the bombardment, pedestrians were advised to walk on the north and east sides of streets; they were cautioned also against remaining on the top floors of buildings during a bombardment and against gathering in crowds.

Good Friday

Friday, March 29, promised to be the desired uneventful quiet spring day so fitting for the usual religious ceremonies. No shells had fallen in Paris since Monday. No one knew the reason for this, but the hope was that the silence would continue. The three-day respite had been a real relief and had permitted the people to shake themselves out of the nightmare of the previous week. But at 3.30, when the long afternoon services were in progress, the three hours of service in comparative darkness, symbolic of the three days which Christ spent in the tomb, a shell struck along the Voie des Charbonniers, in Montrouge, beyond the city. No one was hurt. At 3.55, twenty-five minutes later, one burst in Châtillon, again over the city and near a place called 'la Pierre Plate.' Neither of the explosions was heard in most of Paris proper. People were certain that another day would pass without any shells. At about four o'clock the funeral service for a woman killed in the bombardment of Saturday had been finished in the cathedral of Notre-Dame on the island. At the church of Saint-Gervais, a magnificent stone structure in the Place Saint-Gervais opposite the Hôtel de Ville and only a block from the Seine between the islands, the worshippers had finished the three hours of service and were kneeling in prayer. The place was crowded. It was just 4.30. Suddenly the

PILE OF STONE, CHAIRS, AND TIMBERS IN
THE CHURCH OF SAINT-GERVAIS

PILE OF STONE AND TIMBERS WHICH
FELL FROM THE ROOF

BROKEN VAULT OF THE CHURCH OF
SAINT-GERVAIS

THE BOMBARDMENT CONTINUES

hundreds of kneeling worshippers were startled by a terrific crash overhead, an explosion. A projectile had struck the roof. Those looking up quickly saw a stone pillar crumpling, beginning to fall. Then the stone vault supported by this pillar began to crack, crumple, and in a second scores of tons of stone, some blocks weighing half a ton, were pouring down upon the mass of people. To try to escape was futile. In a twinkling the cathedral resounded with the crashing of the roof, the impact of the masses of stone, the shrieks of the injured and dying. Those not caught in the fall made a rush for the doors, for blocks and fragments of stone continued to fall. The scene was indescribable.

Immediately the frantic work of rescue began. As rapidly as possible the injured were taken out; then the wrecks that had been human beings were uncovered from the mass of stone that filled the nave of the cathedral, in places more than six feet deep. Soldiers, French and American, ambulance and Red Cross workers, civilians, the clergy, all laboured like mad, heaving off the great blocks of stone; this even while more stones were falling. Gradually the dead and dying were uncovered, and, receiving the blessings of the Archbishop of Paris, were carried past the bowed onlookers. Pools of blood were everywhere, over the floor, the steps in front. Eighty-eight were dead, nineteen men, sixty-seven women, and two children, and sixty-eight more were injured. M. Clemenceau and President Poincaré arrived quickly to see what assistance the Government could render.

Among the dead were General Francfort, M. Henri Stroehlin, of the Swiss Legation, Mlle Bartin, daughter of the Belgian Consul-General, French, British, American civilians, a few soldiers. Several of the worshippers who were assisting in the work of rescue had seen a friend seated some distance in front of them, a young woman only recently married. She was under the mass of *débris*, and as the stone was cleared away the only recognizable mark by which she was finally identified was her engraved wedding-ring.

At 5.45 another and the last projectile for the day struck in the Rue de Fontenay, near the Bagneau cemetery in Montrouge. Again far over the city and no one injured. Four projectiles for the day, three of them over the city, neither killing nor injuring anyone. And one in the city proper, with such tragic results. What curious humour in the pranks of Fate! That the one projectile should strike a vital supporting pillar in a great church, at the very time when it was filled with people and they kneeling in prayer! What would have been the sensations of those handling the great gun had they been able to observe on a screen beside the gun three minutes after the roar of the discharge a motion picture of the crumpling of the cathedral arch, the panic of the people, the great mass of stone piling up where a few seconds before had been people quietly kneeling?

Saturday, the 30th

The surmise in the Artillery office on Friday night was that the four shells of the day were shot from a new gun. The three entirely over the city and one almost on the target seemed to indicate, when one compared this performance with that of the previous Saturday, that a new gun was being used. At 7.15 Saturday morning a projectile struck in the Rue Falguière, near the Nord-Sud underground station, killing four and wounding twenty-three of the crowd hurrying to work. The conclusion of the night before seemed correct. From then on through the busy day projectiles fell regularly at intervals varying from 10 to 50 minutes, averaging 25, until 3.23 P.M., when the twenty-first and last burst. A fragment of the third shell, at 8.10, bore the marks 13 ∴—that is, shell No. 13 of Series 3. Ten people were killed during the

BOULEVARD RASPAIL AND RUE DE RENNES, MARCH 30, 11 A.M.

MATERNITY HOSPITAL, BOULEVARD DE PORT-ROYAL,
APRIL 11

PÈRE LACHAISE CEMETERY, MARCH 25, 3.48 P.M.

THE BOMBARDMENT CONTINUES

day and forty-seven wounded. No alarm was given. The business of the city continued without interruption; transportation of all kinds remained in service. The bombardment was as regular, as sustained, as on the previous Saturday, the casualties almost the same, but the effect on the life of the city vastly different; so quickly do people adjust themselves to new conditions, however difficult or tragic.

The shells of Saturday, March 23, bore the marks of Series 1. On Sunday markings of Series 1 were found on some shell fragments and of Series 2 on others. The grooves in the copper bands of the two differed in width. This indicated two guns in action. On Monday morning there were three of Series 1 and two of Series 2. After a puzzling long silence of eight hours another of Series 1 arrived. The shells of Good Friday and of Saturday were from a new series. Most of them burst far over the target; almost certain indications of a new gun. What had happened to the other guns?

The people of Paris finished the day, fully expecting on the morrow, Easter Sunday, a repetition of Palm Sunday, when they had been shelled all day long. But there was reason, nevertheless, for more cheerful feelings. The great offensive was slowing up; the threatened breakthrough had been averted; there seemed more hope for the future since the armies were all under one command, and General Foch, with his background of brilliant achievements on the Marne in 1914 and later in Flanders, the chief commander. Heavy fighting was still in progress, the rumble of the guns was still heard in the quieter hours of the day, but the Germans were making but slow progress and at terrible cost. And the weather bureau predicted rain. Never would it be more welcome than at this time, to mire in the artillery, transports, supply trains, which the Germans were trying desperately to bring up to the support of their infantry.

III
THE LONG-RANGE GUNS

EARLY March was a period of intense activity in the German Army. The severest portion of the winter was past. December had been a month of vicious weather. Life in the trenches was hardly to be endured. The men were freezing. Morale was low in all armies. The winter had not been so severe as that of 1915–16, but there were not many on the Front who had gone through that winter. Men, soldiers, are expendable—very. No previous war had demonstrated that so forcibly. Under the arrogant tactician and active commander of the armies, Ludendorff, men were just so many bags of sand to stop bullets, or machines to go forward and shoot guns, jab bayonets, and dig trenches. The German soldiers were beginning to realize this, and the reaction was setting in.

January had been less severe, balmy even at times; February was rainy, cold, raw, but men were hardened to that. But March was beginning, except for the three days of rather general snow, as February had ended, with all the signs of a beautiful spring. The barometer of morale rose rapidly. Good reason. The Colossus of the north-east was out of the way. The Russians were fully occupied with revolutions, internal strife. So practically all of the divisions on that front had been released for duty in the west. Two new armies had been created, the Seventeenth under Von Below from Italy, and the Eighteenth under Von Hutier from the east. Von Below had taken over the line north of Von Marwitz' Second Army from Cambrai almost to Lens. Von Hutier took over the line south of Marwitz

THE LONG-RANGE GUNS

from about six miles north-west of Saint-Quentin to a point slightly south of La Fère. Hutier's army was the right of the Army Group of the German Crown Prince, and that of Marwitz was the left of the group of the Crown Prince of Bavaria.

Men on the Western Front had had plenty of rest; not much home leave, however; dangerous for soldiers, making them discontented with the rigours of service, the filth of the Front. They had had frequent snatches out of the trenches, play in back areas or labour in forwarding the mountains of supplies that had been moving westward for months.

How the supplies piled up along the Front in March! In the armies of Von Hutier, Marwitz, and Below, before Amiens, and in the Army Group of the German Crown Prince on the Chemin-des-Dames—railway-supplies, ammunition of every description, barbed wire, miscellaneous supplies, food. No thought of any retirement on the Western Front. Why should there be, with all the new divisions released from the Russian Front, and the old western divisions recruited again to strength?

The very air was charged with expectancy of big things. The War would end during the summer in a glorious and complete victory for the German armies. Hindenburg and Ludendorff had assured the Reichstag of that in February. The French and British armies were low in morale. They were low in man-power, no longer able to man all their batteries and accessory services fully. It was absolutely necessary for them to keep the trenches filled and a certain number of divisions of infantry in reserve for emergencies. During the winter the French had broken up nearly a hundred battalions. They had demanded that the British take over additional frontage, and, with nearly 200,000 fewer men in his army than a year before, Haig had taken over forty miles more of the line. General Gough's Fifth Army had taken that additional section, and stretched they were, to the point of raggedness, to cover it. All of this was known in the German armies. It was known also that a large number of the great railway guns kept parked at Camp Mailly had been turned over to the American Railway Artillery Reserve; that American batteries were being equipped with 75, 155 Schneider and GPF guns, and that the British were turning over any number desired of 8- and 9.2-inch howitzers. So this was the psychological time to strike; during the spring and summer, before the American armies, which had been much talked about but not seen, could arrive, receive their training, and get into action. It would not do to tarry long, for no matter how raw and untrained the American soldiers had been until recently, they had a reputation for unusual adaptability, resourcefulness, and recklessness. There was every assurance that they could not arrive in force, be trained, properly equipped, and organized before autumn. It would be all over before then.

With such prospects, Russia defeated, Roumania out of the way, old divisions fully recruited, many more from the east in reserve, a total of two hundred in line and in reserve on the Western Front, fine spring weather, and mountains of work to do, the morale barometer naturally rose to new heights. The report, rumour, guess, was bandied about on the Front that at the proper time Ludendorff intended to smash one of the British armies, possibly the Fifth, before Amiens. It was strung out so thinly, was in the worst condition to sustain a smashing blow. Then the German Crown Prince would descend on the French between Soissons and Rheims in a sharp, crushing blow. Another British army, perhaps the Fourth at Ypres, would follow the way of the Fifth, and the time would have arrived as a result of the drawing of the scant reserves of the Allies from their already exhausted centre to assist the Fourth Army in the north, suddenly to drive a wedge through to the coast between the French and British. And then when

THE LONG-RANGE GUNS

the armies were separated either could be destroyed first, as conditions seemed to advise. They could not shift reserves then. A beautiful plan in prospect was this, the field armies phase of the campaign. And there seemed little possibility of failure to accomplish it.

Nowhere was there more intense and enthusiastic activity than down in that corner left in the line after the retirement of early 1917 on the Somme, the corner about the city of Laon: the Laon Corner. Not so great activity in this region in piling up supplies, for this would be the pivot for the first two offensives. But something new was here. The third phase of the year's campaign was to be the continuous straffing of the civilian population behind the lines. There was to be no respite. The beginning had been made on January 30 on Paris, which was to be the central objective. Thirty 'planes had succeeded in dropping 141 bombs containing nearly four tons of explosive on and about the city. And when the 'planes crossed the line to bomb other towns the alarm was sounded in Paris lest the 'planes be headed that way. Much joking was done over the predicament of the Parisians, their discomfiture night after night when they were warned to get out of bed and hasten to the cellars, and the 'planes went to Châlons, Nancy, Amiens, instead; a great joke. Eighty-two bombs were dropped on Paris on the night of March 8–9, and eighty-eight on the night of March 11–12.

But the real surprise was coming, and the men labouring on the slopes of the little Mont-de-Joie along the Rheims-Laon-La Fère-Amiens railway, just north of the village of Crépy-en-Laonnois, were spurred to greater activity to finish all their preparations before the orders could be given for the first of a series of the war-ending offensives. The Germany Army was going to give the world its biggest surprise, in the shelling of the city of Paris from this point. On April 28, 1915, the important harbour and city of Dunkirk came under shell-fire from a 15-inch naval gun.

THE PARIS GUN

That was a great surprise. At the beginning of the War 6-inch rifles with their ten-mile range were considered adequate for all field service. There were the huge siege guns, of course, the mobile 17-inch German mortars that had quickly destroyed the ring of supposedly impregnable forts about Liége between August 4 and 9, 1914. But the world had known of great bombards, mortars, for centuries. It was the long-range firing in field warfare that caused the surprise. When it was determined that the Germans had actually mounted one of their newest 15-inch naval guns practically in the fields, actually on the edge of a small wood beside the village of Luegenboom, and were shelling Dunkirk with it at a range of 23.5 miles, this was regarded as the limit of range for field warfare. The French Army began early in 1915 to mount their 8-, 10-, 12-, and even 14-inch naval and sea-coast guns on railway carriages. They accepted no mounting that was not quite mobile. But the 15-inch Luegenboom-Dunkirk Gun had continued to hold the record for range, and it was certain that no one dreamed of a range in excess of thirty miles for any kind of service, even sea-coast, where guns of any weight may be used, carriages of any variety, and massive emplacements of steel and concrete. From the first the German Army had led in the use of heavy long-range field artillery. Other armies had been quick to see the advantage and follow.

It was not surprising that the men from the Navy and artificers from Krupp's, busily at work north of Crépy in the Laon Corner, were driven at their tasks by the greatest pride and enthusiasm. Their *entrée* was to be a climax of surprises, the last great, spectacular, dramatic surprise. They felt all the more pride in the achievement in that so many seemingly insurmountable difficulties had been mastered. Early in 1916, when Dr von Eberhardt presented his theories and calculations to Director Rausenberger, a veritable genius in the designing of artillery, it

THE LONG-RANGE GUNS

seemed that a range of sixty miles could be attained with available powders, and a gun that could be made on existing machines. It was a daring exploit, the dream of a physicist, appreciated and accepted by the more practical genius, Rausenberger. Then came the conferences with the Admiralty Ordnance officers, Admirals Rogge and Gerdes, in Berlin. Did they see any use, any need, for such a gun? They did, of course, but more was needed. Did the Army High Command, meaning General Ludendorff? He did also; in fact, contrary to his custom, he was enthusiastic. So work was begun on the designing of all parts of the final unit, gun, carriage, projectile, and powder containers. All went beautifully until the end of 1916 when, to the consternation and dismay of all concerned in Berlin and at Krupp's, a telegram came instructing them to increase the range of the gun to seventy-five miles. That was easy to say, but it might be in the class of miracles. But the Somme retreat had been decided upon, and there was no choice. A way was finally found to attain that end, and more, eighty miles. By the summer of 1917 this gun was finished and taken to Mappen for testing. The question was raised and discussed many times as to whether this extreme range and the unique method of attaining it would have been realized had it not been for the Somme retreat and Ludendorff's telegram instructing them to increase the range to seventy-five miles. The difficulties experienced with the projectiles were unexpected. The first, fired in July, was an utter failure. Several new designs tested in September were equally dismal failures. A beautiful gun and no projectile. A radically different design of projectile was tested in November. It was a failure, but the idea seemed to hold out hope. Modified forms of the November shells were tested in December; there was more hope, and real success was achieved in January, just in time.

But work had been in progress in the field in the preparation of the positions, emplacements, and all the accessories since the previous September. Unusual optimism, to begin the preparation of emplacements for a gun when the first one was barely finished and the projectile for it an utter failure. But the men of any army must be kept busy somehow. That is one of the great problems in the army during war as well as in times of peace, keeping the men busy, contented, during the periods of inactivity. So work had been in progress for six months. There was serious question indeed as to whether information of this unusual preparation, excavating, had not been passed around through Belgium to France meanwhile. French peasants living all about had observed the building of the railway lines and knew of the excavating. They appeared stupid and uninterested, but it was a fully appreciated fact that little happened on the German side of the lines that was not quickly, somehow, reported to the other side.

The choice of the Laon Corner for the super-guns had a very definite connexion with the need to increase their range from sixty to seventy-five miles. As the lines were in January 1916, the sixty-mile range was ample, and afforded some choice of positions for the gun. After the retirement on the Somme in 1917 there was only one position where adequate concealment could be secured along an existing and favourably located railway line, even with the increase in range of the gun to eighty miles. Such guns and their parts must be transported on standard railway lines and must be emplaced near them. The only possible positions were in the Laon Corner; and the choice there was sharply limited. It would not be wise to work such guns at their extreme range; they would wear out rapidly enough under the most favourable of conditions. And it was necessary to emplace them in the densest and oldest wood available for effective concealment. There actually was no choice of positions. The eastern slope of the Mont-de-Joie in the Saint-Gobain Wood was the only possible place. This was dangerously close to the lines and easily within the range

THE LONG-RANGE GUNS

of French railway guns that could be emplaced to the south on the Soissons-Rheims railway line or to the west on the

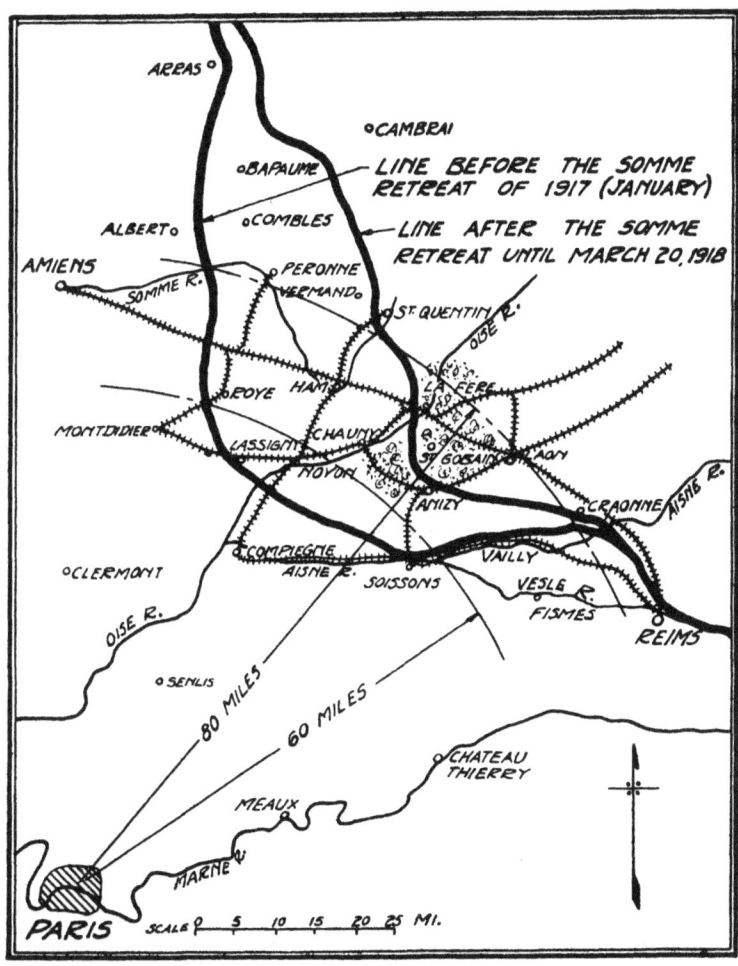

THE GERMAN LINES BEFORE AND AFTER THE SOMME RETREAT

Noyon-Chauny line or the Chauny-Anizy-Soissons line passing through the Basse Forêt de Coucy which would afford fine concealment for such guns. Cannon of such value as these new long-range rifles should never be placed

THE PARIS GUN

within so short a distance as seven miles of the lines as they would be here; but the combination of circumstances demanded the risk.

Three separate positions were prepared. The one begun in September was in the rather sparse and young growth wood known locally as La Sapiniers. The installation track branched from the main Laon-La Fère line at the Crépy station, crossed the Crépy-Couvron road, and led along the northern edge of the wood or southern edge of a partial clearing along the main railway line. Here a branch was led off to the north-west into the clearing. This was to mislead air observers. The ties for this were laid on top of the soft ground. The main branch passed on through to a point where the wood was dense and the trees highest. Only those trees directly in the area of the track were removed. It was hoped that the track beyond the false branch that led into the clearing could be concealed. A considerable clearing was necessary about the emplacement, about seventy feet wide by nearly a hundred and fifty feet in length, the long edges of the rectangle pointing toward Paris, almost due south-west. The track from the main line to this emplacement, which was called No. 1, in order of construction, was about half a mile long, and beyond the false branch it was most carefully camouflaged. The track was laid on a heavy bed of stone to support the exceedingly heavy loads that were to be brought in. Fine slag was then spread over the ballast and ties, and boxes or sockets of wood put between the ties and outside the track all along the way. Freshly cut saplings would be set in these sockets every few days. It was hoped that the path of the curved track would thus be obscured from air observation. Wherever possible, the taller trees were drawn together over the track with wires.

Within the main clearing and near the north-eastern side a pit was dug, about thirty-five feet square and fifteen feet deep, for the concrete emplacement. The making of this

Position No. 1

The Branch Railway leading to Position No. 1

THE LONG-RANGE GUNS

was a tedious job. Its interior was octagonal in shape and in several steps, a total depth of ten feet. Two rings of anchor bolts were embedded in the concrete, and a steel base ring on which the gun-carriage would rest and turn was bolted to the concrete by these. This ring, twenty-seven feet in outside diameter, was in six parts, which were fitted together so perfectly that there were no perceptible joints. The raised portion between the outer and inner rings of bolts was very perfectly machined to permit the traversing, or turning, rollers to roll on it with the least effort.

Heavy concrete shelters were constructed to the right and left of the emplacement with their tops barely above ground. The tops of these were more than four feet thick, advisedly strong, for they were to house ammunition and the gun crew too in emergencies, and there must be no question of their adequacy. These and the steps to their entrances were covered with branches to conceal them from the air. Another shelter was constructed of the trunks of saplings in the wood to the right for the battery personnel in emergencies.

Branch tracks were led off to the right and left from the main track about three hundred feet from the emplacement. As these neared the clearing, they were made parallel to the central track, were about twenty feet to the right and left of it, and continued about eighty feet beyond the emplacement. The central track passed directly over the centre of the emplacement and a hundred feet beyond. Far more time and care were spent on Emplacement No. 1 than on the others because, as the first conception and to serve the first planned gun-carriage, it embodied pretentious plans. The gun that would be operated on this emplacement could be trained on Amiens, Compiègne, Meaux, Coulommiers, Châlons, Soissons, and many other towns as well as on the principal target, Paris. The emplacement and carriage permitted this.

More tree-boxes were provided along the tracks inside the main clearing, and from the trees on either side wire netting covered with grass, broom, and strips of cloth or paper was stretched, practically covering the space. This was most necessary, for the location of the gun must not be revealed. All knew perfectly that once the guns began firing the enemy air observers would be over only too quickly searching for them.

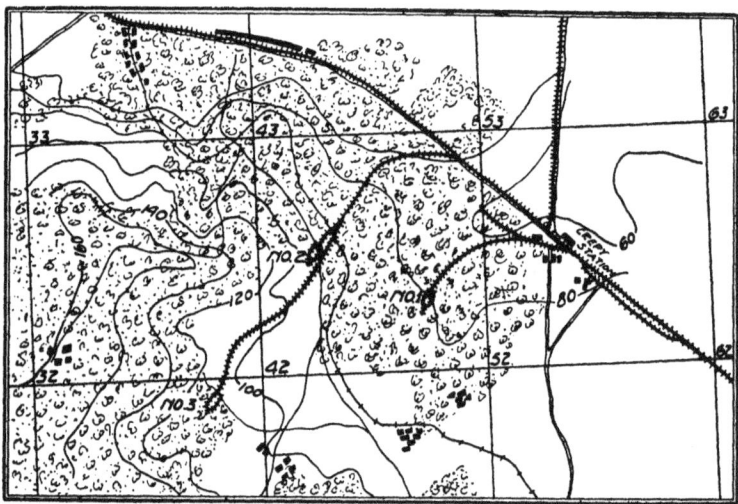

THE THREE GUN POSITIONS AT CRÉPY

The second branch line for the other emplacements was led off from the main line about half a mile farther north, just as it began to pass through a short section of wood. The same care was taken to conceal all of this branch that was taken with the vital part of the first. It curved around through the wood toward the south-west, gradually climbing the gentle slope of the small mountain. At the end of about half a mile a short line was run off to the right and parallel with the main branch line for several hundred yards to a position not far from the large clearing. The main branch continued on to the clearing, across it, gradually climbing

THE LONG-RANGE GUNS

till it entered the wood on the far side. Just within the wood it terminated at the third emplacement. It was a little over half a mile from the main track to No. 2, and about a mile and a quarter to No. 3.

The same lateral tracks were provided at No. 2 as at

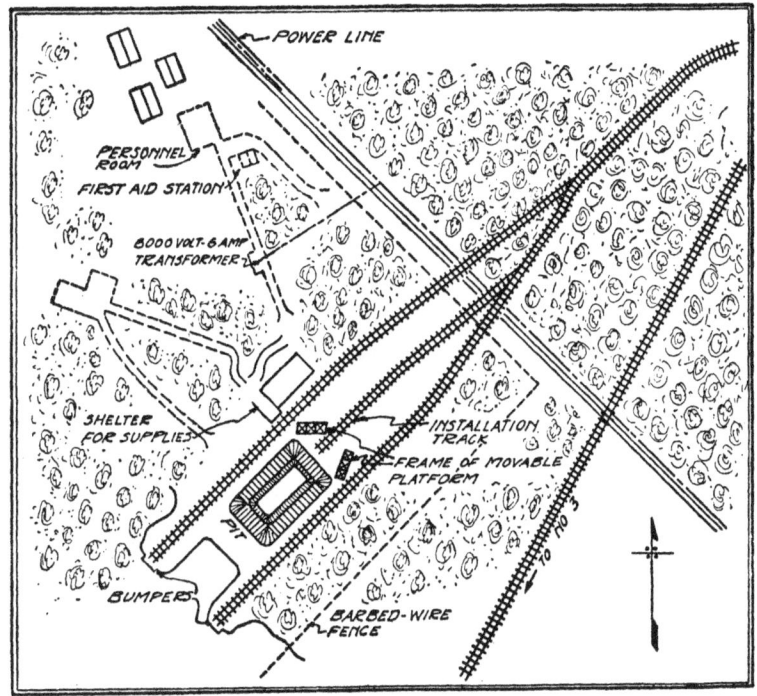

DIAGRAM OF EMPLACEMENT NO. 2

No. 1. The pit for this emplacement, however, was a rectangle about fifty feet long, thirty-five feet wide, and eleven feet deep. The approach track passed over a hump on the side of the hill where the lateral tracks branched off, and the three passed down grade at a slight angle to the emplacement. The slope of the mountain was so sharp at this emplacement that it was necessary to make about a six-foot cut on the north-west, or uphill, side for the one track; this made it possible to lay the downhill track

THE PARIS GUN

without any filling. Earth bumpers were provided at the end of each side-track. The central track terminated at the far side of the emplacement.

It had been decided since the construction of the first carriage, the one intended for emplacement No. 1 in La Sapiniers, that a simpler type of carriage would suffice. The pits at Nos. 2 and 3, which were identical in shape and dimensions, would therefore house heavy timber structures instead of massive concrete as at No. 1. Timber platforms had been found quite satisfactory for the 13.5- and 16-inch railway-guns in the French Army for several years. It was only necessary to provide labour and adequate lifting devices, cranes, to install them. The construction of heavy concrete emplacements on a battle front entails the greatest of difficulties. Since it had been decided more recently that Paris would surely be the only target, a simple carriage, so designed that it could be traversed a few degrees to compensate for the effect of the wind, which would vary in force and direction from day to day, would suffice. Such a carriage could be mounted on a timber platform.

The problem of providing shelter for ammunition and men was solved easily. The slope of the hill at No. 2 was about one foot in five. Tunnels were dug into the side of the hill to two spacious chambers thirty feet underground that would afford comfortable housing and ample protection. Two entrances were provided for each, and a portion of the one to the north was fitted up as a first-aid station. The transformer for the electric current that would be used in operating the guns and carriages was installed in one of the shafts leading to the north chamber. The gun, when at zero elevation for loading, would be some twenty-five feet above the base. A loading platform of such height that the breech of the gun would be just chest high to the men, when at the loading angle, was therefore necessary directly behind the gun. A permanent platform of the same height as the loading platform was constructed of

THE LONG-RANGE GUNS

wood on the hillside, and the narrow gauge track from the ammunition storehouse, the south chamber, terminated on this. A gang plank was provided to connect the permanent with the loading platform.

An old road had passed exactly across the emplacement. That was closed, and a new road, not much more than a path, was run on down to No. 1. The electric-power line paralleled this path, and a barrier of barbed wire was constructed along the road and for a distance south-west along the railway line to No. 3 to keep out inquisitive people. Army personnel in the neighbourhood would have to be kept away, and the men of the batteries kept within bounds to prevent them from spreading information about the guns.

Great care was taken to conceal the railway track leading across the clearing to emplacement No. 3. It was about a hundred and twenty feet higher than the main railway line where the branch left it. The cross ties in the half-mile across the clearing were spread over with earth and the rails with paper cloth and burlap to conceal them from the air. Inspection from the air showed this to be an effective scheme of camouflage; more effective, indeed, than the trees in boxes along the tracks in the wood.

The third emplacement was almost identical with the second. The pit and timber base were of the same size, and the approach and side-track similar. The ground was soft on the downhill side of the emplacement, so it was necessary to support a portion of the installation track on that side on piles. On the uphill side galleries were driven into the hill to four chambers. Each had two outlets so that the personnel might not be entrapped by a cave-in. The southern chamber was for ammunition.

A path or narrow road led on up the mountain about a third of a mile past another underground chamber with two entrances, a pump to supply water, and a shelter of sapling trunks, to a headquarters building constructed of sapling trunks, timbers, and boards. This was for the officers and would be used as General Headquarters. It was close to the highway which branched off the Crépy-Foudrain-La Fère road on the southern mountain ridge, and led over the northern ridge back to the same main road. The telephone-line from Army Headquarters was connected with these quarters. A gallery was provided in the side of the hill near Headquarters for emergency use.

Both emplacements were well camouflaged with grass-covered wire-netting. Wood cleats were nailed on the trees on either side so that men might climb up and fasten the wire in place or take it down for firing.

All this work, which represented no small achievement of labour, had been in progress all the winter, and by March was completed, or nearly so. Even before the beginning of March the work of installing the gun-carriages and guns themselves was busily going on; men arrived daily, highly skilled men from Krupp's, battery artificers and navy personnel, to operate the guns. All of the work had been under the supervision of the Navy, which was familiar with such guns. Navy personnel in Army uniforms. Admiral Rogge, who had been supervising the whole work for two years, was assigned to command. Commander Kinzel was assigned to the ballistic command. These guns were far too important and valuable to be treated as mere field-cannon.

One installation was to be completed as early as possible, so that if the Army preparations were completed when the weather forecasters announced a probable two weeks of fine weather and the first offensive was ordered one gun at least could go into service. Gun No. 1 was the logical selection.

The first cars to be pushed in on the La Sapiniers branch contained the five parts of the gantry crane required to install the carriage and then the gun. The two special trucks were unloaded and placed on the side-tracks where they branched off from the main track. The two legs of the crane were then unloaded, set upright on the trucks, and bolted fast. They were then pushed forward to the emplacement. The bridge was brought up on its car, raised and fastened to the tops of the legs. This bridge, or crossbeam, contained the usual carriage, which could travel backward and forward. Great steel cables, capable of lifting the huge load of the gun, could be let down from the carriage to raise the loads from the cars. The power for all this was supplied on the line from the transformer at emplacement No. 2.

The gun-carriage arrived in numerous parts. The two sides were separate. Then there were the connecting transoms, the base traversing rollers, elevating gear, motors, the huge sleeve or cradle which would hold the gun and in which the gun would slide back in recoil at each shot. The rollers were placed on the steel base-ring already bolted to the concrete; cages, or bearing-rings, were then assembled to the rollers to keep them properly spaced and to carry the superstructure. The upper bearing-plate was mounted on the rollers and fastened to the spacing-rings. The sideframes were set on and bolted to the base-plate and the transoms between. This made of the carriage a unit as rigid as though it were a single steel casting. It towered above the emplacement, a thing formidable in itself. Then the great cylindrical cradle, with its recoil and recuperator cylinders beneath, was mounted on top with its trunnions fitting perfectly in the bearings on top of the side-frames. The elevating mechanism came next, then the trunnion-caps, and finally a careful adjusting of all parts to see that there was no binding. The Krupp men were justly proud of this huge mechanism.

The final item for assembly was the gun, the great achievement. No such gun had ever been seen before. It had been made from one of the Navy's newest 15-inch 45-calibre rifles, but now it was almost double the original gun in length. It had been tubed down to 8.26 inches,

THE PARIS GUN

and the extension of the tube beyond the 15-inch gun made the new gun a strange-looking device. This, transported on its special cars, was run up to the emplacement, carefully raised by the crane, slipped through the cradle, and its great breech-lug bolted to the recoil and recuperator pistons.

The final step in the assembling and adjusting was a careful bracing and straightening of the long tube by means of what resembled one vertical, or strut, and the connecting-links of a suspension bridge mounted on top of the gun. This was to prevent even the slightest drooping or bending. The most careful bore-sighting was necessary to insure that the axis of the ' Jack's Beanstalk ' was a straight line and not a curve. Perfect fitting plugs with tiny holes through them were placed in the muzzle and the breech, and two rings with cross-wires in them were placed in the interior of the gun. When the cross-wires were in line with the holes in the end plugs the axis of the gun was straight. This was a laborious process, but absolutely necessary. A smooth-bore muzzle-section had been ripped off at the proving ground for failure to brace and straighten the tube. If not braced it drooped nearly an inch in its entire length.

While all this fitting and adjusting were in process ammunition was brought in and carefully stored in the massive concrete shelters. The projectiles were such tiny things, particularly so when one compared them with the monstrous carriage and gun from which they were to be sent off into space. Each was in its separate crate to prevent the slightest damage. Great brass cylinders, or cartridges, filled with powder were also brought in, each also in its special crate. Then there were cans of powder, silk fabric to make powder-bags, gauges, rammers, supplies of oil, grease, all that goes to make up a complete unit of so elaborate a kind. A platform with a special hoist was erected at the rear of the gun for the loading.

Some officers, one of them a geographer and reserve

THE LONG-RANGE GUNS

officer, were busy at night and by day determining with the utmost accuracy the true north line, and from this the exact direction of the line through the centre of the base of the carriage and the centre of Paris. When this was determined the base-ring was engraved with an index mark which would serve as the zero mark in aiming the gun.

Similar work was in progress at emplacements No. 2 and 3; but there the carriages were different: there were no concrete bases, no steel roller paths, no traversing rollers for turning in a complete circle if desired, as at No. 1. In each case there was merely a great steel base-plate with a simple pivot, resting on timbers, and the carriage on this. The zero point of the carriage had been carefully marked in the shops. The geographers determined the gun-Paris direction again, as at No. 1, and placed a zero mark on the base-plate. Each carriage was provided with its compass or azimuth sight to check exactly the gun direction; this lest any settling of the timbers threw it out of line unknown to the crew.

Work was finished at emplacement No. 1 early in March, and Grand Headquarters was so notified. The erection of the carriages at No. 2 and 3 was still in progress. Some apprehension was felt on March 6, a beautiful day, when French 'planes were discovered overhead; reconnaissance 'planes, and observers were taking photographs. Nothing was moved, men remained under cover while the 'planes were about, lest their motions betray any unusual activities. Trees were not yet in all the sockets, in very few of them, in fact, but it was hoped that the other precautions would prove effective. Fortunately the nets were all in place over the emplacements.

Other work than that of erecting the guns had been in progress. Anti-aircraft guns were installed in the wood on the north side of the main railway line where the No. 2–3 branch left it. Other batteries had been placed along this

THE PARIS GUN

branch at about the centre of the large clearing, and still others along the narrow gauge railway line running north from Crépy past emplacement No. 2. These were in the clearing near some houses where the railway line passed through a projecting tip of the wood. All of these batteries were carefully camouflaged.

Smoke-pots were placed all about in the Laon Corner so that the emplacements might be effectively obscured no matter what the direction of the wind. Telephone lines were run from Battery Headquarters to a number of heavy field-batteries emplaced in this region. Battery Headquarters was connected by telephone with each of the Paris guns.

As soon as the work of installation at emplacement No. 1 was finished early in March the gun crews began their training. Training was certainly necessary, for the procedure was distinctly unique. Seemingly every unit of the guns and carriages and ammunition was freakish; the gun interminable in length, with a smooth-bore section, and the whole tube elaborately braced to keep it straight. The carriage was nearly twenty-five feet high. The projectile was a relatively tiny thing with narrow copper bands far separated, and the shell itself enlarged in advance of each. Grooves were cut into the steel, making the shell literally a screw. In practice the shell, which, though small, weighed 228 pounds, was brought from the storehouse in a tray on a special carriage. The tray was then lifted by a winch to the loading platform twenty feet up, the tray locked to the breech of the gun, and the rammer-head fitted carefully to the base of the projectile. The shell was then pushed forward through the long powder-chamber, and when it reached the forward end it was slowly turned until by the 'feel' it was known that the raised portions of the shell, the screw-threads, had entered the grooves in the bore of the gun. Never such a procedure as this before. The need for this care would make the service of the gun

THE LONG-RANGE GUNS

slow. The projectile was not rammed in practice, for it would not be easy to remove it. When later a real projectile would be put in it would be fitted just as carefully and then rammed hard so that the 'lands' of the gun (the raised portions between the grooves) would bite hard into the forward copper band. The projectile would then remain in place when the gun was elevated to its extreme angle for firing.

The crews also practised loading the powder-charges. There were three: two bags and a metal cartridge. The charges in the metal case and the one bag were fixed in weight, but the weight of the other bag would vary according to the state of wear or erosion of the gun, and numerous other considerations. All of the projectiles must leave the gun with as nearly as possible the same velocity if they were all to drop on the same target. But, as shot after shot would be fired, the terrific heat of the exceedingly dense gases would soften the thinnest of films of steel of the walls of the gun, especially at the forward end of the powder-chamber; the stream of dense gas passing over these surfaces would then scour away the metal to such an extent that each new projectile that was put in would stop or jam just a little farther forward. Thus each succeeding projectile would have a slightly shorter distance to travel in the gun. If, then, the fiftieth projectile were to leave with the same velocity as the first it would be only by virtue of the fact that it had been pushed harder in its shorter travelling-distance. Hence the necessity for the variable third section of the powder-charge.

By the middle of March the gun crews were well trained to their new duties; they were expert in handling the gun, in gauging the point at which the next projectile would seat so that the variable powder-charge could be quickly weighed out and bagged, in handling the projectile, entering the metal-base powder-case, and in elevating and setting the gun at exactly the right elevation. Everything seemed

THE PARIS GUN

ready everywhere along the Front; guns 2 and 3 would be in a few days.

On the 20th news of the long-expected order passed like a flash through all the armies, and, just before four o'clock the next morning, the usual first day of spring, the German artillery all along the front of Generals Below, Marwitz, and Hutier, from the Laon Corner north past Arras, began a five-hour preparation for the first colossal offensive. Speculation about the object of the first offensive had been correct. The armies of Generals Gough and Byng must bear the brunt, and were very poorly prepared for it. It had been repeatedly said in the British armies during the winter that " The Germans dare not take the offensive, and will not, for if they do and do not win they will lose the war." And so confident of this had they been that they had not taken many obviously desirable precautions. The artillery forward of the Paris Gun region about Crépy took part, and such a drum-fire of crashing, booming, and muttering cannon had not been heard before.

As if to satisfy the impatience of the Paris Gun crews who could not see why they should not have been permitted to join this overture of artillery, the orders came from Grand Headquarters during the day to begin firing on the 23rd. The climax, the reward for all the labour, was at hand. More drilling of the gun crews during that and the next day, for the rumour and hope that the Kaiser would come and inspect the guns in action was confirmed. He would come down from Headquarters at Avernes, whither he had come in his special train some time during the past few days. The crew of No. 1 must be perfectly trained for so special an occasion.

There was more discussion of certain features of the bombardment; particularly observation of the effects in Paris. Numerous daring aviators had already volunteered to fly over and observe if the shots reached the target and, if possible, the effect. There were agents in Paris too;

THE LONG-RANGE GUNS

perhaps they could observe and report. But it was decided that it would be too dangerous to try to observe from 'planes, and unsatisfactory. And spies could learn but little in a short time. If the expected effect were realized the Paris newspapers would be full of it. These would go to Switzerland the day of printing, and each day it would be possible to learn thus of the previous day's bombardment. This was far from ideal, but it could hardly be bettered. The serving of the great guns would become monotonous, and that usual stimulus to care in handling them, knowledge quickly of the effects, would be lacking, but it could not be helped. The officers would have to be doubly careful and vigilant.

The ballistic officer and his assistant calculated repeatedly all of the corrections that must be made, and made so carefully, in handling the gun. What a laborious job it is to calculate all of the corrections that must enter into the aiming of the great rifle that is to shoot at a target that cannot be seen, nor the effects observed ! The target is merely on the map. Here the gun and there the target. It was bad enough for the twenty-three mile Luegenboom-Dunkirk Gun. But for these guns it was far worse. On the evening of the 22nd the calculations were again checked carefully in Headquarters on the top of the hills. Off in the east and to the north the artillery flashed and rumbled ceaselessly. The great concentration of divisions had rolled over the line and over the British Fifth Army. For the time all was going beautifully. On the morrow the Parisians would be treated to something new. The great air raids of the 8th and 11th had shaken them thoroughly, and false raid alarms almost every night since had kept their nerves raw.

Down in the lower wood and over along the slopes of the mountain the gun crews were resting after their strenuous labours. Some of the officers and men sat out in the open in the frosty air listening to the furious rumble of guns and admiring the beauty of the perfect starlight night. Down the slope and in the meadows all was dark and silent, except for an occasional supply train passing on the main line.

But those calculations. The ballistic commander of course had the range-table, which had been computed most carefully from the test firings at the proving ground. But that merely gave the weights of the powder-charges for the various ranges and for each successive position of the shell as the gun became worn. A most unusual table even so. This gun was to be operated at one elevation only. Each time it was elevated for firing it would be set at 50 degrees. No matter what the range, always an elevation of 50 degrees. The range would be changed by varying the weight of the powder-charge. This was analogous to zone-firing for short cannon, mortars, and howitzers, but even with such cannon the elevations were changed.

And here lay an interesting story in itself. It was just on this point that Professor von Eberhardt spent so much time, made such laborious calculations, and presented his results to his chief, Dr Rausenberger, early in 1916. He concluded that if one were to shoot a projectile of sufficient weight through the low, dense layers of air at a high initial elevation, and it were possible to give the projectile an initial velocity of about a mile per second, it would very quickly, twelve miles up, come into air so rare as to offer a negligible resistance, and the projectile would then have approximately the desired elevation of 45 degrees that Galileo had proved correct for the maximum range in a vacuum. The projectile would go on up, gradually turning over from the pull of gravity, and descend finally into denser and denser air to the earth, having travelled more than three-quarters of its horizontal distance, or range, in a virtual vacuum. He thought this should give an unusual range, *provided* the initial velocity of about a mile per second were possible. This had been found possible; and the elevation of the gun to give the greatest range was 50 degrees.

Ganz geheim.　　　　　Nr.

Schußtafelauszug

für die
lange 21 cm Kanone
in Schießgerüst

mit Sprenggranaten L/4,5 m. Bdz. u. Jz.
(mit Haube).

Gewicht des Geschosses: 104 bis 106 kg
　„　der Sprengladung: 6,85 kg (Fp.1)
　„　„ Ladung in der Hauptkartusche:
　　　70 kg R. P. C 12 (1230 × 20 8).

Die Schußtafeln sind aufgestellt für 761 mm Barometerstand. Unter Barometerstand ist derjenige am Geschützaufstellungsort und nicht der auf Meeresniveau reduzierte zu verstehen.

Berlin, 1918.
Reichs-Marine-Amt.

FRONT PAGE OF FIRING-LIST FOR ONE OF THE 8·26-INCH GUNS AT CRÉPY

THE LONG-RANGE GUNS

The first item in the calculations, the range, was fixed. But even here there was something unique in artillery operations. For all normal field-artillery firing the earth's surface is a plane. But not for these guns. So great were their ranges, and for the range in question—that is, to Paris—that the distance from the gun to the centre of Paris, a straight line beneath the surface of the earth, of course, was nearly half a mile shorter than the map distance, which is the distance on the surface of the earth. The earth, a sphere, had to be regarded as what it is, and the straight-line distance beneath the surface between two points on its surface had to be computed. This was the distance with which the gun and its projectile would be concerned. And then the density of the air—that is, the reading of the barometer—and the temperature, the direction and velocity of the wind, the temperature of the powder, which was stored underground where the most uniform temperature would prevail. The final correction was more weird than that of the range—that is, for the compass direction. So great was the range that a correction had to be made for the rotation of the earth, and this varied with the compass direction in which the gun would be fired. If, for example, it were desired to fire on a target seventy-five miles due south, it would be necessary to aim, or 'lay,' the gun on a point east of the target. At the instant the projectile was fired it would be rotating about the axis of the earth at the speed of the gun. Seventy-five miles south the distance round the earth in a plane perpendicular to its axis was greater; a point there travelled more miles per second and, as everywhere on the earth, from west to east. When the projectile had travelled south the distance of seventy-five miles the point due south of the gun had moved on east. So to strike a point due south it was necessary to compensate for the differences in speed of rotation of points north and south about the earth's axis by aiming the gun east of the target. If one were to fire north it would be necessary to aim west of north, for in that case the gun would be travelling faster than the target.

Dr Rausenberger and Dr Von Eberhardt, who had arrived during the day, had carefully inspected the guns and carriages. They had come out from Essen to witness the initial firing, to observe the behaviour of the guns, and particularly to study the effects of the first day's firing. It was expected that the one day's firing might half wear out a gun; it would literally wear out from erosion while one looked at it. The guns were so expensive, so slow of manufacture, that every possible effort would have to be made to conserve them and to increase the life of the later ones.

Saturday, March 23

Every one connected with the Paris Gun Headquarters and No. 1 gun was astir even earlier than usual on this morning. Breakfast for all was quickly disposed of; few were interested in it. This was the great day for which all had been labouring so long. The culmination of all the trials, labour, disappointments, successes: the climax. The officers and visitors hurried down the mountain slope from Headquarters and over to No. 1 in La Sapiniers when it was barely light. All the country, the mountain-top as well as the valley, was covered with a light fog obscuring distant views, and shutting out the sun and the sky; ideal for the bombardment. Neither airmen nor balloon observers could see anything.

To the north and east that ceaseless and at times increasing volume of artillery fire rolled, muttered, and rumbled as though a multitude of violent thunderstorms were in progress. The offensive was still 'going nicely.' The Hutier tactic was working like a charm, successive waves of fresh divisions rolling forward and leapfrogging each other through and over the British lines. It looked as though Amiens might be taken.

Reduzierte Schußweitentafel für 50 Erhöhung
:i 761 mm Barometerstand, Schußrichtung SW
und 15 Pulvertemperatur.

Reduzierte Entfernung km	Anfangs- geschwin- digkeit m	Seiten- verschie- bung $^1/_{16}$ Grad	Fall- winkel Grad a. $^1/_{16}$ Grad	Flug- zeit Zeit	Endge- schwindig- keit m
128	1646	49	55^6	182,0	763
126	1635	49	55^7	180,3	756
124	1624	49	55^9	179,1	749
122	1613	49	55^{10}	177,8	741
120	1602	49	55^{11}	176,6	731
118	1590	49	55^{13}	175,4	721
116	1579	49	55^{15}	174,2	713
114	1568	49	56	173,0	707
112	1556	49	56^2	171,8	702
110	1545	49	56^4	170,5	698
108	1535	49	56^6	169,6	693
106	1524	49	56^9	168,7	688
104	1513	49	56^{11}	167,7	683
102	1502	49	56^{14}	166,6	677
100	1491	49	57^1	165,4	671
98	1480	49	57^3	164,1	665
96	1468	49	57^8	162,7	659
94	1456	49	57^{11}	161,2	652
92	1444	49	57^{15}	159,6	644
90	1431	49	58^3	157,9	636
88	1419	49	58^7	156,1	628
86	1406	49	58^{11}	154,2	619
84	1394	49	58^{14}	152,0	610

RANGE-TABLE FROM FIRING-LIST FOR ONE OF THE 8·26-INCH GUNS

THE LONG-RANGE GUNS

To the south-east, seventy-five miles away, lay the great city of Paris; beginning its busiest weekday, the people irritated over another raid alarm during the night, but still feeling secure with the French lines intact from La Fère around the Laon Corner and east past Soissons and Rheims.

The gunnery officer, with his expert technicians, made a careful and final minute examination of the great gun. So many times they had done this, but one can never quite satisfy himself that so valuable a weapon is in perfect condition. The test powder case entered perfectly; the firing mechanism worked perfectly; the elevating and traversing mechanisms were in perfect order; the azimuth and elevation instruments, delicate affairs and easily injured, were taken from their cases and fitted to the carriage and to the socket connected with one of the cradle trunnions.

The orientation and ballistic officers were busy checking their calculations of the firing data. It would be horribly embarrassing if the first shot were to miss Paris through a blunder in the calculations. It was frosty, and the powder was a degree under temperature; so a 50.5-kilogram forward charge was ordered. Cold powder does not build up to pressure so rapidly, so a slight extra charge was necessary. The middle and base charges weighing 75 and 70 kilograms were fixed, already made up. The forward charge was quickly weighed out, bagged, and ready. All were kept in the storehouse until needed, to keep the temperature at the proper point.

It was rapidly approaching seven o'clock. The weather forecasters thought the fog would hold for a part of the day, but one must not take unnecessary chances on being seen. The discharge of the gun and other guns in the corner would be heard over the line only seven miles off, and 'planes would be up all too soon. The commanding officer therefore ordered the smoke-pots to the north lighted so that there would be a good screen over the whole corner in an hour. The gunnery officer called up the batteries

THE PARIS GUN

north and south to inquire if they were ready; they were, and were standing by for his signal. Those guns would set all French sound-ranging instruments jiggling so violently that the discharge of the great gun would be undecipherable on their record charts.

The order for loading was given, and all sprang to with a will. The projectile was hauled over on the ammunition track, hoisted to the loading platform, and its tray locked to the massive gun-breech. The crew that had done this in practice so often fitted the rammer carefully to the base, slid the projectile forward to the end of the powder-chamber, carefully turned it to fit into the grooves in the gun, and then, with a mighty heave, rammed it home. The powder-charges were already coming up to the loading platform; the first was slid into the powder-chamber, then the second; each was pushed forward into place with the rammer. Then two tiny pressure gauges were fitted into special sockets in the wall of the chamber, and the brass-cased base-charge was put in. The gunnery officer with his sergeant inspected every move critically; the order to close the breech was given, and, with the turning of the crank, the huge block of steel moved across, sealing in the projectile and powder. The block was locked in place, and the crew scrambled down from the platform. The sergeant inspected and set the firing mechanism and signalled " All's ready " to his officer. At once the switch was closed, and, with the hum of the elevating motor the great gun began to rise to its firing position.

What an impressive, awe-inspiring sight! The massive carriage, twenty-five feet high, and a gun whose length equalled the height of the average ten-story building slowly raising its muzzle far above the tree-tops. All of this in a clearing in a wood, early on a foggy morning, with a death-dealing instrument to be sent to far-off Paris in a few minutes. How could one describe the emotions? Were they those that would be experienced as the switch is about to be closed in a death-chamber for an execution; or as a great battleship is ordered into action? Perhaps both.

The gun was up; every one was out of the way who had no special function. The elevation was carefully set, checked by a special quadrant and by a second gunner. All was ready. The gunnery officer had all batteries on the 'phone, and when he received the final signal that the elevation had been checked he called to all to stand by for the order. At exactly 7.17 he gave the order on the 'phone; instantly heavy guns, north, south, and west, fired practically in unison; in a second the order to the Paris Gun sergeant. With a terrific, crashing roar the great gun belched forth a huge cloud of orange-red smoke and incandescent gas. The projectile had gone. The great gun recoiled violently in its cradle, came to rest, and then slowly slid forward into battery.

At once the elevating motor was set going, and the gun slowly descended to be inspected and loaded again as before.

Meanwhile the seconds ticked off as the projectile mounted to unknown heights in its flight toward its target. From a position of rest in the gun it had been set into motion with violent twisting and pushing. A million pounds pressure had been exerted on its base while it travelled up the gun. There had been a terrific straining to set it turning at the rate of a hundred revolutions per second before it left the gun so that it would remain head on throughout its journey. In a fiftieth of a second it left the muzzle of the gun at a velocity of 5260 feet per second, a mile per second, and with the energy of 8,000,000,000 foot-pounds. As the projectile emerged into the air it encountered a pressure of two thousand pounds from the force attempting to stop it. In twenty-five seconds it was twelve miles high and in air only one-tenth as dense as that at the surface of the earth. It had lost heavily in velocity getting through that layer of dense air; from 5260 to 3000

THE PARIS GUN

feet per second. And the temperature had dropped below anything experienced on earth, at least to 70 degrees below zero. In ninety seconds it was at its maximum height, twenty-four miles, and turning over. There was no air to speak of up there. For at least fifty miles of its range it travelled in a virtual vacuum. The velocity at the top of its path had dropped to 2250 feet per second. And then it began its downward journey. It gained steadily in velocity, until at the twelve-mile level it had regained the 3000 foot-seconds it had before. But there began the real resistance to its flight; its velocity increased slightly, 75 foot-seconds, and then it began to slow up even while falling.

At the gun officers were studying their watches; 150 seconds; 160; 170; in just a few seconds, at the 176th, at some place in Paris that projectile would strike and burst. With what effect? Not for forty-eight years had the great city of Paris been shelled. Not since 1870, when the besieging German Army fired more than a million solid shot, some hot, and spherical shell into the city. In a few seconds it would again be a city bombarded by German guns. Perhaps in that great city from which the projectile was now only ten seconds, eight seconds, distant, certain people were walking toward a corner, to walk into the projectile or out of danger. One hundred and seventy-six seconds; 7.20. The projectile had burst.

Before the cloud of smoke from the discharge had floated away over the trees the elevating motor was bringing the gun slowly down to its loading position. Two of the crew at the breech crank slid the great block slowly to the side. As was expected, the brass case of the base-charge had been almost melted away; the base was thick and heavy, and most of that remained. But it would not be possible to use these cases again, as with the ordinary gun. As soon as the case was removed there was a rush of air through the bore that swept out the remaining gases. The bore was hastily inspected, the pressure gauges removed and tossed down

THE LONG-RANGE GUNS

to the waiting ballistic officer, and, after swabbing out the powder-chamber, the crew at once entered, placed, and rammed the next shell. As soon as it had been rammed they measured the distance from its base to the breech face of the gun with a special gauge provided for that purpose. This was a part of the procedure in calculating the weight of the next charge of powder. No addition would be made to the charge of powder for the first four and a half inches of advance of the point of stopping of the shell. But as soon as the advance equalled 4.5 inches the powder-charge would be increased by 2.2 pounds. Then when the advance had progressed 100 millimetres, or 3.94 inches, further, and for each hundred millimetres thereafter an additional kilogram of powder would be added. So the measuring of the point of stopping of each shell would be an invariable part of the procedure in loading and calculating the powder-charge.

Again was the gun unique. In no previous gun had such instruments as pressure gauges been employed to learn the probable point in range at which the projectile struck and to correct the calculated weight of the powder for the next charge. The gauges were quickly opened, and the tiny cylindrical pellets of copper removed and measured with a micrometer gauge. Those pellets had been cut from bars of copper which had been compressed under a definite pressure. The pellets had been machined carefully to the diameter and length which they had before the gun was fired. When the gun was fired the terrific pressure of the gases in the gun passing through a tiny hole in the end of the gauge, a hollow cylinder of steel, forced a piston within down on the copper, crushing it slightly. The new and reduced lengths of the copper pellets then indicated the maximum pressure of the gases in the gun for that shot. From the range-table it should have been 59,000 pounds per square inch for the corrected range of 67.1 miles. But the gauges said that the pressure had been only 53,800

THE PARIS GUN

pounds. This was perhaps to be expected; a cold gun. Seven and a half pounds extra powder were quickly added to the variable powder-charge, and the bag sewn up for loading. The crew then fell to with enthusiasm to finish loading the second charge.

Meanwhile the ballistic officer continued his calculations to learn where the first shot had probably fallen. He found that it had probably burst at a distance of seventy and a quarter miles from the gun. This was plotted on the map and found to be up in the north-east section of Paris proper, probably in the region of the Boulevard de la Chapelle or Quai de Seine, provided, of course, that it had not deviated far to the right or left. Not at all bad for the first shot from a cold gun. Perhaps the extra powder would land the second closer to the centre of the city. It was not probable that there had been much deviation to the right or left, for there would be but little drift to these projectiles. Since the rifling of the gun had a right-hand twist, the projectile rotated in a clockwise direction, considering it from the rear; but the atmosphere through which most of its 92-mile path passed was so rare that there could be but little of the usual drift or deviation to the right for a right-hand rotation.

The unique device, the pressure gauge, which revealed to the gun crew approximately where each shot had fallen almost as soon as it had struck, was a fair substitute for the air observer's reports in its effect on morale. It was an indispensable accessory in conducting the fire of so unique and valuable a weapon. As the crew scrambled down from the platform after loading the second round they examined the map eagerly and with enthusiasm over the result.

A second crashing roar, and another projectile was on its way. It started at just 7.37. Twenty minutes to depress the gun, remove the powder-case, pressure gauges, calculate the correction to the powder-charge, load, elevate, and fire; not so bad. Perhaps this could be reduced to fifteen minutes; the shots would then be close enough in time to keep the nerves of the people well on edge.

Naturally speculation was rife as to the effect. Had such a shell fallen in the Pottsdamer Platz in Berlin, what then? In twenty minutes another at the Schlesischer Bahnhof; then another at the Admiralty. The tendency was, of course, to magnify the effect. But Paris papers would reveal that on Sunday.

The pressure gauges indicated that the second shot had struck only a mile and a half short of the target; near the Gare du Nord or the Gare de l'Est, allowing for no lateral deviation. The gun was warming. The third shot, fired at 8.2, showed a lower pressure than the second, so the powder-charge was again increased. The next shell fired at 8.14 may have fallen close to the Seine, perhaps on the Island. The gun was now beginning to show marked signs of wear; nearly three inches initial advance of the projectile; surely never so difficult a weapon to deal with; always calculations, corrections, compensations. Such erosion as this in the same calibre of field-pieces would cause heart failure to the battery commander.

Within an hour the service of the great gun was becoming a matter of routine to most of its crew. Not so, however, to the ballistic officers; calculations without end; each time the examination of the pressure gauges, measurement of the state of wear of the gun, checking of the powder temperature, barometer, wind. A different weight of powder-charge for each separate shot. The seventh shot at 9.1, with an appreciable overcharge, showed a high pressure. The projectile probably fell four miles beyond the target, outside the city walls. Nothing could be taken for granted with this gun.

Everything was going perfectly in the entire organization. The 210-mm. camouflage guns located at various places about the Laon Corner were ranging on various objectives on the French side; this to give the impression of the purpose of harassing them, of destroying roads and depots. But they were firing at the instant of fire of the big gun; or a second or two before. This must have been puzzling to the Frenchmen. A thin curtain of smoke hung over most of the corner, an effective screen if the mist should dissolve at noon, as had been the case during the previous few days. The gun crew managed to average close to fifteen minutes per shot. The longest intervals hardly exceeded twenty. The camouflage guns easily kept up to that; they could make it five if desired, and, working in divided shifts, even two or three minutes.

By eleven o'clock the battery had got off fifteen shots. The last was fired at 10.52. This was excellent service, and the ballistic officers' map showed a good record. The crew were feeling the strain, however, and the rapidly wearing gun was sizzling hot. Surely the Parisians had been 'straffed' sufficiently to produce something close to panic. The commander ordered the firing to be stopped. The crew repaired to lunch with far more will than they had considered breakfast. A detachment from another battery cleaned the gun thoroughly, and the officers and Krupp technicians gave it a thorough examination, using special lights and mirrors to inspect the surface of the powder-chamber and the bore of the gun farther forward. The continuous use of the gun at fifteen-minute intervals for the fifteen rounds had had its effect. The point of seating of the projectile had advanced more than a foot, and from now it would continue to advance more rapidly. The gun was about one-fourth worn out. Probably no more than sixty rounds could be fired from it. There was no lack of animated conversation at the officers' and men's messes; the greatest enthusiasm was manifested over the map record so far. Those who had laboured so long for this day felt the keenest satisfaction over the results. Rausenberger, Eberhardt, Rogge, Kinzel, each felt a special sort of satisfaction because of his share in the achievement.

THE LONG-RANGE GUNS

During lunch-time word was received that the Kaiser would arrive about one o'clock. The resumption of firing was therefore delayed, and everything about the gun was put in perfect order. He arrived with others from Headquarters before one o'clock, and examined the whole installation with keen interest and satisfaction, and remained for the first few rounds beginning at 12.57. Not many gun crews had had the honour of serving their pieces under the eye of the Kaiser, a long-remembered privilege for this crew. He departed after several rounds had been fired to inspect the other emplacements.

By 1.30 the sky began to clear of the mist, and from the top of Mont-de-Joie one could see French balloons hanging in the sky all along the line to the south-west. Observers were searching the corner for signs of the guns. Some French 'planes came over, and fire was held for an hour till they were driven off by the anti-aircraft guns and German combat 'planes. A final shot was fired at 2.42, after an interval of an hour. The mist had cleared away by this time, and only the smoke remained to screen the guns. Firing was stopped for the day, and the crew cleaned the gun thoroughly. Firing would be resumed in the morning. If all went well No. 3 would join in.

SUNDAY, MARCH 24

With almost identical weather conditions firing began at gun No. 1 at 6.47, a little earlier than on Saturday. It was Palm Sunday. People would be going to Mass at about this time, and there would be services here and there in Paris all the morning; the people attending these services, and those in their homes all over the city, in fact, would hear distinctly the explosions of the projectiles on this quiet morning. The next shot was fired from gun No. 3, and thereafter the guns alternated. The interval was reduced from fifteen to ten, and occasionally to as low as six minutes.

THE PARIS GUN

Everything went more smoothly than was anticipated. But then, after such elaborate preparation, things should go smoothly. Firing was stopped at noon, slightly later than on the first day, and both crews hurried to lunch, the officers to theirs. All the morning they had been expecting a report from Headquarters on what was said about the bombardment in the French newspapers.

While at lunch the Admiral was called to the telephone to talk with Headquarters. Every one was expectant; it must be news. "The French papers report a heavy bombardment of Paris on Saturday by some German long-range guns. No such range as these guns seem to have has ever been known. The life of the French capital is completely demoralized. . . . The battery is instructed to continue the bombardment."

The Admiral's face reflected the news as he listened to the report. The crew were hilarious when he told them the details; they must drink to such success. Wine and glasses were produced and the toast drunk, "*Hoch!*" Hardly had the glasses been filled a second time, however, when the crash of something which had exploded in the meadow below set the windows rattling. How could it be? But there was no mistaking it, a projectile of the heaviest calibre, 12 inches or larger. It could only have come from a French railway-gun, and it struck midway between guns 1 and 3. This was to be real war, then, for the Paris Gun batteries. The opponent had struck back, and accurately, within thirty hours of the first shot. But how could he have learned of the locations? Each mutely asked that of his neighbour. With all the elaborate precautions of camouflage of the railway curves, the camouflage guns firing accurately all day on Saturday and to-day, the smoke-screen—how could it be? Had he any information before Saturday that enabled him to emplace guns in anticipation of some surprise from this region? If not, how could he have located the positions since Saturday

THE LONG-RANGE GUNS

morning, moved up such a gun, emplaced it, and begun firing so quickly? One hazarded the only plausible guess. The long-drawn-out work of excavating and building the railway lines since September must have been reported to France through Belgium by local peasants whose opportunities to see the work had been excellent. That must be the explanation.

Another heavy shell crashed farther over in the clearing. This was no joking matter. 12- to 15-inch shells at five-minute intervals, and as close as those two, were not to be taken lightly. The Admiral called a conference to decide what to do. It was decided to cease the bombardment for a few hours and to observe carefully where the shells fell. Perhaps it was only guesswork on the part of the French. Distinctly lucky for the French, but most unlucky for the gun crew. Shortly after three o'clock a heavy shell struck a tree near No. 1; it burst immediately, and a hail of fragments flew in every direction. The burst was so close that dozens of the fragments caught members of the crew, and six were seriously wounded, among them the gunnery officer. Tragedy at the gun end of the bombardment had come much sooner than anyone had anticipated.

German air observers searched the region south of the corner during the afternoon, but French 'planes were out in too great force to permit them to get far. They did not learn anything about the location of the French gun or guns.

At 5.43 one more shot was fired from No. 1; a tentative shot to see if it would draw the fire of the French gun. It could not be possible that they had any listening devices across the line that could distinguish the discharge of the big gun from those of the great number of large-calibre field pieces firing at the same time. The shot drew no answering fire. The French gun had been silent for an hour or more. Firing on Paris would be resumed in the morning.

THE PARIS GUN

Monday, March 25

Firing began early again, the first shot being fired from No. 3 at 6.47. The pressure gauges indicated that it fell short, slightly more than a mile and a half. The second was fired from gun No. 1 ten minutes later, at 6.57. This was not quite so good, three miles short. Too many projectiles were falling in the north-eastern section of the city; they should be evenly distributed if the bombardment was to have the desired effect. The third projectile, again from No. 3, at 7.7, must have fallen almost on the target, as the fourth and sixth on Saturday. The next from No. 1, with an interval of only five minutes, at 7.12, fell far short, nearly five miles, out in that growing collection north-east of the city proper. This made the ninth out there. Gun No. 1 was beginning to act very erratically. In a few minutes the crew of No. 1 heard the expected discharge at No. 3. At 7.37 they got off their own shot; the lowest pressure yet, six miles short; it may have fallen as far out as the suburb town of Drancy. Hardly had they fired when there came over the telephone the appalling news that No. 3 had blown up; what they thought was a shot a few minutes before had in reality been a serious calamity.

When the order to fire the third round from No. 3 was given there was a blinding flash at the breech, a deafening roar, and paralysing concussion. The whole massive breech was blown off. Men of the crew were hurled about as so many sticks; seventeen were killed or wounded. In fact, there were only a few who were not hurt. This gun had a picked crew from the Krupp works. All had been going so smoothly at both guns that the crews had been remaining about the guns when they were fired. The guns were so long that no discomfort had been experienced from the high pressure of the gases issuing from the muzzle. The gunnery officer of No. 1 was telephoned to cease firing. Meanwhile, however, the No. 1 crew had got off their shot at 7.37.

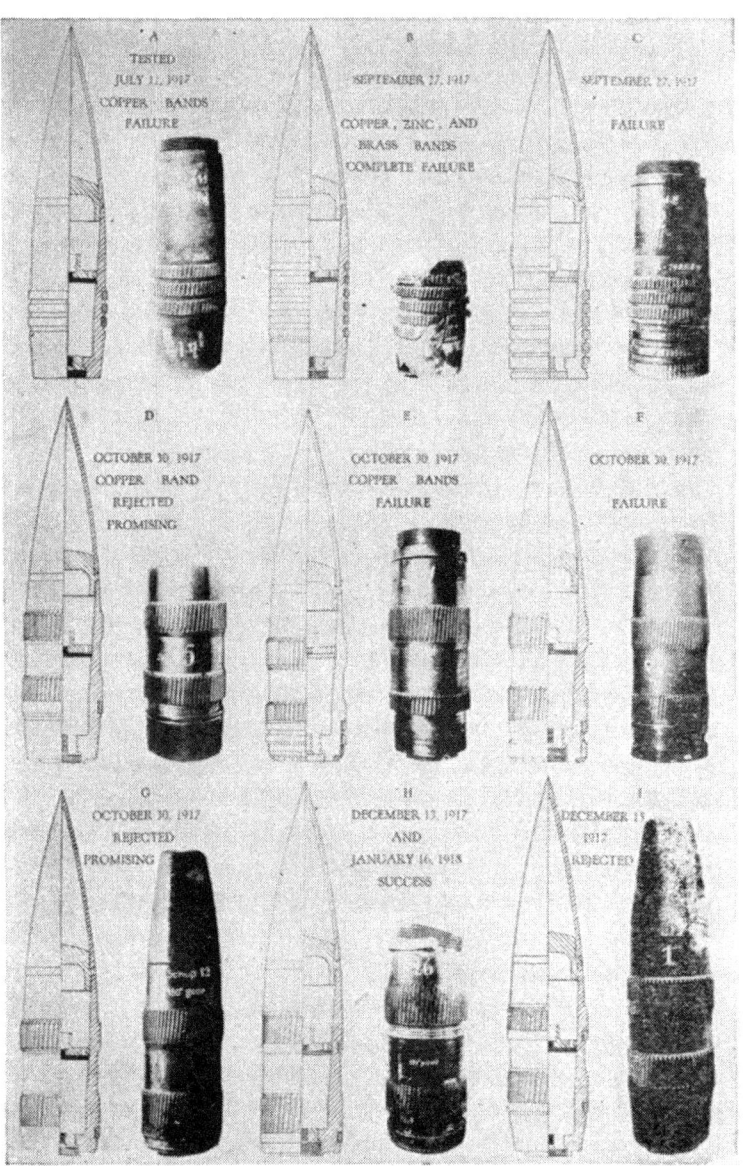

THE EVOLUTION OF THE PARIS SHELL

THE LONG-RANGE GUNS

The few uninjured and less seriously injured about No. 3 carried the wounded into the underground quarters for first aid. Later they were taken down to the men's quarters at No. 2, where the battery medical station had been fitted up. Five men were dead. The business of 'straffing' Paris was taking its toll at this end earlier than had been expected. Air bombing, even the bombardment by artillery that had begun on Sunday, had been thought of, expected even, but no such calamity as this. And to add to the effect of this calamity, the French guns were already at it, and the great shells were dropping here and there with alarming promise of one finally landing on one of the emplacements themselves. Each detonation threw up a huge geyser of earth, or the woods reverberated with the crash, and one could hear the falling of the trees that were uprooted or broken off. The Fates had turned the tables in this game with a vengeance.

It was decided to discontinue firing from No. 1 until a thorough inspection could be made of No. 3 to learn, if possible, the cause of the premature explosion. Perhaps the projectile had not been rammed hard enough, had dropped back on the powder when the gun was elevated for firing. Then when it was driven forward it jammed at a slight angle, or the rifling of the gun and the projectile did not mesh. And, if so, the powder pressure had instantly built up to 10,000 atmospheres or more, and what remained of the powder at that point practically detonated, as T.N.T., an unfortunate habit of powder under very high pressures. It seemed more probable that the projectile had dropped back on the powder. That could and might happen again. From now on the crews would have to take to some bomb-proof cover. It was possible, too, that the steel from which the Series 2 shells had been made was softer or harder than it should be, and that the fatal shell had crushed or cracked in the gun. The remaining shells of this series would be discarded.

THE PARIS GUN

After lunch, when the French guns were less active, No. 1 was again ordered into action, and a shot was fired at 3.45. The pressure developed indicated that it had fallen nearly two miles short. But the French guns were at once busy again, more than busy. Apparently more guns had joined in. The seventh and last shot of the day, the fifth from No. 1, was fired at 6.27. This was much later than the last shot of either Saturday or Sunday. It fell nearly four and a quarter miles short, probably outside the walled section of the city.

A council was called during the evening to consider the problems which had developed. Just when all seemed to be going so smoothly a host of troubles had arisen. Gun No. 3 was out and the carriage damaged. Practically all of that crew were killed or injured. The French guns had the range and location with remarkable accuracy, and it was only a matter of a short time until one of those 12-inch or larger projectiles would drop on No. 1 emplacement, kill the crew, and demolish the gun and carriage, or both. And No. 1 gun was consistently undershooting the target; it was not sending its shells within that portion of the city where the effect on morale would be the greatest. It was decided to abandon both positions and to get gun No. 2 into action as soon as possible. Shells from the French guns had not been falling dangerously close to that position yet. There was no knowing how the French artillery was operating—whether from sound-spotting or not; certainly not from balloon or aeroplane observation. How grudgingly the decision to abandon position No. 1 was made! So much labour spent on it; the concrete base, heavy concrete ammunition shelters, months of time. But apparently it had to be done. Such is war.

Elsewhere in the Army and in the Navy events were progressing most satisfactorily. Things were going so well with the German armies and so badly with the British that Ludendorff was expecting the supreme calamity, the divi-

THE LONG-RANGE GUNS

sion of the British and French armies, on Monday; a clean break-through which would stop the exchange of reserves. The submarines were taking a fearful toll of Allied ships. It was learned later that on this same day the threat of the desperate and perhaps fatal calamity, a division of the armies, had forced Clemenceau and Lloyd George, Haig and Pétain, to do what common sense had dictated long before, to agree on a unified command for the Allied armies. Foch was chosen for the supreme commander.

All haste was made during the next few days, Tuesday, Wednesday, and Thursday, to evacuate position No. 1. The gun was taken out, placed on the cars, and started back to the Krupp works to be rebored. It might then be used again, and it ought to have an appreciably longer life. Also it ought to shoot more consistently. Probably it could not be used at these positions, however. The carriage was dismantled also; then the installation crane, and all was as it had been a month before. The ammunition would be transferred to position No. 2 later. On Tuesday the French guns, certainly more than one by this time, blasted up the region pretty generally with their heavy shells. The work of dismantling No. 1 to the accompaniment of the heavy shells bursting here and there in the wood and out in the clearing was none too pleasant.

Affairs on the Front did not continue so well as the progress of the first five days had promised. Foch had been made Generalissimo on Monday; somehow he had made what was left of Gough's army hold; Fayolle had held on the southern side of the salient. The British were fighting like fiends, simply refusing to retire a kilometre farther. French reserves were damming the breech so rapidly, attacking so furiously, that the weary Germans at the tip of the spear could not make headway; and they had outrun their provisions, their artillery support; the roads were fearfully torn up. The perfect weather continued, beautiful moonlight nights, but there was desperate fear of the inevitable rains. "If only guns 1 and 3 could have kept on going at Paris all the week," said every one of the Paris Gun crews. "What damnable luck!"

The work of dismantling guns No. 1 and 3 had been nearly completed by Friday; there was need for speed at No. 1. Air reconnaissance during the days of silence of the guns had revealed activity in numerous places on the French side. More railway-guns had been brought in. Some smaller French field-guns were being emplaced quite close to the line. If the French had been firing on Sunday, Monday, and Tuesday with any accurate knowledge of the exact locations of the active guns, it were as well to get clear of positions 1 and 3 at once.

On Friday morning, Good Friday, the technicians reported No. 2 so nearly in firing order that it could go into action in the afternoon. There had been too long a break in the bombardment already; a great psychological advantage had been lost through two unforeseen tricks of Fate. The gun was in order by noon, and, preceded by more of the endless calculations of firing data and with new and ample precautions to protect the crew against a repetition of Monday's calamity at No. 3, the first shot left for Paris without mishap at 3.27. No. 2 was operating at an effective range of 74.4 miles, almost the same as No. 1, which was 74.5 miles. The gauges revealed a high over-pressure; the shot probably fell beyond the city. In twenty-five minutes the second shot was fired, at 3.52. Again a super-pressure, higher than the last; the projectile must have fallen about three and three-quarter miles over the target, not so far from the seventh shell fired at 9.1 on the previous Saturday morning from No. 1. The deliberate overcharges were sending the projectiles over the target, which was desired, but too far over. It must have surprised the people over there to get two projectiles in succession when they had had only one a day before.

The pressure for the third shot, more than half an hour

THE LONG-RANGE GUNS

later, at 4.27, was just right to put the projectile on the target. Services were probably in progress in several of the churches in that region, and if the people within the city had not heard the explosions of the two projectiles that fell beyond the city a goodly number must have heard the last one. Those in the churches would go in all directions within an hour and report it, the renewal of the bombardment. But almost with the firing of the third round a heavy shell burst out in the clearing; then others at short intervals, bursting too far away to do serious damage, however. The fourth and last shot was fired at 5.42, after an interval of more than an hour. The pressure was again high; sufficient to send the shell over the city. The ballistic officer suspected that they would pay heavily in a shortened life of the gun for these high over-pressures. Guns can ill stand such treatment, abuse, as it actually is. Firing ceased with heavy projectiles landing at short intervals all about in the clearing and wood. All short, however, giving the assurance, most welcome, that the French gunners had not learned yet that the afternoon's firing was from a new position. There was good reason to believe even that they did not know of the location of No. 2 at all. They had been noticeably ranging on No. 1 in most of the firing; it was a good thing that that position had been abandoned. Short-interval firing would be resumed on the following morning.

The evening report from Grand Headquarters revealed that the breech in the Allied line before Amiens had been dammed. The German Army was making but slow progress there and at heavy cost. So long as the first stage of the great offensive was in progress, however, Paris would be bombarded constantly.

MARCH 30

Another Saturday—but how much had happened since the last! Early on the previous Saturday morning all crews were up before time, eager to hear the roar of the first shot;

THE PARIS GUN

the great day toward which all had been looking. The German armies were rolling over their opponents; the division of the Allied armies seemed certain. On this Saturday two of the three emplacements had been abandoned; one gun was worn out, another had burst, and a crew had gone with it. One gun had been worn out in testing projectiles at Meppen; so the gun on No. 2 carriage was the fourth of the total of seven. The battery group was under constant shell-fire, not yet at No. 2 position, but uncomfortably close to it.

The first shot of the day was fired at 7.12, only a few minutes before the time of the first of a week before. Others followed at intervals of from ten to fifty minutes through the noon hour to the last at 3.20. Perfect firing; one could not hope for more perfect service from a crew, nor for more uniform results from a gun. There was an excellent grouping of bursts about and just over the target; a few had fallen short; two were short of the city itself. A few fell in the north-east section of the city which had been so badly bombarded during the first two days.

Heavy shells from the French guns and a shower of what seemed to be 6-inch shells had been coming over all day. The latter were more annoying than the former, for apparently the battery of four or more 6-inch guns, as it appeared from the number of projectiles, was ranging all over the clearing and wood. Those guns, with their limited range, had to be very close to the line to reach this point.

A council was called at the end of the day to decide upon some vital questions. First, the guns were wearing out at an alarming rate. Three were completely gone at the 8.26-inch calibre, and the one operating on No. 2 carriage was apparently half gone with only twenty-five rounds fired. The second question was with reference to the growing volume and accuracy of counter-battery fire. The day's experience with the French 6-inch guns, which had a life of at least 3500 rounds each and could be served rapidly,

THE LONG-RANGE GUNS

pointed to a not distant day when they would be showered with literally hundreds of such projectiles. Some of them would certainly land on and about the No. 2 position, which could not escape detection indefinitely. It was necessary, of course, to continue firing throughout the present offensive, which might last for another month.

There were only three spare guns for use in this region. When the guns were rebored to 9.1 inches the weight of the projectile would be increased to 273 pounds, the calibre length of the gun decreased, and the range would certainly be reduced. How much, no one knew. No test firing had yet been conducted from a rebored gun. The reduction would certainly be as much as five kilometres, however, and perhaps more. So the rebored guns could not be used from position No. 2, which was 74.4 miles from the target. Apparently there was no alternative but to reduce the daily firing to ten or fewer shots. It might be possible to devise some ways of causing those ten to harass the Parisians as much as the twenty, and more, fired already on the three most active days. Perhaps if a few were fired in the morning, a few in the afternoon, one or two late at night, one at midnight, the desired effect could be realized. Care would have to be taken about night firing, however, to avoid detection from the flash.

And then about the counter-battery fire. The distance from the front was about seven miles. It required about four seconds for the projectiles to travel from the lines to the Crépy battery. If observers at the line were connected directly by telephone with the gun position they could call a single word warning each time they heard a heavy projectile or a volley of 6-inch shells go over. The time for the warning to come over the 'phone would be negligible, and if the receiver sounded a horn at once every one would have time to throw himself down where he stood or to step behind cover in the remaining three seconds. If one lies flat on the ground the worst that is likely to happen from a bursting

THE PARIS GUN

shell, unless the shot strikes beside one, is to be showered with earth and perhaps tree-branches. This seemed the best precaution; the only possible one, in fact.

Some Paris newspapers finally reached Headquarters. Among them was the interesting Sunday edition of *Le Matin*, with an article by a M. Charles Nordmann, and a map showing the probable location of the guns. All the week the absorbing and unanswered question at the battery had been: How had they learned so soon where the guns were located? The map in *Le Matin*, drawn not twenty-four hours after the first shot had been fired, located the batteries definitely in the woods of Saint-Gobain, where they certainly were. There was no statement concerning those details which the French artillery certainly had, however, when they fired the first shot at noon on Sunday. None of the later papers contained so much detailed information as those of Sunday and Monday. Obviously the censor had prohibited the publication of the more vital and interesting information.

On Saturday afternoon information was telephoned from Grand Headquarters that on Friday a projectile had struck a church in Paris, and in some manner about sixty people had been killed and many more wounded. Reference to the record of Friday showed that only one shot had fallen in any locality where a church could have been struck, at least a church in which there could have been so many casualties; that was the third. The map-plotting from the pressure records showed that the third shot could and might have struck in the neighbourhood of the Ile de la Cité. There were half a dozen churches in that region, among them the great Notre-Dame, the church of Saint-Gervais, just across the north channel of the river, another up at the Louvre, a fourth over in the Boulevard Saint-Germain. The French papers discreetly omitted the name of the church.

Only three shots were fired on Easter Sunday, all between

THE LONG-RANGE GUNS

two and three o'clock in the afternoon. This was in accordance with the plan to reduce drastically the daily firing, but to fire a few rounds every day to maintain the menace.

Four shots were fired on Monday, April 1, but at intervals quite different from those of the day before. The first was fired at 12.32, and a second at 1.13. Three hours later, at 4.5, the third was fired, and the last at 7.12. Arrangements had not yet been completed to carry out the second of Saturday's decisions; that concerning warnings from front-line observers, of shells passing over. The necessary telephone lines would be completed quickly, however. The gun crew would then be subjected to less serious risks. Heavy 12-inch and many 6-inch shells continued to strike all about, making life most uncomfortable, to say the least. And during the day, while a crew of men were transferring ammunition from the concrete shelters at No. 1, a heavy shell, probably 12-inch, struck squarely on the north-eastern rim of the concrete gun foundation. It tore up half the steel ring, broke up the concrete, bent the great anchor-bolts, and the back-fire of fragments spattered the south-western side. A hail of fragments of steel passing above the concrete caught the labour crew working about the entrance to the ammunition store, killing six and wounding seven others. All possible speed would have to be made in getting the telephone line into operation so that warning could be given and such calamities averted.

Grand Headquarters telephoned that Paris papers had announced a general funeral on Tuesday afternoon for the victims of the projectile which struck the church on Friday. The battery would therefore not fire during Tuesday afternoon.

Three projectiles were fired on Tuesday morning, one in the evening and three on Wednesday morning. In spite of diligent searching by airmen and sound-rangers, the French 6-inch battery had not yet been located. Its firing was

THE PARIS GUN

annoying. 6-inch shells were small compared with the 12- and 14-inch, but they were not to be ignored, particularly when they came over in volleys and without warning.

The gun was silent on Thursday and Friday. The god of luck seemed distinctly displeased. The wonderful weather that had prevailed since the great offensive began on the 21st broke on Tuesday. The spring rains had begun with showers on Sunday and Monday. How it rained, poured! Everything dripped. Mud, mud, mud! The divisions out in the great salient that had grown so rapidly during the first few days had even threatened on the 25th to burst wide open, but had expanded less and less rapidly since those weary, exhausted divisions made a last effort on Thursday to prevent the great advance from dying out, but to no avail. The resistance had become too much for them, however; their artillery and provisions were too far behind, the roads in terrible condition, though till Tuesday at least dry. The downpour simply mired them in, and on Friday General Ludendorff called off further operations sharply. No need to waste men further in this quarter. The supply services had a sufficiently difficult job to get provisions, wire, railway materials, out into the salient with the line stabilized; the rain and mud made everything doubly difficult and added not a whit to the morale of the men at the Front.

The number of French shells increased daily. Apparently there were several 12-inch and several 13.5-inch railway guns down toward Vailly, and at least a battery of four 5.7-inch long field-guns close up under the line. The shell fragments that had been found and measured were of those calibres, and the rates of firing indicated those probable numbers of guns.

The telephone line from the Front was completed by Saturday, the 6th, and, beginning shortly after eleven o'clock, 11.17, nine shots were fired. Six were in rapid succession between eleven and two o'clock. Another was

THE LONG-RANGE GUNS

fired at 2.47, the eighth at 5.27, and the last quite late, at 11.27, the latest so far.

The performance and condition of the gun showed that it was worn out, so only one more shot was fired from it; on Sunday, the 7th, at 1.57. The projectiles were seating nearly six feet in advance of the position of the first when the gun was put into commission on Good Friday afternoon. Forty-eight projectiles had been fired from it, and the last half-dozen had fallen too far short. The high pressures of the first day had certainly shortened the life of the gun; but perhaps those long shots had been worth while. One of them certainly took a heavy toll, the one that struck the church of Saint-Gervais. The gun was condemned, and the next three days, Tuesday to Thursday, were spent in removing it and in putting in a new one. Foggy weather prevailed all of this time, so the crew was free of annoyance from air-bombers. There was good reason for a new gun at just this time, and as much speed as possible was made.

On Tuesday morning, the 9th, the second stage of the first great offensive was launched in Flanders. The Third and Fifth British Armies of Byng and Gough had been so mauled in the offensive just finished that they were practically out of the running, especially the Fifth, which was in the worst condition at the beginning and invited disaster. It was now the turn of Horne's First Army north of the Third, the Fourth Army about Ypres, and Plumer's Second farther west. If those could be so hammered up that it would require months for them to be reconditioned, fully supplied, and recruited, then the British Army as a whole would be out of it for months. They would be hard put merely to maintain a line and could not send reinforcements to the French while they in turn were being hammered into the same condition. Ludendorff might hope for a breakthrough, but he knew that that was a dream; modern armies such as his and Foch's weren't to be beaten in that way. One or the other had to be worn out, all reserves consumed, all divisions so worn down that their reserve of vitality, their will to hold, to endure punishment, would finally be at such a low ebb that a mighty effort by the stronger on some part of the line of the weaker would find little initial resistance, and there would be no reserves to dam the break. Both he and Foch knew that it would end that way. Ludendorff could not afford to delay, to play a waiting game, for he had all the reserves he would get; he knew that Foch would soon have almost unlimited reserves from America. He was therefore playing a waiting game. Ludendorff hoped to win during the summer. He had to win then if ever. Foch knew that if he could hold out through the summer he certainly would win in 1919.

So every element of the German Army had to play its part in the great game of 1918; the game of wearing out the whole British Army and of so harassing the French civilian population, the French capital, and the French armies that when the British Army had been broken the French would quit. When it became known on Monday at the Paris Gun that the next blow was imminent, that information was a deciding factor in condemning the gun then on carriage No. 2, and all possible speed was made in getting in a new one. As in March, the new gun was ready, and firing on Paris was resumed on the second day after the opening of the offensive. Six shots were fired from the new gun on Thursday, the 11th, between 3.47 and 6.57 P.M. All were well-placed shots, too, from the story of the pressure gauges; most of them were on or over the target. The average range was 75.1 miles, five-eighths of a mile greater than that to the target. This had been the general experience with new guns; uniform high pressures, and most of the shots within the city and fairly close to each other. It was when the guns were half worn out, the projectiles seating between two and three feet forward, that they began to shoot so erratically. The plan decided upon some days since, that of firing fewer shots per day, was held to even at the

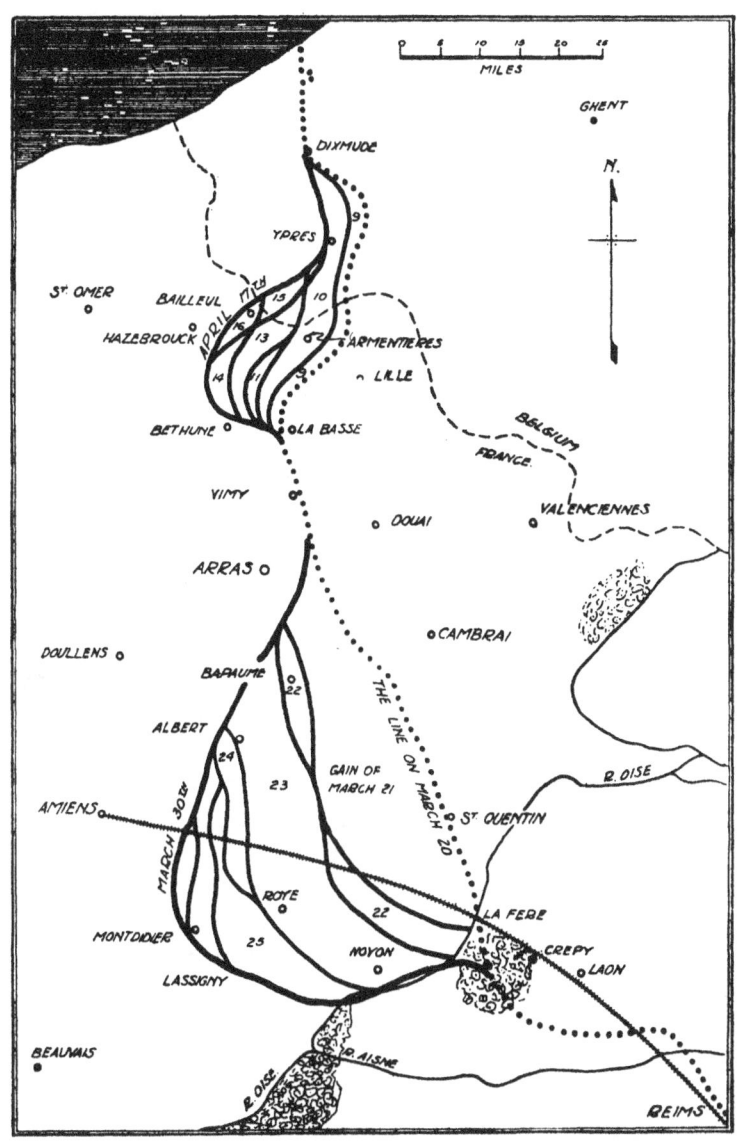

THE NEW WESTERN FRONT, 1918

THE PARIS GUN

beginning of this new offensive. Three were fired between four and five o'clock and three more between six and seven.

On Friday, the 12th, all the country emerged from its blanket of rain and fog, and one saw the sun again; not always so welcome as one would suppose, however, for French observation and reconnaissance 'planes were over most of the day, and the observers apparently were directing the firing of the 12- and 13.5-inch guns at Vailly. Those guns were viciously active all day long, and on this, as on several other of the clearer days, literally hundreds of shells of all calibres came over. The observers at the Front were busy all day calling the warning, and the men about the battery, while serving it, were more than busy in dropping or getting under cover. It was estimated at the end of the day that as many as seven hundred shells had come over. In spite of this, the crew fired three shots between 6.55 and 8.7 in the morning, three more from 11.57 noon to 1.12 P.M., and a seventh at 8.7 in the evening. This kept up the hammering of Paris, bunched the shots for maximum effect there, worked for the safety of the gun crew, and kept down the total number to save the gun.

On Saturday, the 13th, with the offensive still in full swing, Mont Cat of the chain of small mountains in the north having fallen during the day before the German advance, the battery fired but four shots, from 6.42 to 7.47 in the evening. The French guns had been going heavily all day, and it was plain that the air observers who had been over in such force on Friday had made good their long-awaited opportunity. They had found the location of No. 2, which they had not located before. Shells had fallen all about in the vicinity of the carriage during the day, but none had yet struck it.

Another plan was followed on Sunday. There had been but little night firing so far. It was too dangerous. The vivid flash of the discharge above the tree-tops could be

THE LONG-RANGE GUNS

seen easily unless there were a mist or fog. This night seemed safe, however; enough mist to conceal the flash in the seven miles to the Front. Four shots were fired between 12.17 and 1.15 A.M. Three more were fired in the afternoon at 1.46, 2.36, and 3.32; an hour apart. This must have demonstrated the unharmed existence of the battery to those on the French side who may have hoped that it had been badly damaged. It seemed that more guns had been put in and a real organization effected on the other side, for on Monday the battery area was deluged with shells. No firing at all was done that day, but, beginning at 12.52 A.M. on Tuesday, six shots were fired within two hours. Three more were fired in the late afternoon. That was another busy day for the observer; hundreds of shells came over. Bailleul and Passchendaele, up toward Ypres, were taken.

After two days of silence three shots were fired late on Friday afternoon, and two on Sunday evening, the 21st. The second offensive was dying out, and the fifth gun was almost worn out.

Wednesday, the 24th, was marked in the German Army calendar as the day on which their own tanks were used for the first time. It was in a renewed attempt on Amiens. One shot was fired on Paris that day; in the late afternoon. It fell short of the city. On the next day, however, the gun came to life again with seven shots, scattered well through the day, the first two at 7.7 and 7.27, four more at 11.57, 12.31, 1.12, and 1.57, and the seventh at 11.22 P.M. Mount Kemmel, with some six thousand French prisoners, was taken during the day. The German Staff had not known that there were any French forces in that region.

Two shots were fired on Friday afternoon, two early on Saturday afternoon, and three on Tuesday, the 30th, at 6.32 A.M. and 5.12 and 7.12 P.M. A general attack was launched all along the Lys front during the day to break

THE PARIS GUN

if possible the growing resistance of the British armies with their French reinforcements. It was French reinforcements which had been captured, hardly on their arrival at Kemmel, on Thursday. The general attack was promptly checked, however, by the heavily reinforced opposing forces, and the aggressive activities were called off sharply on Wednesday, May 1. Three rounds were fired on Paris that morning, the first at 1.12, the second at 8.1, and the third at 8.36. All were short, far short. The fifth gun, the first great offensive, and the first phase of the bombardment of Paris were finished. The gun had fired sixty-four shots and was worn out.

Orders were received at once not only to cease firing, but to evacuate the entire position. That was a welcome order; the position had become well-nigh intolerable. A new one had already been selected in the newly won ground toward Amiens. It would be closer to Paris and out from under the formidable concentration of French counter-battery guns all about the corner. There could therefore be nothing but relief over the order to vacate this position that had seen so much grief to the personnel. One gun had burst. Two gun positions had been rendered untenable in the first week; the third had recently become almost equally so. More than a score of men had been killed by the explosion of gun No. 3 and by exploding shells. Many more had been wounded. The daily bombardment from heavy and medium French guns had become so furious at times that almost a hundred would fall within an hour. It was estimated that a total of at least five thousand shells had fallen in the five weeks. Quite naturally there was nothing but huge relief over the prospect of moving to a new position which could not be so easily reached, if at all.

In spite of the grief experienced by the Paris Gun battery they shared the satisfaction, elation even, evident everywhere on the Front, and back at home as well, over the universal success so far achieved. The field armies had

THE LONG-RANGE GUNS

done magnificently; a British army had been destroyed; three others had been badly used up. The Allies had lost over 200,000 in casualties and prisoners; fifteen of their precious divisions. Mountains of supplies, field-shops and depots, had been captured. The submarines, so it was reported from the Admiralty, were blocking the transports from America, had sunk half a million tons of shipping in March and April, and were preventing American troops from getting over. And the morale-breaking campaign was going perfectly. Eight air raids on Paris since January in which 318 bombs had been dropped on the city. And 183 shells had been fired into the city since March 23. Well-authenticated reports said that more than half a million people had left Paris since January; the city resembled a besieged fortress, and the belief that the morale-breaking campaign should be concentrated on Paris had been amply justified. There was no longer any doubt in their minds but that they would win the War before winter.

IV

THE SECOND BOMBARDMENT

The Marne Offensive

Shortly after one o'clock on Monday morning, May 27, people all along the way from Rheims, Fismes, and Soissons to Paris awakened with a dread feeling of apprehension to hear the sharp crashing or the booming of guns and exploding shells and feel the vibration of the earth and their houses, according to their distance from the lines. The Allies had been caught napping. Their reserves were concentrated in the west, about the Amiens salient, and Ludendorff had struck in the south instead. Along this line from the Laon Corner east past Rheims the Allies' line was held by the French Sixth and Third Armies of Generals Duchesne and Mecheler. Seven divisions of these armies, three of them British, were on that portion of the Front which was directly in the path of the attack. All of these were weary, worn divisions that had been pummelled unmercifully in the March and April offensive before Amiens and north in Flanders, and were here to rest, in what had been considered a quiet, safe sector. On Sunday afternoon it had been learned from prisoners taken on the front of the 11th Corps of the Sixth French Army that an attack was coming. The army commander was notified, but beyond spreading the news into the divisions on the line and warning them of the danger nothing was done.

The divisions in the line found themselves smothered under high explosive and gas. The bombardment lasted for three hours, and when at four o'clock it was switched

THE SECOND BOMBARDMENT

to a creeping barrage there wasn't much left of the Allied defences. Twenty-eight fresh divisions of German shock troops, most of which had been out resting and refitting since the middle of April, and about a hundred of the huge tanks that had appeared for the first time in the attack on Amiens of April 24, advanced irresistibly over this devastation. The whole Front was so drenched with gas that the advancing men were compelled to wear masks, ludicrous boar-snouted things with staring eyes, that, together with the huge fort-like tanks, made of the attackers something out of a madman's imagination. There was nothing for the thin Allied line to do but retire, leaving machine-gunners here and there in favourable spots to mow down sections of the advancing Germans. All of the roads south of the line were again choked with refugees fleeing with their bundles, carts, cattle, when it was hardly day.

The one o'clock bombardment had broken with particular fury on the great railway-guns about Vailly, those that had been put in between March 24 and April 13 to shell the Crépy long-range gun positions. All of those guns were still in position, for it was not yet known whether the Crépy guns had been moved or not, though they had been silent since May 1. May 3 had been a beautiful clear day, and French airmen had taken more photographs. These revealed nothing, however, that had not been seen on the photographs of April 11 and 12. At even so late a date as May 16 General Maurin, commanding the general artillery reserve, in which was included the 305- and 340-mm. guns, had already arranged and agreed to notify the Paris Defence Service of the firing of the Paris Gun at once, as the sound-rangers on the Front should detect its now well-known sound. Just what would or could be done with this information had not been decided. Since the amusing drum and whistle alarm of March 25, no alarm of any kind had been sounded, and it was felt long before the end of April that there was no need to sound a warning. It would avail nothing and could, and probably would, do harm.

There was no doubt but that the Vailly guns had been carefully and accurately spotted by German observers, for a veritable hail of heavy shells fell on and all about them. It requires an hour or two to get the 305's free of their steel-track foundations; not much time seemingly, but with the shells, gas, and high explosive falling on and all about the mounts, half of the crews were killed in the attempt to get them free, and then they failed. Had they got them free it would have been necessary to bring up a locomotive to pull them out, and without doubt that would have had its boiler punctured and in turn would have blown up. The men laboured valiantly, recklessly, but in vain. Finally they tried with sledge hammers, bars, anything made of iron and heavy, to damage the vital parts so that they would be useless when captured.

For the 340's there was no hope. Those carriages must be placed on heavy sub-track timber foundations, and the front and rear trucks removed. It required at least half a day under the most favourable conditions to remove one of them. So they were hammered up as thoroughly as the hail of exploding shells would permit. There were no thermite shells on hand, cans of powder aluminium, and iron with which the guns might have been destroyed very quickly and completely. No one had anticipated any necessity to destroy these guns to prevent their capture. From now on thermite shells would be a standard and carefully checked item of battery equipment for all heavy guns; when put in the gun-bore and ignited the mixture burns with such terrific heat as to melt and burn the steel and destroy the gun.

In Paris the rumble of the guns could be heard more distinctly than on March 21. It had an ominous sound, coming from the east. Though the Front had been quiet for a month, Parisians had not been made to expect an

THE SECOND BOMBARDMENT

Allied offensive; they knew, in fact, that they were not yet able to wage one. So this was another blow from Ludendorff. There was time to print in the earliest papers some slight news as to where the blow had been struck. It was between Soissons and Rheims, on the famous Chemin-des-Dames. But there were no details.

Hardly had the first of these papers appeared when, at exactly 6.30, there was an explosion in the Rue Cabanis, at the asylum of Sainte-Anne, three-quarters of a mile from the southern wall of the city—a projectile from the long-range gun. The first in twenty-seven days, and again without doubt a part of the programme of the offensive starting in the east; no one was hurt. At 6.45 another struck over the city, in Montrouge. A third burst at 7.9, far over the city in Fontenay-aux-Roses. That killed one. Five more followed in rather rapid succession, before 8.30. The eighth, which struck in the Rue Linné, killed two and wounded eleven pedestrians.

After an interval of an hour and twenty-one minutes, at 9.45, a projectile fell out in Montrouge; followed at short intervals by six more before 11.30. The eleventh projectile, which fell in the Rue du Montparnasse, south of the Luxembourg Gardens, wounded five people. The fifteen projectiles killed four and wounded twenty.

Hardly had the bombardment begun when men from the Municipal Laboratory and Artillery Headquarters began to visit the successive places struck to examine the damage, gather fragments, and observe new phenomena, if any. Long before noon it was determined that the projectiles were larger than those of March and April. It seemed they were about 9.45 inches in diameter, and so they were designated in the reports. The construction was different also. The rifled sections seemed slightly longer, and the base had been modified. The raised lip about the fuse hole in the base had been changed to have a cone shape with a base angle of about 30 degrees. Then the three rows

THE PARIS GUN

of projections about the bottoms of the grooves for the copper band had been changed; obviously to provide the bands with a better grip about the projectile. The copper bands had the same width as those of the previous projectiles. The number of grooves cut in the shell was the same as before, sixty-four. The conclusion in the Artillery office from all of this was that the original guns, which they had for some time believed, from considerable evidence, had been made by retubing 15-inch naval guns, had been rebored from 8.26 to 9.45 inches, and rifled with the original rifling tools. This could easily be done by providing merely a new and slightly larger rifling-head or tool-holder for the bits which cut the grooves.

The confusion amounting almost to a rout on the right of the French Sixth Army, within whose area the Vailly guns and many of the sound-ranging units had been located, made it impossible even to attempt observations on anything so minor at the time as the long-range gun. Their front, as that of the Third Army with its worn British divisions full of raw recruits, had crumpled as a house of cards in a gale. But on the left of the Sixth Army and the whole of the Tenth there was not the pressure of an offensive, and the sound-ranging units on the front of the Tenth Army in the centre, around Noyon in particular, were free to give attention to such matters. They were able to spot several shots before the end of the morning, and could even hear the sound of the firing at times between the continued cannonading to the east.

There was not necessarily an immediate indication in Paris that the gun location had been changed. A plotting of all the bursts at noon indicated a surprising state of affairs, however. It was the first time in the twenty-four individual days of bombardment that every single projectile had burst beyond the target. This could of course be by design, and perhaps it was. But it did not necessarily indicate a new gun position. The few shots spotted by the

THE 305-MM. RIFLE ON THE BATIGNOLLES RAILWAY CARRIAGE
The gun which began shelling position No. 1.

340-MM. RIFLE ON THE SAINT-CHAMOND RAILWAY CARRIAGE

THE SECOND BOMBARDMENT

Tenth Army rangers, however, came from the Bois de Corbie, south-east of Ham, and from a point approximately half a mile east of the roadside village of Beaumont-en-Beine and four and a half miles north-east of Guiscard. This information came into the Artillery office in Paris through Provins in the afternoon. Reference to the map showed this position to be about 68.75 miles from the target. There was no railway line near nor through that wood, but the line from Laon to La Fère on which the Crépy guns had been brought in passed on across the original front to a junction at Tergnier, thence north-west through Ham on its way to Amiens. If the Germans had run a branch from this line as far south as Beaumont they certainly had not shirked labour. The railway line skirted a wood for more than a mile at Mennessis, north of Tergnier, and if they were getting themselves away from the Vailly counter-battery guns, which must have been the only reason for the move, that wood would have been quite out of range and at the same time slightly closer to Paris. But the reasons for the selection of the Bois de Corbie would be discovered in time. Some 340's were promptly ordered up to Ribécourt on the Compiègne-Noyon railway to be emplaced in the wood to the west of the railway. At this point, which was about as close to the Noyon-Montdidier front as was safe, the range was sixteen miles, well within the range of these guns. Several days would be required to emplace them.

While the Parisians had been going about their business on this Monday morning with relative indifference to the bombardment, about which they could do nothing anyway, things were going disastrously to the east of Soissons. By six o'clock in the morning the most advanced German columns had climbed the sharp rise to the top of the formidable Craonne plateau, the famous Chemin-des-Dames, and were streaming down the gradual southern slope. To the east of the plateau they had met but little resistance, and their initial active front from Anizy east to Craonne, unit by unit, was literally running a race with itself for the first objective, the Aisne river. By noon the centre had gone half-way, a thing impossible had there been any real resistance. When one reckoned the advance by noon it was plain that the rate of progress was the rate at which soldiers, bearing heavy packs and for a time toiling along in gas-masks, could walk in fields, on roads, mopping up as they went. All opposition had been literally smothered under the terrific initial bombardment with the tremendous amount of gas sent over. Early in the morning the British divisions were crumpled in, even generals were killed, wounded, and captured, so complete was the surprise and so rapid the advance.

All along the line west past Noyon to Montdidier, and east past Rheims to Toul, the heavy bombardment which between Anizy and Craonne had switched to a barrage, continued hour after hour; one hour most violently with volumes of gas, then an hour of high explosive. This to give the pretence of a possible advance in those sectors and to prevent any hurried shifting of such reserves as might be back of those parts of the line. Even far up in the north at Ypres a bombardment was in progress, and local jabs were made at the line for purposes of diversion. The bombardment east and west was continued throughout the day and the entire night.

By noon the divisions that started at four o'clock in the morning had reached the Aisne at Vailly. By eight o'clock in the evening the centre had reached the Vesle at Fismes, and had crossed it just east of that city. Their entire front had surged forward from Coucy-le-Château, north of Soissons, to Courcy, north of Rheims. Still there was little if any opposition to their progress. Some of the bridges over the Vesle had not even been destroyed. And the roads south from all parts of the line were crowded with refugees, the most pathetic of war's victims; old men, women, children, all trying to escape and to save a few of their posses-

THE SECOND BOMBARDMENT

sions. Mingled with these were wounded soldiers, gassed, crippled, some displaying blood-soaked bandages, some hobbling on improvised crutches. A semblance of a rearguard covered the progress of this motley crew, going south.

The first shell of Tuesday, the 28th, burst at 5.40 in Bagneux, almost as far over the city as the farthest two shots of Monday. A second burst at 5.54 in the Place Saint-François-Xavier, south of the Invalides, in front of the church. A third fell at 6.4 in the Rue Cantagrel, in the thirteenth *arrondissement*, not far inside the city walls and a quarter of a mile from the river. There was an interval of three hours then before the fourth fell, in Bagneux, where the first had struck. There were no more until 12.10, noon, when one burst in the Terrace de l'Orangerie in the Tuileries Gardens; the first so far to fall north of the river. Curious performance, this, of the 9.45-inch gun, consistently over-shooting the target, or perhaps it was deliberate overshooting by the crew to give the people in the southern part of the city and outside a first-hand dose of artillery warfare. Assiduous solicitude on their part, perhaps for the complete education of the Parisians. Another followed in an hour, striking on the Quai de Jemmapes, not so far from the Gare de l'Est. The next, in nineteen minutes, fell in Pantin, short of the city. It seemed that the distribution was deliberate. It was hardly possible that a gun could have such a dispersion as to shoot a projectile far over into Bagneux and then, three shots later, one eight miles shorter, into Pantin. That would be a total dispersion in range of 12 per cent., something that just was not done by a proper member of the artillery family. And was not this the aristocrat of them all? No, it was certainly deliberate.

And then, beginning at 5.15, there fell a series of three, one far east of the city in Romainville, where two had fallen on April 6 and 13 respectively, one in the Rue Bisson, near the Boulevard de Belleville, close to the eastern wall, and the last at 5.53 in the Avenue Jean-Jaurès, just inside the walls in the north-east corner of the city. A most erratic bombardment, thought the artillerists who had plotted the locations of the ten successive bursts as they were telephoned in throughout the day. Two projectiles far over the city, two decidedly short and to the left of the target, and the remaining six all about the city. Both days' bombardments were unique.

The 340's ordered up to Ribécourt on Monday were reported as on the way. It might be several days before they could be got into position and ready for firing. Air observers had got over during the day, but only at such a height as to make clear observation almost impossible. The whole area about Corbie Wood was thoroughly organized by this time, and the distance in from the Tenth Army line was such as to make reconnaissance a most hazardous undertaking.

A Ray of Hope

Elsewhere other things had been happening. At 6.45 in the morning, at almost exactly the tip of the great Amiens salient, at the town of Cantigny, about three miles northwest of Montdidier, an American force went over the top for the first time in an offensive operation. An Allied offensive in the face of an offensive; primarily a morale tonic, one that was sadly needed. The 28th Infantry, with the 26th in support, executed the coup. In a brilliantly sharp and well-executed action they took the town, mopped it up thoroughly, and dug in beyond it. In spite of its quite limited extent, this offensive operation had a peculiar significance at this time that gave it a prominence that was decidedly out of proportion to its physical dimensions. The front was a mile and a quarter. There were about four thousand Americans engaged, including the support. The planned and accomplished gain in depth was but limited, something over half a mile. The significance and

THE SECOND BOMBARDMENT

heartening part of it was that it had been planned and carried out by the new recruits of the Allied armies, the Americans, at a time when the enemy was practically at the flood-tide of his successes. And they had done it with a dash, a finish of technique, and such a relentlessness of purpose, such a sharpness of accomplishment, that the action itself stamped them at once as possessing the qualities of first-class combat soldiers. Somehow, and perhaps it was not strange, the idea had been spread abroad in the previous months that the German armies were invincible, German strategy faultless, the German soldier irresistible.

The great German steam-roller Army, operating according to the Hutier plan, had simply rolled over the opposing forces as tanks over barbed wire. And this was the low tide of Allied reserves. They practically weren't. Great Britain was said to have a home army of a million men, but it was said also that the continuation of the Lloyd George administration in power depended on keeping that home army at home. Therefore they were not reserves ; the British Army had no reserves. Neither had the French. They had gone up the scale as far as they dared, down as far as they dared, had even cleaned out the diseased, the partially maimed, the Apaches from Paris, and had herded them into the line, had abandoned some of their heaviest artillery, had filled their shops with women, all to release men for the line and the reserves ; but even so they were drained dry. The Germans called it ' bled white.' So neither army had the slightest hope except in the Americans, who had not yet been tried out in offensive warfare.

It was true that during the March offensive American engineers at work on roads and railways behind Gough's Fifth Army had dropped their digging tools, had got into the fray with the retiring British regiments, and had not only acquitted themselves with credit, but had, with their exuberant enthusiasm, greatly heartened the sorely discouraged and battered Tommies. Infantry regiments had been in the

THE PARIS GUN

line, from Toul east, for a long time, almost all the winter, in fact, and were just now getting heavy punishment. Other units had been in reserve in numerous places, had even been brigaded with French and British regiments after General Pershing had put all American resources at General Foch's disposition on March 28, when the emergency seemed, and was, desperate. But in no case yet had they demonstrated what they could do under those circumstances when a staff must plan offensive movements down to the last detail; when all of the host of vastly different units of an offensive or aggressive fighting machine must take these plans and carry them out according to schedule; must execute the job sharply, with dash, confidence, with appreciation of, and at the same time contempt for, obstacles, difficulties; must finish it with a truly professional touch and a completeness that puts it without question in the past as a creditable accomplishment.

That was what the 28th Infantry did at 6.45, and that was why at this desperately discouraging time it meant so much more than an operation of that magnitude would ordinarily mean.

The details of that engagement, which by evening the Paris newspapers were beginning to play up even with headlines for the benefit of a discouraged populace, were quite simple. The 1st Division, a part of which executed this offensive, came to France in the previous June; a division largely of raw soldiers, not by any means prepared for service. They arrived wearing even the broad-brimmed southern campaign hats and canvas leggings. They had undergone rigorous training in base camps, and had been practically reclothed—short overcoats, wool uniforms, iron hats, hobnailed shoes, gas-masks. They had copied much from their Allies, but in most respects they had remained themselves. For example, the 'doughboys' did not believe in fighting in, nor from, trenches. Neither did their commander. Trenches were merely temporary shelters and not

THE SECOND BOMBARDMENT

ditches in which to live. So they kept up their training in open warfare. Then Americans had believed for more than a hundred years that a rifle was meant to be used in hitting a target and not merely as a handle for a bayonet. When American doughboys and officers were told that soldiers on either side walked about in relative safety a hundred yards or more behind the front trenches they could not understand it and doubted if it were true. The rifle range of any American camp is a noisy place all day long, and there were no finer rifles in the world than American-made rifles. Added to the natural result of those two was the fact that practically every boy in the American Army had owned a rifle of some sort, air or 22-calibre, or both, during at least half of his twenty years, and his marksmanship had always been a matter of pride to him. Thus, though he had so much to learn to become a veteran soldier, in one respect he would always excel, in the use of a rifle. And the certainty of his ability to defend himself with this instrument, the knowledge that he had a good rifle, could always hit a man at a hundred yards, and four out of five times at two and three hundred, made of him a soldier quite certain that he could take care of himself, could take what he was ordered to take, and could then hold it. But French and British staffs weren't sure of this. In fact, they did not believe that marksmanship with hand-rifles had much to do with success in war.

In January the 1st Division had gone into the line north of Toul. The Germans discovered them quickly and gave them little rest; shelled them continuously, raided them repeatedly. But Germans did not come above ground near the line in that sector while the 1st was there. The few who did were promptly shot.

The 1st Division was relieved at Toul on April 1 by the 26th, and moved round to Chaumont-en-Vexin, north-east of Paris, for a hasty and belated training in open warfare. It left here on the 17th to replace the

THE PARIS GUN

162nd French Division on a front of about three kilometres in the Cantigny sector of the French First Army. It finished taking over the sector on April 25. Here it had an excellent opportunity to employ all it had learned about defensive warfare, for all about this great salient the Front popped, sputtered, and boiled as an angry volcano threatening to blow up again at any moment. The Germans harassed the Americans night and day with artillery fire of all calibres, and trench-raiding was frequent and formidable. Soon the Americans were as proficient in raiding as the Germans. They learned that they had before them, among others, the 271st and 272nd German infantry regiments whose companies averaged 160 men each.

The American position was not easy to hold. It seemed better to advance and take from the Germans some strong positions on higher ground. This would deprive the Germans of an advantageous jumping-off place in any new offensive toward Amiens, would ease the pressure on the Americans at this point, and would make easier an Allied offensive here if one could be undertaken.

The 28th Infantry under Colonel Ely, one battalion of the 26th Infantry under Major Theodore Roosevelt, Jr., for support, and detachments of French tanks and flame-throwers were assigned to the job. The most careful and elaborate plans were worked out and even rehearsed in anticipation of the event. Trenches similar in plan to those occupied by the Germans in the little town that had been Cantigny on the higher ground were laid out in the rear of the lines. Sand-tables showing the topography, woods, objectives, strong points, houses in Cantigny that might possibly serve later as American machine-gun shelters, were prepared and laboriously studied. The most exact plans and orders were made to cover every minute detail, time-tables for the bombardment, and rolling barrage. Then for three successive days in the previous week the 28th Infantry rehearsed the assault in detail upon the

THE SECOND BOMBARDMENT

prepared terrain to the rear, till every officer and man knew perfectly the part which he was to perform, the route by which he was to advance, and the exact objectives which he was to reach.

On completion of this training every company commander with a second company officer and two non-commissioned officers made a daylight reconnaissance to compare the actual terrain with the ground on which they had been rehearsing, and to select the visible objectives on which to concentrate when the assault began.

Then the night before the day set for the final preparations and the assault arrived. But meanwhile, on Monday morning at one o'clock, another storm had broken; the Germans had begun another great offensive. This became known during the day, but there seemed no reason why it should interfere with the 1st Division's plans. They had set 'zero' or 'H' hour for 5.30 A.M., Tuesday, May 28, and that it would remain. The 38th Infantry and the battalion from the 26th entrucked for the front lines at 12.30 and by 3 A.M. were practically all in position in their jumping-off trenches. Twelve French tanks were on hand, French flame-throwers to mop up the cellars, French 'planes for reconnaissance, a detachment of American engineers for pioneer work on roads and trenches. For the preliminary bombardment and barrages there were about 250 pieces of artillery, both American and French, ranging from the 75- up to the 280-mm. Each man of the assault companies, all in line by 4.57, was equipped with his shelter-half, rifle, 220 cartridges, two hand-grenades, a rifle-grenade, a flare, sandbags, two days' rations, two canteens of water, and a pick or shovel.

Promptly at 5.30 the 250 guns opened up on Cantigny with a roar. The walls yet standing crumpled quickly. This was continued for an hour, and at 6.30, when the gunners suddenly pulled back their line of fire to the initial line of the rolling barrage the Germans in the area had been reduced to the same state of paralysis to which they had reduced the French and British to the east twenty hours before.

The infantry went over behind the barrage which lifted a hundred yards every two minutes; they remained as close as fifty yards to the barrage. The enemy was completely bewildered in face of the tanks, the bayonets, for which they traditionally ' had no stomach,' and the flame-throwers. Most of them did the only thing left them; they surrendered, in groups and singly. The few who showed fight were shot. Two hundred and seventy-five dead were counted. In an incredibly short time, less than thirty minutes in many places, the objectives beyond Cantigny were reached, most of the town had been mopped up, and the temporary victors faced the really difficult job of consolidating and holding what they had gained. They began to dig in promptly.

When the companies of the 28th had gained their objectives and began to dig in, a situation had developed that in certain of its aspects was comic, very funny, though neither of the combatants in the duel saw anything funny about it; decidedly not. It was tragically serious to both. First, the American division had carried out an order perfectly. The order had directed them to gain certain terrain, some important high ground, and the point of the salient. But the order had a bigger purpose than that. It was to learn what the untried American staffs and soldiers would do on the offensive at this time in their period of training. There was a lively possibility, one might even say a certainty, that the ability of the Allies to last through 1918 would depend on the Americans; that much would depend on them in defensive warfare alone. There could be no thought of any large offensive except on the strength of a seemingly absurd number of American divisions; not dozens, but scores, perhaps hundreds. And they would have to be tried out in an independent offensive operation

THE SECOND BOMBARDMENT

somewhere some time. This was the somewhere and some time. The Americans sensed that. So when they went over at 6.30 and had dug in by 7.30 they had bitten off a chunk that they dared not spit out. It had to be chewed and swallowed. They had to keep what they had taken, no matter how difficult it might prove. The taking had been easy, less than a hundred casualties. But the holding proved terrible.

Then, on the other side, the Germans had a problem. They were staking all on winning this summer. It was now or not at all. It had been advertised in the German Army and all over Germany that the submarines were preventing the Americans from getting over. " They were not in France in sufficient numbers to count. Those in France were raw, unequipped, unfit for any except easy defence sectors." All propaganda, of course, but most necessary propaganda. Germans at home and in the field were as sick of the War as were the Allies. They were kept at the terrible job only by the assurance that this time they would certainly win. There must be no gloomy aspects to that rosy picture. That, translated into front-line language, meant that if the Americans were put into any Allied offensive or tried one by themselves they were to be dealt with promptly, harshly, and so completely as to make good the assertion that Americans did not count, either in quality or quantity. At 7.30 the Americans were furiously consolidating shell-holes, shallow communicating trenches, and stringing barbed wire in front to hold something which they had to hold and which the Germans did not dare let them keep. A fine promise of a nasty squabble over a relatively unimportant bit of terrain.

Under a veritable hail of shells, machine-gun and rifle bullets, the consolidation went on. The third American assault wave behind was busy under as great difficulties in consolidating three points, one in the wood, 200 yards east of what had been the town, one in the wood north-east of it, and the third in the cemetery of the town. Each was garrisoned with a platoon of infantry provided with automatic rifles. Telephone wires were strung, and cut by shell-fire almost before they were working. One American sergeant successfully wriggled over the top so many times to repair cut lines that the Germans, who at a distance could see him through their glasses, gave him the name of the " Black Snake of Cantigny."

Just two hours after the town was captured the Germans' first counter-attack was seen coming over from the Alval Wood. They followed a barrage, the accuracy of which was carefully checked by their airmen. But they made the mistake of staying nearly 200 yards behind it; the Americans had been only fifty behind theirs; dangerously close, but worth the risk. So when the barrage had passed over the American line there was plenty of time for all not too seriously wounded to size up the situation and act in concert. It takes an appreciable amount of time for a man to walk a hundred yards. When the German assault line was a hundred yards away, at least a minute since the barrage passed over, the Americans opened fire in a single burst. Automatic rifle-fire that was moderately accurate and hand rifle-fire that was deadly. Hardly a man pulled a trigger but he brought down his advancing German. In a flash almost five hundred Germans were down, killed or wounded, and those unhurt were fleeing toward Framecourt Wood.

This was the first of seven such assaults made in forty-eight hours, in the same manner, with the same result. And during all of that time the Germans shelled Cantigny and all about it so violently with gas, high explosive, and shrapnel that in the end practically every man of the regiment was a casualty; many serious, some not so serious. At the end of this time the Germans were in another predicament. In the beginning they had not dared permit the Americans to keep the gain. After seven unsuccessful

THE SECOND BOMBARDMENT

attempts to retake it, after shelling the area so furiously that from the air it looked like one of those pock-marked pictures of the moon as it appears through a great telescope, they dared not continue their counter-attacks for fear of additional bad effect on morale if they should continue to fail. Seven failures were already too many.

On the American side, despite the terrific casualties, the effect was of incalculable value, not only to the 1st Division, but to all American divisions and to their Allies. Stock in the American Army went up like a rocket. They were even at this stage of their training first-class shock troops. Too reckless, perhaps, but the almost unlimited supply of them compensated for this. General Foch at this desperate time saw from the demonstration, and several more soon to come, some hope shining through the gloom that the Allies could hold out through 1918. The gloomy Parisians got from this local success the only cheer that could counteract the disheartening pictures drawn by the refugees swarming in on trains from the east.

In the eastern theatre the situation was desperately discouraging. By the time darkness had fallen on Monday night the Germans had taken the Aisne bridges, crossed the river, and reached the Vesle at Fismes. Early Tuesday morning they were pressing south on a still more extended front both east and west. In the centre they were encountering no resistance worth mentioning. Before noon they had crossed the Vesle as far west as Braisne. By evening they were on the very edge of Soissons, and were closing in on Rheims. In the centre they were south of Mont-Notre-Dame and Saint-Giles and straddled the Vesle at Jonchery-sur-Vesle.

Concern over the situation was approaching hysteria in Paris. The papers, *communiqués*, were making the very best of it, but the gravity of the crisis could not be concealed. Paris paid but little attention to the offensive on Monday. A fatalistic belief seemed to prevail since the checking of

THE PARIS GUN

the March and April offensives that somehow the Germans could be held until the Americans were over in sufficient force to turn the tide. But it was obvious on Tuesday that what amounted to a break-through had been achieved.

A break-through it practically was. The German Army had made two trials of the Hutier plan, the whole great human machine was thoroughly organized for and accustomed to it, their man-power was at its height, while that of their opponents was at its bottom. And though Ludendorff had not expected it, he had caught the Allies entirely unprepared on this front. Their artillery preparation had been almost perfect, and their execution of the advance hardly less perfect. On Tuesday evening they literally had no opposition before them. Every road south of the area was choked with refugees. Trains had been bringing hundreds of them into Paris all day, other trains were hauling them more directly south, away from the Paris zone. They were not desired in Paris. The problem there was already sufficiently complicated. Very soon the vitally important Paris-Château Thierry-Épernay-Châlons railway, following the Marne river, would be under heavy artillery fire; communications would be broken. The German line at Mont-Notre-Dame was already within heavy-gun range of this railway.

Though they could do but little, perhaps nothing, to dam the flood in the centre, Generals Foch and Pétain were beginning to take vigorous steps to make the German gain as precarious, as difficult to hold, and as dangerous as possible for those who would try to hold it. It had been concluded on both sides that the War was not going to be won by the mere accident or hard-won accomplishment of a break-through. Modern armies tear up things too thoroughly on the starting of an offensive to permit any but the infantry to move with anything like concerted speed. The whole machine does not move; the Front runs entirely out of touch with its supplies in its eagerness, in the

THE SECOND BOMBARDMENT

practical necessity, to get forward quickly. Being composed of human beings, the Front then has its limit of endurance. Replacements stream after those on the Front, roads are choked with men, just men going and coming; and in the confusion, the gradual organizing of the supply system under these new conditions, respite is given the enemy, if he has any reserves, gradually to narrow the advancing front, cover the gap, and finally the force of the wave is spent. The problem of supply is so much easier for those on the defensive; they simply use an existing system. If they must retire, they do so toward, into, and through the supplies at their second and third lines of defence.

The most serious concern of Generals Foch and Pétain was therefore not over the rapid advance of the German front, no matter what alarming significance it might and did have to the public, to the capital, which saw the German Army advancing on it as in 1914. They were vitally concerned and feverishly active in executing that old tactic of stabilized warfare, of keeping the corners past which the advancing armies were streaming from melting away as the earth on the edges of a break in the banks of a river. If they could make the original corners 'stay put,' or nearly so, then the Front might take care of itself.

The first projectile from the Paris Gun on Wednesday morning, the 29th, burst at 6.25, in the Rue du Bac, south of the river, not far from the Boulevard Raspail. In fourteen minutes another burst between this and the Invalides in the Rue Barbet-de-Jouy. One person was wounded here. These two bursts were not a quarter of a mile apart. Coming so close, both in time and distance, they added to the alarm of the news in the morning papers and caused people in that region more than unusual concern. The second projectile of Tuesday, at 5.54, had burst at a point quite close to the second of this morning.

There were no more shells until the afternoon, when two fell; one at 1.30 in the Rue de Vaugirard, a mile and a quarter from the second in the morning and not far from the southern wall of the city; the other at 1.50 in the Rue de Berri, just off the Boulevard Haussmann, on the north side of the river. One person was wounded by the projectile that fell at 1.30. There were relatively few fatalities from the shells of these few days, but damage to property constantly: a roof blown off here, the fronts of several rooms blown out in a building, a small shop demolished, the machinery in a factory bent and broken. The damage was not by any means comparable to that wrought by the fewer number of air bombs.

The morning papers contained an interesting mixture of news. They played up the American success at Cantigny more fully and elaborately than those of the previous evening. They did not hesitate to exaggerate. They presented the best possible light on the desperately serious situation on the Sixth and Third Army fronts, between Soissons and Rheims. " The French regiments are retiring in good order. . . . The Front is intact. . . . Reinforcements are being rushed to the scene. . . . Refugees are being taken care of. . . . Few prisoners have been taken by the Germans." But rumours that counteracted this optimism were spreading. Refugees exaggerated the gravity of the situation, if anything. And a rumour of danger always gathers more alarming details as it is passed on. The people of Paris were becoming genuinely alarmed. There was already some talk of moving certain activities away from the city. People were not working efficiently. Every one knew that the official news had been drastically censored, so what was one to believe? The papers said that the situation was in hand, there was nothing to be alarmed about; rumours, which are so enticing, said the opposite. And the long-range gun kept pounding away, the sirens screeched out their alarms night after night, sometimes more than once. It was no wonder that people were getting out of the city as though a pestilence prevailed.

THE SECOND BOMBARDMENT

The afternoon was free of shells from 1.50 to 6.20. Then there was a fairly rapid succession of eight. The first fell short of the city, in Pantin. After fourteen minutes another burst half a mile from the target, on the north side of the river. It killed one person. At nine o'clock one struck entirely over the city in Montrouge. These three made a veritable procession in seven-league boots. After forty minutes' silence one fell in the Avenue de la République. In fourteen minutes another burst in Châtillon, a six-mile jump. The next, at 8.7, struck in Montrouge, over the city, but not quite so far. Another burst in Montrouge eleven minutes later; three for them during the day. At 8.24 the last shell fell in Châtillon. It wounded five. Four shells in succession had struck beyond the city.

Information was received in the Artillery office that the 340's had arrived at Ribécourt by way of Compiègne, and that all possible speed was being made in getting them emplaced. Even working continuously under the most favourable conditions, such a mount cannot be made ready for action in less than two days, and sometimes it may require four or five. There was every incentive to speed in this case. No one could tell when this portion of the Front might become active again; it was expected soon. American Headquarters had just reported to General Herr's office that five 14-inch railway carriages were on the way over, and that these guns had a range of 22.8 miles. It would be possible to shell the Cugny or Beaumont position with those guns, therefore, from any point of the Compiègne-Noyon railway south to the city of Compiègne itself; and likewise from any position on the east and west Compiègne-Soissons railway including Compiègne and Soissons.

On the night of the 28th when the advancing German line reached and passed the Vesle from its junction with the Aisne west of Vailly, east past Fismes to Jonchery, the French machine-gun units which were maintaining the rear-guard action thought they detected signs of a halt of the

THE PARIS GUN

German divisions. They concluded on Wednesday morning, however, that they had been mistaken, for the entire German line was on the move again; slowly at first, but soon with greater speed than the day before. The Soissons and Rheims corners which had been held so stubbornly by the French began to crumble before the violent efforts of the German infantry and artillery. Before evening Soissons changed hands. Rheims was in grave danger; the Germans were easily within sight of it. The German line had advanced during the day on a front of sixty miles to a maximum depth of ten miles in the centre where they were within four miles of the Marne by evening. They had captured three hundred additional square miles of valuable terrain, more than a thousand square miles in three days. Almost all of the Allied effort, resistance, was being applied to hold the Soissons and Rheims corners. But the question of the centre was becoming both alarming and acute. It had to be stopped somewhere; for if the Germans could widen the salient sufficiently, those French and British units so tenaciously holding the corners would find themselves in intolerable salients and would have to retire, thereby giving the Germans just what they wanted—a great hump of a salient without dangerous indentations. General Maud'huy on the west with his Eleventh Corps was holding well in spite of terrible punishment and terrific pressure. The reserves most readily available for stopping the centre were Americans. The 1st Division was already in line at Montdidier and busy, so probably the 2nd and 3rd would have to be called upon. Some of these might have to come in on the western side too, to prevent the Germans from widening their front and pinching off Maud'huy's Corps at the Soissons Corner.

On Thursday, the 30th, the Paris Gun commander repeated his plan of Sunday, April 14. The first shell burst out in Pantin at 2.40 A.M. There were no more then until 7.4, when the first of a group of four fell practically at the

Pavement inside the Pillars at the Rear of the Madeleine

Tunnel beneath the Pavement at the Rear of the Madeleine

Hole through the Pavement of the Madeleine opening into the Tunnel beneath

THE SECOND BOMBARDMENT

corner of the Passage Miollis and the Boulevard Garibaldi. As had been almost invariably the case when a shell burst at such a time of the day and near a Métro station, this one caught a crowd of people on their way to work. It killed eight and wounded two. The next three, at 7.20, 8.34, and 8.58, did not even wound anyone. The second of the group, or third of the day, fell over the city in Kremlin-Bicêtre in the garden of the city hall. The next, number four, fell just inside the walls in that region, and number five, the last, passed over the city and burst nearly four miles west of number three. There were no more then for twelve hours. At 8 P.M. exactly the sixth for the day burst only a quarter of a mile from the last in the morning, in Issy-les-Moulineaux; the seventh, at 8.20, a mile from this, in Vanves; the eighth, at 8.39, in the Avenue de Breteuil, south of the Invalides. It caught another crowd on the pavements, killing four and wounding two. A fragment of this shell bore the designation, 68•: shell No. 68 of Series 1 of the larger projectiles for rebored guns.

The ninth and last for the day struck the Madeleine. It passed between two of the pillars at the rear, struck the pavement about midway between the pillars and the church wall, and exploded instantly. A fragment struck and broke off the head of a figure of St Luke in a niche in the wall. The force of the 273-pound projectile striking the pavement at a velocity of 2200 feet per second and the force of the instantaneous explosion broke and blew a hole through the stone pavement and roof of the brick tunnel beneath. Fragments scarred the walls and pillars, but fortunately there were no casualties. It produced considerable excitement in that crowded locality, however, the large square in front, with the bus and Métro stations in the Boulevard de la Madeleine. This was always a busy place. A fragment of this shell bore the number 41•.

The plotting of the bursts for the day gave the artillerists more food for thought. At the end of the day forty-six of the larger projectiles had fallen in and about the city, all presumably from one gun. From examination of the shell fragments brought into the Municipal Laboratory and Artillery offices it appeared that the lands of the gun were hardly half as badly worn from the forty-six shells as were those of the last 210-mm. gun used in April, when the gun had fired forty-eight rounds. The extreme life of each of the guns that had fired from Crépy had been about fifty rounds. It was obvious that those guns had been worked at the absolute limit of endurance of metal, the steel of the gun, and almost if not beyond the limit of reliability of powder as to rate of burning and consequent pressures. The 9.45-inch cannon was operating more as a cannon should. The battery surely had much better control over the shooting; the wear was materially reduced. Prisoners had reported that the Crépy guns had an extreme range of eighty miles. Whatever the Germans had done to get that range, obviously they had reached the limits possible from present-time human ingenuity and known powders.

It was quite plain then why the Germans had moved their gun. The reduction in range seemed so insignificant, from 75 to 68.3 miles. But that slight reduction, together with the reboring of the gun to a slightly larger size, had apparently doubled the life in rounds that could be fired. When they moved they had also got away from the Vailly guns, which, by the way, would not have troubled them since those guns were taken on Monday, the first day of the new offensive. Perhaps they knew when they stopped on May 1 where the next offensive would begin, and had had no thought of the Vailly guns in their move.

The battery commander of the 340's at Ribécourt reported that the guns were about ready; they surely would be on Friday.

The situation on the front between Soissons and Rheims had become desperate, and threatened to become worse. The Germans had swept to the Marne during the day, and

THE SECOND BOMBARDMENT

by evening they held the northern bank from Brasle just outside Château-Thierry east for six miles to Jaulgonne, at the tip of the second sharp north bend of the river. The Paris-Nancy railway was cut; a serious blow to the transportation system feeding supplies to that front. So desperate had the situation become for the Allies even by midday that more reserves had to be called upon to help dam the centre

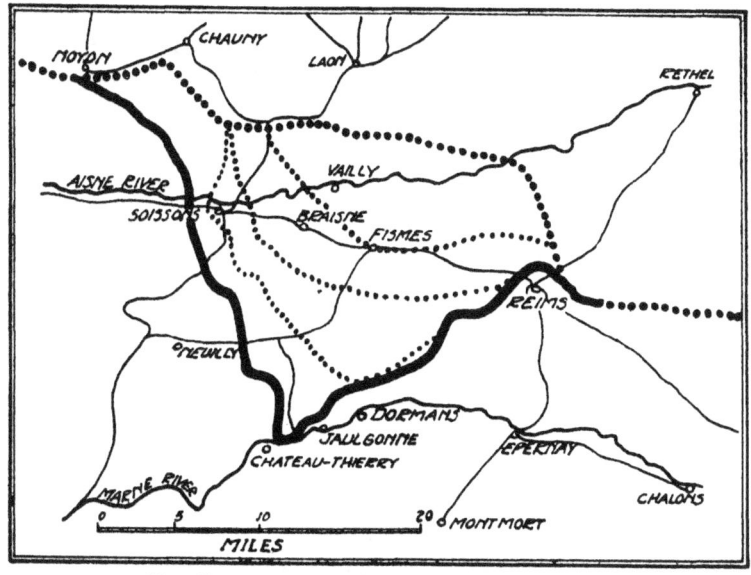

THE FRONT ON THE EVENING OF MAY 30, 1918

and hold the divisions that were expected to begin at any hour a furious attack on the western wall of the salient to compel the French divisions holding on to the Soissons Corner to retire. The line west of Anizy broke down as far as Noyon, though at Soissons but little further advance was made.

The 2nd American Division was just finishing its celebration of American Memorial Day at its camp at Chaumont-en-Vexin, in the region of Beauvais, north-west of Paris, when General Bundy received an order from General Foch directing him to entrain the division at once and proceed to the region of Château-Thierry. The entire division was *en route* by night.

The 3rd Division was far to the south-east of Château-Thierry, 112 miles, at Châteauvillain and La Ferté-sur-Aube, a short distance to the south-west of Chaumont, the American Headquarters. General Dickman, commanding the 3rd, received orders at about the same time as General Bundy to hasten to the Marne at Château-Thierry. The orders were more complicated than those of the 2nd, however. The 5th Infantry Brigade (General Sladen), consisting of the 4th and 7th Infantry and the 8th Machine-gun Battalion, was to be attached to General Degoutte's Sixth French Army, and they were assigned to the passages of the Marne from Château-Thierry east to Dormans. The 6th Infantry Brigade (General Crawford), composed for the emergency of the 38th Infantry and half the 9th Machine-gun Battalion, was assigned to hold the Marne passages from Dormans east to Damerie under General Marchand, 10th Colonial Division of the Fifth French Army. The remainder of the 6th Brigade, the 30th Infantry, and half the 9th Machine-gun Battalion were assigned to the support of the 5th Brigade at Château-Thierry. The remaining unit of the division, the 7th Machine-gun Battalion, was ordered to entrain at once for Château-Thierry. The other units would entrain the next day. The machine-gun battalion was *en route* by evening.

The shell which burst at the back of the Madeleine at 8.59 was not to be the end of the day for the Parisians. At 11.30 the sirens started their screeching, and people sought shelter at once. It proved to be another real raid. Six 'planes had been detected crossing the lines. In the next hour, despite the furious barrage put up by the anti-aircraft guns, they succeeded in dropping six bombs on the city. One of them, a 660-pound bomb, set the whole city vibrating. The deepest cellar does not prevent one from hearing and feeling the explosion of such a bomb. Another

THE SECOND BOMBARDMENT

of the six weighed 220 pounds. The remaining four were 22-pound bombs. The " All's well " was sounded by one o'clock, and the weary, harassed Parisians went back to their beds for a few hours of sleep before the next day's work and inevitable bombardment by cannon should begin.

May 31

The first shell of Friday, the 31st, which burst far out in Dugny, along the Chemin de Gonesse, at 8.10, was not heard in Paris proper. A fortunate circumstance for the sorely tried populace. The news in the morning papers was sufficiently alarming. " German infantry have reached the Marne." A repetition of 1914. The grey horde had been turned back then by Foch's brilliant lunge through the centre and Joffre's great attack in the west by the army rushed thither from within and all about Paris in every imaginable conveyance. Where was the army, the reserves, that could repeat that now? The papers tried to be optimistic, but when it was admitted that the Germans had advanced from the Chemin-des-Dames to the Marne in four days optimism sounded cheap; it had a false ring. It was so thin a veneer over the really gloomy situation as to have just the reverse of the intended effect. One doubted everything printed. If the Germans were at the Marne, what was to prevent them from encircling the French armies between Soissons and Paris and advancing on Paris itself?

The second projectile fell in Aubervilliers at 8.45. The third struck in the same district at 9.40, and not more than a quarter of a mile away. The next fell at La Courneuve, between Aubervilliers and Dugny, at 10.25. There were no more then till 1.28, when the fifth burst just inside the walls in the extreme north-east point of the city. This was the only explosion that was heard by any considerable number of the people within the city. The sixth and last burst in Le Bourget, on the Paris-Compiègne road, at 1.47. It was almost as far short as the first. The artillerists who were following the bombardment were greatly puzzled to comprehend the reason for the totally different performances for this day and the day before. There was no evidence to be found on the fragments of projectiles of the day, the tell-tale grooves in the copper bands, to indicate why the six projectiles had fallen not only short of the target, but five of them short, and far. short, of the city itself. On Thursday seven of the nine projectiles fell over the target, four entirely over the city. The only reasonable explanation seemed to be that the battery commander had deliberately reduced the powder-charges to undershoot the target and scatter the projectiles about more. The majority of the projectiles since May 27 had fallen over the target. It did not seem reasonable that the gun which had been so consistently overshooting should all at once without intention on the part of the battery commander consistently undershoot, and so far under.

Not a single casualty from bursting projectiles was reported during the day. Experience in April had shown that this was apt to be the case when projectiles consistently fell so far short of the city in the less densely crowded districts. There had been eight such days to date, six in the first bombardment prior to May 1, and May 30 and 31 of the second bombardment.

The first of the 340-mm. French railway-guns moved up to Ribécourt got into action during the day and fired regularly on the mean point indicated by the records of the sound-rangers. The Sound-Ranging Section No. 10 had already secured observations on six shots. The instruments of this unit were well located only 13.7 miles from the supposed gun position and were well oriented. Sound-Ranging Section No. 8 had secured observations on ten shots, but this section was more than 15.5 miles from the supposed gun position, and was not well located for

THE SECOND BOMBARDMENT

observation. The various points located by them were so much more dispersed than those of Section No. 10, probably as a result of their more unfavourable location. It seemed best to use the mean point located by Section 10. A second 340 was due to get into action on Saturday.

The German armies of the Crown Prince began the expected attack on the western walls of the great salient during the day in an attempt to break down or encircle the Soissons Corner. So great was the pressure that the French divisions were compelled to retire all along the line from Soissons to the Marne. The reduced depth of gain, however, as compared with that of the day before, gave evidence both of the spent condition of the German troops and of the desperate efforts of the French to hold. The Germans got as far as the edge of the Villers-Cotterets Wood. They made no further gains on the Marne except at Château-Thierry, where they took the section of that city north of the river.

The 7th Machine-Gun Battalion of the American 3rd Division, which entrained on Friday afternoon from Châteauvillain, had travelled most of the 112 miles by Saturday afternoon and had detrained on the roads south of Château-Thierry. In spite of the fact that they had travelled thirty-six hours without sleep, they made a forced march of the remaining distance at once, and when they plodded into Château-Thierry at six o'clock they walked into German shells already bursting in the part of the city south of the river. The weary French troops were struggling with the advancing Germans in the streets of the northern section of the town. The Americans hastily found positions for their guns which would enable them to sweep the main bridge in the centre of the town and the river-banks up and down stream. One gun crew crossed to the northern side of the river and found an advantageous position that would enable them to cover the retirement of the French across the bridge. During the night the greater number of the French infantrymen passed across the bridge and through the American lines. Several hundred remained on the north side, however, to help oppose the German advance to the bridge as long as possible.

The infantry of the American 2nd Division, travelling by trucks since 5 A.M., reached Meaux late in the afternoon. The artillery was following by rail. The infantry was ordered to May-en-Multien, seven miles north-east of Meaux, and from there it began a march at midnight to Montreuil-aux-Lions, about six miles west of Château-Thierry on the Paris road, where they arrived, greatly exhausted, soon after dawn. This would be, for the time, their headquarters. The artillery had reached Cocherel, several miles to the west. The division was to remain intact, not to be parcelled out as had been the 3rd, south of the Marne.

Though the Parisians had been spared danger and alarm from the day's cannon bombardment, they were not to get off entirely. Six 'planes were detected crossing the lines, and the alarm sounded by the sirens shortly after ten o'clock. They did not reach Paris, however, and in an hour the retreat was sounded. Again after midnight more 'planes crossed the lines, apparently making for Paris, and the sirens screeched out a second alarm. The second raid failed to materialize also, and the final " All's well " of the night was sounded about 3 A.M. on Saturday.

June 1

To most Parisians, arising after a night of relatively little sleep because of the two raid alarms, Saturday was just another day of anxiety over a situation in the east that they could not fully understand because of the strict censorship on details. Those who presumed to know more than others said they had heard that the German armies were well-nigh within heavy field-gun range of the capital. A little

THE SECOND BOMBARDMENT

further advance and heavy 15-inch shells such as had been falling in Dunkirk for three years would be bursting in Paris. The papers of the morning were no more specific, no more encouraging, than on Friday. Optimistic, of course, but not encouraging. They said that more American divisions were in or going into the line about Château-Thierry.

Fortunately for some of the Parisians, those within the city walls, the bombardment had taken such a turn as to cause them less concern, less anxiety. But those living in the suburbs were anything but comforted. At 6.50 a shell burst in La Courneuve, near the Bernard factory. At 7.30 a second burst closer to the city, in the Rue du Fort, in Aubervilliers; at 9.45 a third, in Aubervilliers. Then at 10.6 one burst far out in the region of Bonneuil, but near the Paris-Compiègne highway. Except for the projectile which fell only a minute after midnight on the morning of April 14, slightly farther north, near Gonesse, this fell the farthest short of any of the entire bombardment, seven miles short of the target and four short of the city.

At 10.25 the fifth shell burst, in Pantin, much closer to the walls, but still outside. There was an interval of two hours then before another burst in La Courneuve. In all this time not one person had been killed or injured. Twenty-two minutes later, at 12.57, the seventh burst in Dugny, farther short of the city than the previous. This was the end of the bombardment for seven hours. The eighth and last projectile for the day fell in La Counreuve at 9.25. Three in La Courneuve for the day. The people of that suburb were reminded by these of the series of explosions in the hand-grenade factories there early in March, with which explosions people mistakenly associated the bursting of the first few shells on March 23.

The artillerists were more puzzled than ever. The grooves in the copper bands of the fragments gathered during the day indicated clearly that the gun was yet possibly thirty or more rounds from the end of its life.

THE PARIS GUN

But every projectile had fallen so far short of the target that there could be no thought of deliberate undershooting. No battery commander would waste so valuable a gun in bombarding market-gardens, far outlying suburbs, villages, if he could send his projectiles into the densely populated section of the city. It began to look as though the rebored gun did not have an appreciably greater accuracy life than the 8.26-inch gun from which it had been made. It looked also as though they had not been able to rebore more than one gun so far. If they had a spare gun it was felt that they would certainly have begun installing it on Friday. Perhaps they would yet replace this one in a day or so.

While the north-east suburbs of Paris were being bombarded during the day, the Germans were consolidating heavily on the north bank of the Marne from Château-Thierry to Jaulgonne. During the night of the 31st most of the French soldiers in the section of Château-Thierry north of the river had retired across the bridge and into the American lines on the south side. For the first time in five weary, crazy, nightmare days they found themselves retiring into a line of fresh reserves. They could drop anywhere and sleep. The Americans needed sleep badly enough, but not so badly as the French soldiers. Several hundred French troops remained north of the river, in contact with the bridge which the Germans were most careful not to damage in their shelling. These French troops with the American machine-gun unit that crossed the bridge the night before held the approaches to the bridge all day long, keeping the streets clear with their machine-guns and automatic rifles. By evening, however, they began to suffer severely from German snipers, and as soon as it became dark most of them retired across the bridge and took up positions on the south side. Shortly after the defenders on the north bank had crossed the bridge French engineers blew up the north two spans. So close were the Germans on the heels of the French and Americans that some of them were

THE SECOND BOMBARDMENT

on the bridge when it was blown up. The machine-gun unit that had not got across the bridge managed to cross the river in the early morning under the protecting fire of those on the south bank. All of the other units of the 7th Battalion were engaged practically every minute of the day in preventing any headway on the part of the enemy in preparing to cross the river. They were under intense shell-fire all day long, had been all of the night before. Apparently the enemy meant to get across.

French reserves were pouring into the corners at Soissons and Rheims all day long. Generals Foch and Pétain had also been strengthening with any other available reserves the western wall of the salient which had been pushed back all along its length on Friday. The Germans were in sight of the northern gate of Rheims, on the Laon highway, when a regiment of colonial troops arrived to help check them. The French trenches circled the very edge of the city. The line on the south of the Marne was still comparatively thinly held, and, had it not been for the natural advantage of the river and its banks to that thin Allied line, the Germans would have been across it already. And unless the remainder of the American 3rd Division arrived during the night or early on Sunday morning it was doubtful if the enemy, who would be in greater force and better equipped by Sunday, could be held. The 2nd Division had been taking up its positions all day long. Since there were no established positions, the division was instructed to dig in on a designated line to hold against the first shock of an inevitable determined attack from the east or north. The 9th Infantry on the right of that division had got into position from west of Bonneuil, near the Marne, through Le Thiolet, on the Paris-Metz road, and for a distance north of that road and on the eastern edge of the Bois de Clerebauts. From here the 6th Marines held the line to Lucy-le-Bocage, the 5th Marines to Marigny, and the 23rd Infantry, temporarily under the 43rd French Division, continued the line to the

THE PARIS GUN

Bois de Neuilly. This position was about eight miles long
and faced toward the north-east. Forward from this line
lay the slopes and crests of a ridge of hills, some of them
heavily wooded, descending to the valley of a little creek,
the Ru Gobert, along which were scattered the villages of
Bouresches, Belleau, Torcy, and Bussiares. On the other
side of this creek the hills rose more sharply. The Germans
were already in possession of them, and their artillery
farther to the rear was already sweeping the 2nd Division positions with heavy high explosive and gas. The
164th French Division was between the right of the
2nd and Château-Thierry, where the line of the 3rd
began. The 43rd French Division was still holding the
line of the Ru Gobert before the left of the 2nd Division, intending to retire from its untenable position through
the Americans as soon as they had got themselves well
entrenched.

The entire situation was regarded everywhere as intensely
critical on this day. There was serious discussion of moving
much of the administration of the National Government
away from Paris. The progress in transferring certain
activities to safer places was materially accelerated. Paris
was approaching the status of an armed camp, a besieged
post of great strategic importance. It was regarded as in
the 'advance zone,' that zone in which rationing, government, life in general, was on a military basis. Day after
day, and all day long, gendarmes went quietly from house
to house, inquiring the occupations of the occupants,
whether they had relatives to the south or west, and advising all who could to put their homes in order, collect their
most valuable small possessions, and leave the city. Transportation west or south was furnished those who could not
easily provide it for themselves. More than half a million
people had already left the city, and in the next few weeks
another half-million would depart. It was not difficult to
persuade people to leave. There was a tenseness in the air,

THE SECOND BOMBARDMENT

an all-pervading anxiety, a general condition of raw, jumpy nerves that made life for those in the capital anything but joyous.

There were numerous reasons for hastening the evacuation of the city. There was every possibility that it would be taken in the next drive. If it were, or if the Germans approached to within heavy field-gun range of it in a four- or five-day drive, there would be just no handling the evacuation. There would be panic, shortage of food; every kind of trouble. Then, too, every element of the entire transportation system from the south and west past Paris to the lines north, north-east, and east was urgently needed to handle just the supplies for the Front, the shifting of troops from one section of the Front to another, the bringing of divisions from southern and western areas, supplies of every description from the base ports. The total Army organization could ill afford at this time to bother about Paris. Wars in the past had been lost because of the desperate limitation of manœuvring power imposed upon the field commanders by the existence somewhere of a city of great value, great fortresses in which large garrisons had been stationed. Were Paris a hundred miles farther south General Foch could breathe much more comfortably.

On this same day General Foch transmitted to the Premiers and representatives of the nations on the Allied side, sitting at Versailles, a most portentous account. He practically told them that the Allies were at that moment virtually at the end of their resources. He reported that the German Army then had 200 divisions which for the time they were keeping filled to strength. The Allies had placed under his command 162 divisions which he was having serious trouble in keeping up to strength. The British had no more reserves; the French had none. He had therefore no choice but to advise them that there was great danger that the Allies would be defeated, would lose the War in the present campaign this summer, unless in some manner the numerical inferiority of the Allies could be remedied in the next two months by the rapid advent of American divisions. He urged with the greatest insistence that the maximum number of infantry and machine-gunners, with necessary small arms, ammunition, and food, be shipped from America in June and July to avert the immediate danger of defeat. He placed the total American force required to avert the immediate danger, to equalize the forces, and finally to turn the tide against the Germans, as 100 divisions, the numerical equivalent of 200 French divisions; a total of 3,000,000 men, with at least 300,000 of them arriving every month during the summer, autumn, and winter. He explained that he was at that time draining his lines ragged in many places to dam the tide at the Marne. If the Germans had sufficient strength to make an immediate attack in Flanders, where there were numerous alarming signs of a preparation on the part of Rupprecht's armies to do so, the British end of the line would very likely collapse, and the Germans would have the Channel ports.

There was only one hopeful point in the whole gloomy picture. Though Pétain thought he had detected an end of the German advance on the 28th at the Vesle, indicating another offensive with limited objectives, the fact now certainly was that the offensive had been transformed into a general engagement; there were for the Germans no limits to the advance except those of possibility. He, Foch, had no choice but to stop them if possible; and to reap something from the catastrophe he and Pétain had been pouring reserves into the corners of the break and had been gradually confining the Germans to that great dangerous pocket as it now stood; Ludendorff would be obliged to wage his next offensive for the specific purpose of breaking down those corners to avert catastrophe to himself. The reserves of the Allies would be there, could meet that thrust; they would not be missed so badly from the thin lines else-

THE SECOND BOMBARDMENT

where, and meanwhile another half-million Americans would have arrived.

The Premiers appreciated the gravity of the situation without any urging. A cable to this effect went to America immediately. An embargo went into effect at once on the shipment of anything heavy, except locomotives, cars, and certain absolutely essential machinery. Every ship's hold would be filled to jamming with men, rifles, ammunition, and food; nothing more.

But not a word of this did the newspapers print. No doubt the German Staff, Hindenburg, Ludendorff, were eagerly scanning the papers at this very time to see if there were any signs of cracking under the strain. Any such sign would be the signal for more furious efforts, would inspire his nearly spent men to still further exertions. German soldiers were as human as French, British, or American; they had their limits of endurance too. Nor did the papers say a word about the evacuation of the city. What the papers did print made an interesting study to those who knew the real situation. In spite of all this camouflage, however, the people of Paris had either a real or exaggerated conception of the gravity of the situation. The fact that they were being urged to leave meant everything. The gendarmes explained but little; they did not know the details, but when one is advised by an authorized public servant on such occasions to put his things in order, gather his most valued small possessions, and get out, nothing more is needed to convince him of the extreme gravity of the emergency. The camouflage of the newspapers then takes on a sinister significance.

That night eleven 'planes were detected crossing the lines, and the sirens, twenty-seven stronger in number than a month before, began their music, commanding Parisians to hunt shelter. Two of the 'planes proved to be the giant bombers which carried a crew of three officers and seven men each. Four batteries of anti-aircraft guns concentrated on one of these which had been caught by several searchlights and forced it down near Betz. At once on landing the crew set fire to it and were taken prisoners. Several of the 'planes got through the barrage, however, and dropped nine bombs on the city, one of them a 660-pound bomb, another of 220 pounds, and seven of 110 pounds each. The city rocked as from an earthquake on the bursting of each of these; violently on the bursting of the heaviest. Two of the smaller bombs burst within a few seconds of each other. The "All's well," which was beginning to be a term of doubtful assurance to Parisians, was sounded by the bells and bugles after midnight. Eleven raids in fifteen days was anything but "All's well."

June 2

Sunday, June 2, was for the Parisians a relatively quiet day. Merely relatively quiet. All of the previous night, all day and all night again, the rumble of the guns to the west and south of Soissons could be heard between city noises. There was no pause to that rumble. On a weekday the noises of the city drowned it. At night it could be heard plainly, and all day on Sunday. For two days people within the city had not been disturbed by the bursting of projectiles. The papers told them, however, that the bombardment had continued. Neither *communiqués* nor newspaper statements were necessary to tell them about the air raids. They knew all too much about those.

The second 340-mm. gun at Ribécourt joined in during the day, firing on the same target as the first, that spotted by Sound-ranging Section No. 10. There were no shells from the Paris Gun during the day.

Along the Marne and up the western side of the new salient vicious, snarling, close-quarter fighting continued all day long. The Germans intended to get across the Marne. The remaining bridges across the river had been

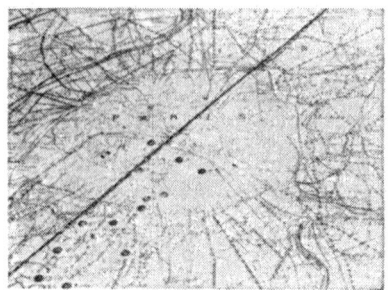

May 27: First Day of the Second Bombardment

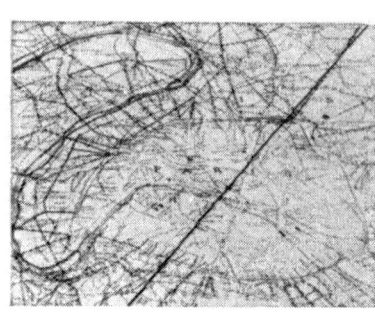

June 11: Last Day of the Second Bombardment

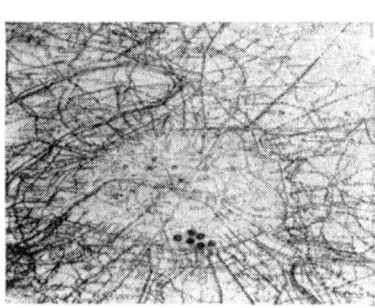

Air Bombs dropped on the Night of June 1

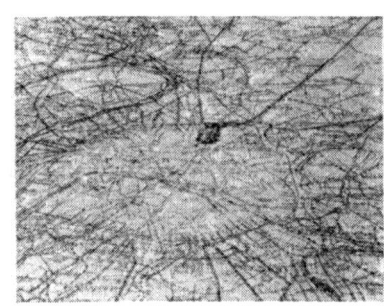

Air Bombs dropped on the Night of June 6

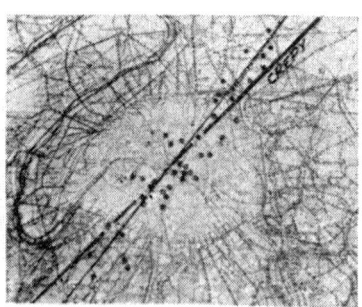

Forty-eight Shells fired from the Third 8·26-inch Gun used at Crépy

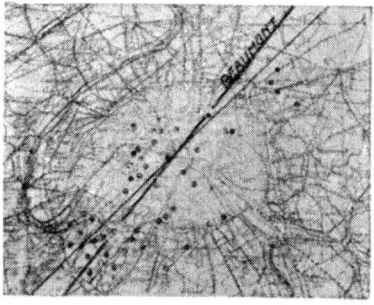

The First Forty-six Shells fired from the 9·45-inch Gun used at Beaumont

THE SECOND BOMBARDMENT

blown up. The defenders south of the Marne were deluged with gas and high explosive. All along the river, from Château-Thierry to Jaulgonne, the Germans tried again and again to get such a foothold on the northern bank as would enable them to sweep out the thin line of defenders on the south side. The remaining units of the American 3rd Division had arrived, and were scattered all along from Château-Thierry to Dormans. The stubborn holding of the Marne by these defenders gave the Army command a breathing spell to dispose of reserves, supports, all along the line. Units of the American 3rd and French 164th Divisions were used for this. They affected complete *liaison* through the 30th Infantry of the 3rd Division with the 9th Infantry of the 2nd Division across the Marne west of Château-Thierry. What supplies came up had to be brought at night, which was made hideous by the never-ending shell-fire, flares, rockets, rattle of machine-guns, drone of 'planes, and roar of their bursting bombs. By evening the German divisions had made a fair advance in the west from the region of Soissons south past Neuilly. But they were meeting the most stubborn resistance, and it began to look as though their progress had been stopped.

June 3

The artillerists were distinctly surprised when shortly before 8.30 on Monday morning, the 3rd, the report was telephoned in that a shell had burst in Aubervilliers at 8.10. It had killed one woman and wounded two others. The assumption of Sunday was wrong. They had not ceased firing to remove a worn gun. The falling of the first projectile so far short as Aubervilliers, five miles short of the target, certainly indicated that they were still using the worn gun that had been in action till Saturday.

The second projectile, twenty-five minutes later, burst in the cemetery in Pantin. The third at 9.20 fell in the

Place de l'Église in Pantin, killing another woman and wounding one man and one woman. Then there was a three-hour respite before the fourth shell burst, in Aubervilliers, at 12.5. That wounded a child. At 1.30 the fifth fell farther out in La Courneuve. It wounded a woman at work in a garden. The last for the day, the sixth, burst in Aubervilliers at 6.20, wounding a man and a woman; ten casualties for the day. Two women killed, and two men, five women, and one child wounded. There was no doubt but that the gun of Saturday was still firing; the tell-tale grooves in the copper bands and the falling of all the projectiles so short made that certain. In all probability the Germans had no more rebored guns yet available.

At Château-Thierry and from there east along the Marne to Mézy the desperate struggle for a passage of the river and to prevent that passage continued. The Germans were now in force all along the river, and the defenders were having a desperate time. The 7th Machine-gun Battalion of the American 3rd Division had been defending the bridge in Château-Thierry and the south bank of the river from there east for some distance since their hasty and timely arrival at six o'clock on Friday evening. By Monday evening they were as near absolute exhaustion as men can be and still fight. Their last real sleep had been the previous Wednesday night. From noon on Thursday till late afternoon of Friday they had bumped along in springless trucks and had carried their heavy machine-guns and ammunition many miles to the river. From then until this Monday evening, more than eighty hours, they had been operating those guns, smoking hot at times, watching and ducking at the explosions of high explosive and gas shells. What sleep any had got had been the hour or more of the sleep of exhaustion when one or another would be relieved for a short period and would drop where he worked or into a trench, and then so deep was that sleep to the tune of rattling machine-guns and bursting shells that they had to

THE SECOND BOMBARDMENT

be kicked awake; they were numb to sound and almost numb to physical pain.

But relief was on the way, to them and their French comrades who had retired into and through them and with whom they had been fighting turn and turn since Friday night. The 164th French Division and all other units of the American 3rd had been put in on both sides of Château-Thierry and east to Mézy. The 30th American Infantry on the left connected with the 9th American Infantry on the other side of the Marne and thence on up the west wall of the salient. These came into the front positions on Monday evening, and shortly after midnight those who had been holding the Marne, particularly about Château-Thierry, retired, getting out by three o'clock in the morning. They carried with them full assurance that their successors would hold what they had fought so desperately to defend. The Germans had to be held at the Marne, at whatever risk to lines that had become thin elsewhere from the drastic drain of supports and reserves.

There was little of a reassuring character that the papers could print on Monday with any hope that the people of Paris would believe it, except two items that smacked of truth. " The line of the Marne is still intact; has been since last Friday evening." And : " More American divisions are in line, along the river, and have been fighting with all the stubborn determination and efficiency that one could hope for from the best and most seasoned veterans." They were told too that there were signs that the great offensive had spent itself. They were sceptical of this.

Before midnight the sirens began their din, routing out of bed those who had dared to retire so early. Seven 'planes had been heard crossing the lines, so there was no choice but to inform the Service for the Defence of Paris at once. The bombers went elsewhere, however, and within an hour the retreat was sounded after the 'planes had been heard returning across their lines.

THE PARIS GUN

Though few, if indeed any, people knew it, events were shaping on Tuesday and Wednesday, June 4 and 5, for what one would be justified in considering the climax of the War; the peak of the prospects of the German armies to win the War. Some might say that the peak was passed with a momentous decision on the evening of May 28 when the German armies had reached and crossed the Vesle. But it remained yet to be determined on that date what the prospects of the German armies would be in their general, unrestricted, limitless objective engagement. On the 30th they reached the Marne. During the next three days they expanded their gains all along the west side of the salient. For several days they had been trying to cross the Marne; they failed. Sufficient of the Allied reserves were now in line to prevent them from crossing. So on Tuesday, the 4th, they turned their attention with redoubled fury to breaking down that stubbornly held western wall and the Soissons Corner.

The Rheims Corner could not be budged. The Germans had got themselves into an intolerable situation. They had either to break down those corners or be pinched out of the great balloon-like salient. Another retreat from the Marne was not to be thought of. The first one in 1914 had not yet been adequately explained to the German people.

People in Paris, however, saw neither any sign of a turn of affairs nor any basis for optimism. The climax they had been seeing develop was more in the nature of that terrible funnel-shaped, dense black cloud that may suddenly appear on the horizon, a tornado. It grows to terrifying proportions as one looks, the sun is blotted out, and then, if one is fortunate enough to be out of its path, he may see it twist, tear, suck up everything that man has built, with people and animals, and fling them about as straws. That was the kind of climax the Parisians were seeing or thought they were seeing, with the supposedly irresistible German Army as the tornado.

THE SECOND BOMBARDMENT

After a three-day respite the bombardment of Paris was resumed on Tuesday, June 4. The first shell burst close to the Est railway-station, in the Rue de Crimée, at 11.20 A.M. The second burst at 12.3 along the Nord railway, three-quarters of a mile from the first. It killed two women and a child, and wounded six women. At 3.30 the third shell struck just east of the Gare du Nord, killing another woman and wounding a child. The fourth, at 4.12, burst not more than a mile from the target, in the Rue Aumaire. It wounded four men, two women, and three children. This was a marked contrast in casualties and effects with the previous three active days when the shells were falling out in the suburbs; four killed, sixteen wounded, much visible destruction of property and serious alarm to thousands of people who heard the explosions of the four shells, as compared with two killed, ten wounded, little visible destruction, and a negligible amount of alarm from the previous twenty shells. No one knew what the German gunners had been doing during the three inactive days. Those gunners certainly knew how vital it was to their phase of the campaign to send the shells in where the effect on morale, resulting from the destruction of property and the killing of people, would be greatest. They had been wearing out a frightfully expensive gun in shooting costly shells that had neither been destroying much property nor killing or alarming many people. Examination of the fragments indicated that they were still using the same gun; the grooves in the copper were getting narrower each day. They were as wide as the grooves in the steel of the projectile when the gun was new. The first projectile of the day, which struck at 11.20, bore the number 71•. All projectiles of this series to date had been marked with a single prick punch-mark, indicating Series 1, but of course of 240-mm., or 9.45-inch, calibre, or supposedly that.

Both of the 340-mm. railway-guns at Ribécourt were busily shelling the position designated by Sound-ranging

THE PARIS GUN

Section No. 10 in the Bois de Corbie. There had been no possibility so far, however, of any satisfactory air reconnaissance to determine where the shells were falling nor to locate the gun. Constant hazy or rainy weather had prevented it.

During the evening the French outposts and advance machine-gun units retired through the American lines from Neuilly-la-Poterie west of Bussiares south toward the Marne. How thoroughly they deserved the privilege of turning over the job for a while! Theirs had been a heart-breaking job, that of holding the horde of well-supported Germans from encircling the Villers-Cotterets Wood and the so-called Soissons Corner. On Monday, particularly late in the day, they had borne the brunt of the front-line attack made by the Germans from the Marne north to Chézy-en-Orxois, when they were trying to dislodge both the 2nd American and the 43rd French Divisions at the same time. The Germans had not made any headway.

At dusk, shortly after the French units had retired through the line, the Germans tried new tactics. They made a concentrated drive on Neuilly-la-Poterie which was the junction point of the 2nd and 43rd Divisions. It was repulsed. At ten o'clock they attacked again with heavy artillery preparation of high explosive and gas. Again they failed, gaining only a temporary hold on Hill 123 from which they were dislodged the next day. During the evening they attacked also Hill 142, south of Bussiares. Here they were badly cut up and stopped by artillery fire.

During the night the weary 43rd French Division on the left of the Marines of the American 2nd was relieved by the 167th. The 164th French, on the right, was relieved by the 4th Cavalry. The 2nd drew in its flanks several kilometres from the Bois de Neuilly to the Bussiares-Champillon road, and the 23rd American Infantry entered the line. The limit of the German advance in that section was fixed that night as it had been several days before on the

THE SECOND BOMBARDMENT

Marne. The Germans would not realize it, however, for some days. Certainly it was to be no tranquil sector for those on either side. An anxious public saw nothing particularly reassuring in the savage, snarling fighting that would go on for weeks in that region.

June 5

No shells fell in Paris on the 5th or on the 6th. A grateful respite. The evacuation of the city continued without abatement, however. There was nothing yet to indicate any hope. The British had lost in March and April all of the hard-won territory on the Somme and in Flanders. In four days the French had lost all their gains on the Chemin-des-Dames. The terrifying advance of the Germans had been stopped for the time; but where would the cyclone strike next, if, indeed, the check on the Marne would hold?

During the day the air-reconnaissance service of the army fronting south of Noyon had its first success in spotting the gun position. It was a beautifully clear day, and they secured a number of excellent photographs that seemed to indicate the gun position without any question. A railway line had been laid from the La Fère-Tergnier-Ham railway at a point west of Annois where a narrow vehicle road crossed the railway. It continued down that road which passed about half a mile west of Cugny and led into the Bois de Corbie. Shortly before it entered the wood a curved spur track had been laid off into the fields to the west. This was quite conspicuous; evidently a supply track. The track then led on down the road into the wood, and immediately a second curve led off to the west of the road. Excellent attempts had been made to conceal this, but the signs of its presence were unmistakable. The point where the line began to curve to the west from the road had not been properly concealed, and the gun position at the end had not been completely concealed. In fact, so clear were the details on the photograph that it seemed one could see the outlines of the gun barrel itself, a long black streak parallel to the direction of the track and in the centre of the obvious clearing at the end. This point was very close to the north-west corner of the wood.

These photographs were most disconcerting to the Sound-rangers, those of Sections 8 and 10, and to the 340-mm. railway-gun battery. The curved track in the wood which they called B was at least a quarter of a mile north of the mean point spotted by Section A. The 340's had been shooting at a point so far distant from the gun position that the gunners must have been chuckling about it ever since the counter-shelling began. The battery promptly switched to the new target, which was still well within their range. It is embarrassing to be deceived in such a fashion. But such is the art of war; some one has to succeed, some one fail.

The fighting about the great salient during the day was characterized by violent shelling on both sides, angry snarling charges of small units of the German 197th Division fronting the American 2nd. These were repulsed with machine-gun and rifle fire and field artillery. The accuracy of American rifle fire made the Germans in that sector thoroughly angry. They had never encountered anything like it before. It was certainly disconcerting.

June 6

On the most violently active section of that long line that bore the name of the 'Front,' the west wall of the Marne salient, things of a different character began to happen. At five o'clock in the morning the 1st and 3rd Battalions of the 5th Marines of the American 2nd Division, together with the right wing of the French 167th Division on their left, charged out through the broken woodlands that clothed the hill-crests north of Champillion in an assault whose

THE SECOND BOMBARDMENT

objectives were the edges of these woods and crests looking down into the open valley about Torcy and Bussiares. They had found themselves in an intolerable position, with the Germans on these crests looking down upon them in the valley, sniping them in the trenches, bombarding them with trench mortars.

They were met by an intense machine-gun and rifle fire, but at 7.10 had obtained all their objectives and were in command of the valley from the coveted hill crests. This advance of the left of the 2nd Division of course exposed its own right flank and necessitated an advance of at least the centre of the division. So at five o'clock in the afternoon the 5th and 6th Marines and the 23rd Infantry assaulted for an objective line extending along the valley from a point a little east of Bussiares to the eastern edge of Bouresches. This was probably the bitterest struggle that occurred during the second offensive. The victorious Germans were getting a dose of their own medicine. They had been warned by the morning's engagement. They could not stand for any reverses. They didn't intend to, especially from Americans. They were prepared for a desperate struggle. And a desperate struggle it proved. Throughout the night among the thickets and tumbled boulders of the Bois de Triangle and Bois de Belleau, to be associated henceforth with the name 'Marines,' the lines surged backward and forward in a conflict as ferocious as any that history had known. The night was hideous with rockets, the rattle of machine-guns, cries and yells of men who cannot be called sane under such circumstances.

Nest after nest of German machine-guns was taken in savage hand-to-hand fighting while the ground behind the American lines, over which supports would have to advance, was torn into no semblance of its former appearance by high-explosive shells. Rockets and flares called for artillery concentration here, a barrage there. The Marines forged ahead steadily all night, but at a terrible cost. The fortunes of the Germans were turning. This advance, local, of little strategic importance, was to continue, and its continuance, its success, the savage determination of the men waging it, was to be the beginning of the heartening of a nation, of the millions yet in the daily belaboured capital, to that desperate uphill struggle of the coming months; a struggle into the sunshine which at this time seemed blotted out.

Though the Parisians had been congratulating themselves on their two-day and two-night immunity from shells and bombs, they held no false hopes of continued freedom from them. They were wise in not expecting much, for at about ten o'clock the stillness of a night disturbed only by the rumble of distant guns and the honk-honk of the horns of the little taxicabs scurrying about in the dark was violently broken by the sudden screech, perhaps more nearly the scream, of the sirens everywhere; a noise so piercing, so all-pervading, that none escaped it anywhere. Twenty 'planes had crossed the lines and were following their usual route to Paris.

The anti-aircraft gunners did their best, putting up a continuous barrage all about the city; the brilliant shafts of light from the searchlights made cubist designs all over the sky, designs animated by the brilliant splashes of light of the exploding shrapnel shells. But some of the 'planes got through in spite of them. In a time hardly sufficient for those in bed to seek shelter the explosion of a great bomb shook the city, a 200-pound bomb. Then two 110-pounders, another 200, and, in the hour and a half, forty 20-pound bombs. Nothing like this had happened since the night of March 11 and 12, when eighty had been dropped. On that occasion they had been dropped all over the centre of the city. On this night twenty-eight were dropped on and about the shops of the Est railway near the station. Sixteen other bombs were dropped in the thirteenth *arrondissement* in the extreme south of the city along the

THE SECOND BOMBARDMENT

Quai de Gare of the Seine. Seemingly the raid had been planned against the railways, the Est and the P.L.M. having received particular attention. This raid more than made up for the previous two days and nights without shells or bombs.

JUNE 7

At 8.30 in the morning the 5th and 6th Marines and the 23rd Infantry had secured possession of Bouresches and had pushed into Belleau Wood to Hill 181 as the fruit of their savage all-night fighting. The Marines were now on higher ground than the Germans who still occupied most of the tangled wood to the north. But the cost of this gain had been fearful. The Americans were still inexperienced in the art of attaining their objectives without reckless disregard of danger. The Marine Brigade had lost twenty-four officers and three hundred men, and the 9th and 23rd Infantry had lost 377 officers and men. The 23rd suffered particularly in repelling a counter-attack of the Germans during the night. During the day the 9th Infantry suffered further casualties when they advanced north of the Morette Wood at the same time that French troops and two companies of the 30th Infantry took the southern slopes of Hill 204 and the village of Monneaux. All this time, the Germans were countering repeatedly and furiously to prevent further advances, to recover lost ground. The only encouraging thing that could be said in published news was that the advance of the Germans had been stopped, and that American and French troops side by side were slowly but surely and steadily pushing them back; on a limited front, but just the fact that the direction of motion had been reversed, that the supposedly invincible Germans were not so after all, was encouraging, and much was made of the fact.

Paris was not to go free another day from shelling. At 11.30 a shell burst between Plessis and Robinson, near the

THE PARIS GUN

cemetery in the Rue de Versailles. No other shell had fallen so far over the city. No one was killed or wounded. The second and third shells fell very close to each other; the second at 11.55, at the corner of the Boulevard Saint-Germain and the Rue Courty, very close to the Seine, and the third fourteen minutes later at the corner of the Boulevard Saint-Germain and the Rue de l'Université. This one wounded a man and a woman. The fourth shell burst at No. 13 Boulevard Voltaire, killing a man and wounding another and a woman.

By this time fragments of the first projectile that had burst so far over the city had been brought into the Artillery offices. It bore the number 62•. And the grooves in the copper were still narrow. The worn gun had not been removed. There had been some other reason for the inactivity of the previous two days. There was further evidence of the continued use of the worn gun at once. The fifth projectile, at 12.50, fell far to the north-east, in Dugny. A new gun would not be dropping any projectiles out there.

There were no more shells then till 8.9 P.M., when the sixth burst still farther to the north-east, in Gonesse. Fifteen minutes later the seventh and last of the day burst at Bonneuil, midway between Gonesse and Dugny.

All day the 340's at Ribécourt had been busily shelling the new position at the end of the camouflaged curve discovered on the air photographs of the 5th.

June 8

At 10.8 on Saturday, June 8, a shell struck and burst in the eighteenth *arrondissement* in the Passage de l'Élysée-des-Beaux-Arts. It neither killed nor wounded anyone. Ten minutes later one burst far out in Dugny, six miles away; again no casualties. There was a two-hour interval then before the next burst at 12.23, out in Saint-Denis, a densely

REFUGEES GOING SOUTH TOWARD THE MARNE ON MAY 27

THE PLACE DE LA RÉPUBLIQUE

NO. 1 RUE DE COURTRY

THE SECOND BOMBARDMENT

built suburb town; this killed two men and a woman. Two hours later, at 2.8, the fourth struck, in Gonesse, and at 4.16 another burst there. There were no casualties for either. It was when the shells burst in the city proper or in such towns as Saint-Denis that they almost invariably took a toll of lives. The sixth and last of the day burst at 7.20 in Aubervilliers. Only one of the day's six shells fell within the city.

The vicious fighting of Thursday night and Friday continued all day Saturday along the American 2nd Division Sector. Belleau Wood was to know no peace nor silence for many days, even weeks to come. Scores of men killed there in the fighting of Thursday night would lie where they had fallen for days. Their comrades had no time for the dead. And some who had taken refuge in shell-holes or in dense thicket and had been killed by high-explosive shells might lie there for months, even years, undiscovered. In a few days that wood smelled horribly.

June 9

Long before the bursting of any shells disturbed the Sunday quiet of Paris or its suburbs another German offensive had started with the usual prelude of hours of artillery preparation, in all respects similar to those of March and two weeks since in May. High explosive, gas, a hail of shells. Again the awakening in the early morning hours to hear that continuous rolling and rumbling of heavy guns. Obviously it was closer to Paris than before, for one could hear it much more distinctly. The Germans had attacked on the Noyon-Montdidier front in an effort to reach Compiègne and to break down the Soissons Corner. This corner was an intolerable threat to them, and, if not broken down at once, it would certainly change the plan of their campaigns. After what seemed an eternity to those under the rain of high explosive and gas, the bombardment

THE PARIS GUN

drew back to a barrage, and Hutier's Eighteenth Army attempted again, employing the famous tactic that bore Hutier's name, to roll over the opposing lines and quickly flank the French armies between them and the Villers-Cotterets Wood. They may have anticipated more difficulty than on the previous two occasions. They certainly encountered it. The Allied High Command would have been more than stupid had it not looked for an attempt in this region to break the corner, once the attempts from within the Marne salient failed. So this line was in no such shape as the line north of the Aisne on May 27. The Germans made headway, of course, but at a rate and at a price vastly different from that of the 27th.

There was no warning, except the preliminary bombardment, of the beginning of this storm. Since the 340 railway-guns at Ribécourt were squarely in the centre of the path of the advance the Germans were among the surprised ones. These guns had not been spotted as had the guns at Vailly, however, and the battery was able to employ the entire day undisturbed by shell-fire in getting the trucks under the carriages and in getting them away on the Compiègne railway. Even so, they had no time to spare, for by night the advancing line was not far from them. This would end their shelling of the Beaumont position of the Paris Gun.

Shells began to arrive in Paris earlier on this morning than during any day for a week, since June 1, in fact. The first burst in Gonesse at 7.55. Another fell in Blanc-Mesnil at 8.25. The same gun was still firing. At 8.55 the third burst in La Courneuve; still no casualties.

A fragment of the shell which burst in Gonesse at 9.46 bore the number 15•. They were still using projectiles from the same lot—that is, Series 1 of the 240-mm. calibre—but not in the precise order that characterized the use of previous series. This fourth shell strangely bore the same mark as the third which fell over the city in Fontenay-aux-Roses at 7.4 on May 27.

THE SECOND BOMBARDMENT

The fifth shell struck in Aubervilliers at 10.20. The sixth, which bore the mark 22•, and the seventh burst in Gonesse, at 11.17 and 11.33; four there in four hours. At 12.7 the next struck in Roissy-en-France, the farthest short of the city so far. The ninth fell along a railway-track in Saint-Denis at 12.28.

There was an interval of three hours then before the tenth burst at 3.39 in Garges, just north of Dugny, and nine miles short of the centre of the city. An hour later, at 4.16, another burst in Garges. The twelfth and last for the day struck within the city at 5.3. It burst in a *café* at the corner of the Rue de Belleville and Boulevard de Belleville, killing one man and wounding nine others. There was a marked contrast between the casualties of shells striking within the city and those falling in the suburbs. This day bore the record for number of shells since May 30.

JUNE 10

So quickly had the French troops got the situation in hand west of Noyon that on the morning of June 10 the portion of the German front that was still in motion was less than half that of the day before. The Germans were able to make headway here only in the centre. General Foch acted promptly, and in the afternoon Mangin's army moved out from the wooded country east of Rollot on the Montdidier-Compiègne highway, caught Hutier's right flank sharply, stopped it, and took prisoners and guns. Mangin's black Colonials were terrible fellows: even the name 'Mangin,' with the assurance that it implied black colonial troops, had become a terror to German soldiers. Those Colonials rarely took prisoners; they regarded them as nuisances, dangerous. Dead men were less troublesome. The Colonials did not mind the 'whiffs' so much as did their white comrades.

During the night, with no moments for rest, the battery

THE PARIS GUN

at Ribécourt had got its precious guns loose and south. A close call.

At 7.55 the first projectile burst against a wall of the Clignancourt Barracks in the Boulevard Ney just inside the city wall on the northern edge of the city. No one was injured. This shell was number 650. But the next in Saint-Denis at 10.25 killed one man and wounded a woman. The third, which burst at 10.45 in the Rue Baudelique, took a heavy toll. It killed one woman and wounded nine others in a shop at house No. 6.

There was an interval of six hours before another projectile fell. It burst in Aubervilliers in the Rue Charon at four o'clock, killing a woman and wounding one man and two women. The last projectile, the fifth, struck between the villages of Stains and Dugny at 7.16; there were no casualties. The total casualties from the five projectiles were three killed and thirteen wounded.

June 11

The active front of the new German offensive was shifted farther east on Tuesday morning in the obvious attempt to press down on the corner about Soissons and put the French armies into a salient more embarrassing than the Marne salient was to themselves. But their going was more difficult than on Monday even. Their fortunes in this region seemed spent for the time. And if they intended striking again in Flanders it behoved them to be quick about it, for the British armies had had a good long opportunity to recoup, to draw in American divisions.

So far as morale was concerned, the barometer was about at the bottom for most French people, particularly in Paris. They could not see any real sign of a turning of fortunes. Every move of the Germans had brought them closer to Paris; the raids and shelling kept up; they were still being urged to leave the city. Indeed, there was every sign about

THE SECOND BOMBARDMENT

the city that more and more preparations were being made for that final tragedy, the evacuation of the city rather than have it destroyed by shell-fire if the Germans should get close enough.

It was small wonder that during the previous month and for the succeeding two Paris was but a skeleton of itself.

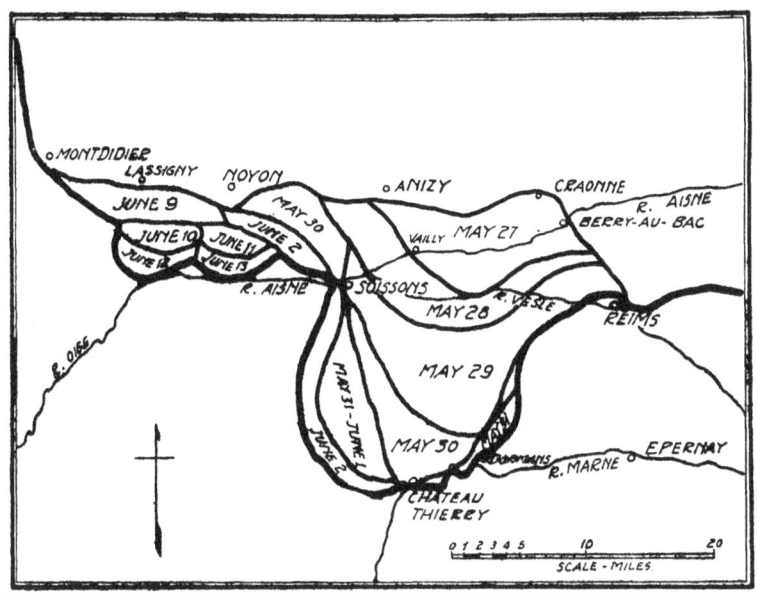

THE GERMAN GAINS FROM MAY 27 TO JUNE 13, 1918

Those who had known it before the War appreciated fully the change. Many shops had been closed. The displays in show-cases, the windows of shops that continued business, were but camouflage; the costly, elaborate things had disappeared. With the possibility of a forced evacuation of the city, with bombing and shelling, it behoved merchants to think of what they would lose in an emergency. Gradually they had shipped west and south much valuable merchandise or had not replenished stock. As for hotels, and pensions, one could have a whole one to himself. One could go to the finest, largest hotels and literally have a floor to himself.

179

THE PARIS GUN

There was no such thing as scarcity of space there, as was almost always the case in times of peace. Hotels were quiet, sombre places at night, reflecting the quiet, dark streets and boulevards. Paris was a good place to get out of, to stay away from, though it still held its old glamour for those who could not easily get there.

There seemed some hope that the day would pass without any shells. But late in the afternoon, at five o'clock, one burst in the Rue Denis Papin in Pantin. It did not harm anyone. A shell had burst at almost this exact spot at 5.48 P.M. on April 16.

The events on the Front during the remaining days of the week revealed that the Germans had ceased offensive operations on their southern front, and must have stopped the firing of their Paris Gun at the time they sent out other orders. The shell that burst at five o'clock on Tuesday, the 11th, was the last of that bombardment.

V
THE BEAUMONT BATTERY [1]

Hardly had the left of Hutier's Eighteenth Army and the right of Boehn's Seventh gathered in and passed Ham and Chauny to the north-west and west of La Fère on the third day of the March offensive before the engineers were busily at the job of connecting the tag ends of the railway line between La Fère and Tergnier. Prior to the 21st La Fère had been on the German side of the line and Tergnier on the Allied side. The Laon-La Fère-Ham-Amiens railway had therefore been torn up for a distance of several miles on each side of the front line. The retirement of the British armies on the second, third, and fourth days of the offensive had been so rapid, so precipitous, that demolition parties were not able to perform the usual thorough job, and beyond Tergnier the railway line was more or less intact. Rails had been removed, switches battered up, in places the roadbed was torn up by German or British high-explosive shells; but it took less time to put the road in condition in such places than across that nearly two-year-old No Man's Land, where few signs of things that had been could still be found. Here the great stretches of barbed wire, stakes, piles of sand-bags, banks of earth, had to be removed, trenches filled in, ties, rails, and ballast brought up; a job of new road-laying.

But the railway had to be put into condition quickly so that the maximum of supplies could be taken forward on this line for the centre of the advancing armies moving

[1] This chapter continues the narrative of the second bombardment.

THE PARIS GUN

toward Amiens. Within less than a week, before the shell that had such dire consequences struck the church of Saint-Gervais on Good Friday, the tag ends had been connected and the line was in use.

The catastrophe to gun No. 3 on Monday morning and the forced evacuation of Position No. 1 during the week under the rain of 12-inch French shells brought about an earlier search for likely new positions than would otherwise have been the case. It had already been anticipated by the ballisticians that the increasing of the calibre of the gun by reboring it to 232 mm., and with the consequent increasing of the weight of the projectiles from 104 to 124 and 126 kilograms would reduce the maximum range of the guns. But as no test firings had yet been conducted, it was not known just what muzzle velocity and consequent range could be attained. There was no question, however, but that the guns should be got out from under the already intolerable French counter-battery fire, to a position where better concealment could be secured and as far as possible from likely French positions, but, at the same time, as close as possible to Paris. Every mile closer to Paris than the present positions could, and probably would, mean an extra two or three shots in the life of the gun, and greater accuracy of fire.

The broken railway-line had hardly been repaired, therefore, before a search was begun for new positions. After passing Tergnier one might select either the line south-west through Chauny to Noyon or north-west through Ham. The Chauny-Noyon line was not promising; the Oise river paralleled it on the south, separating it from the Forest of Coucy and some small isolated forests farther west. The small isolated patches of wood north of the Oise were separated from the railway by the canal, and then, too, they promised poor concealment. The northern railway line was more promising. North of Tergnier, at Mennesis, it paralleled a wood for a distance of three miles; the trees

 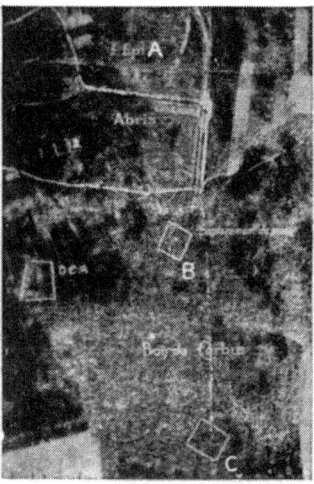

THE SUPPOSED POSITION OF THE
GUN (B), AND THE REAL POSITION (C)

AIR PHOTOGRAPH OF THE BOIS
DE CORBIE: SUPPOSED POSITION (B)
AND REAL POSITION (C)

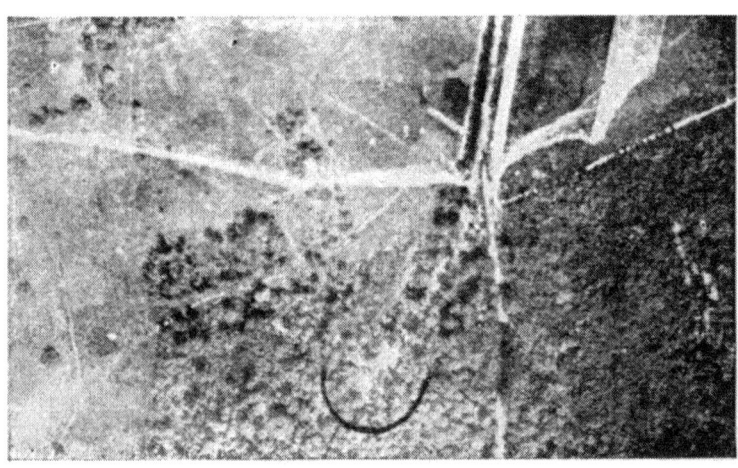

POSITION B FROM THE AIR

were quite close to the track. The narrow road from Jussy just beyond the northern tip of this wood, but on the northern side of the railway, to the little village of Le Fort in the wood and south of Mennesis, ran quite close to the track on the southern side and formed the boundary to the wood. A more convenient place could not have been desired; the closest point of it was 69.5 miles from Paris, five less than the distance from the No. 2 gun which was then firing. South of this wood was the larger Bois de Frières, the closest point of which was 68.4 miles from Paris. On the west side of the Chauny-Saint-Quentin highway was the strung-out Bois de Genlis, about three miles long, but with no point closer than the Bois de Frières. Then west of the Cugny-La Neuville road was the smaller Bois de Corbie, in which well-concealed points as close as 68.6 miles to Paris were to be found. This ended the list of possibilities, unless it were decided to go on to Ham and then south on the Ham-Noyon railway past Guiscard to the Bois d'Autrecourt. But this thought was quickly discarded, for the new front line was less than two miles south of Noyon, and any point in this wood could be more easily and thoroughly bombarded by French guns of all calibres than the positions then in use. Consideration was therefore limited to the Bois de Mennesis, Frières, Genlis, and Cugny. The Forêt de Coucy south-east of Chauny with the railway-lines running through the forest would have been ideal from the standpoint of concealment, but any position within it would be within the ranges of even the ordinary 6-inch guns on the Allied side. The advancing lines had not been able to take all that forest; the southern portion was still in French hands.

The artillerists and engineers continued their studies of the four possible woods during the early weeks of April, while the bombardment was still busily in progress at Crépy and the battles continued on toward Amiens and later to the north about Ypres. They hoped to find ideal or nearly

THE PARIS GUN

ideal concealment both for the approach tracks as well as for the gun positions. Before the reconnaissance was completed test firings of the 232-mm. gun had been conducted at Meppen, and it was discovered that the maximum range that could be expected from it, from the muzzle velocity attained with full charges of powder, would be 70.8 miles; this was a reduction of 8.7 miles from the

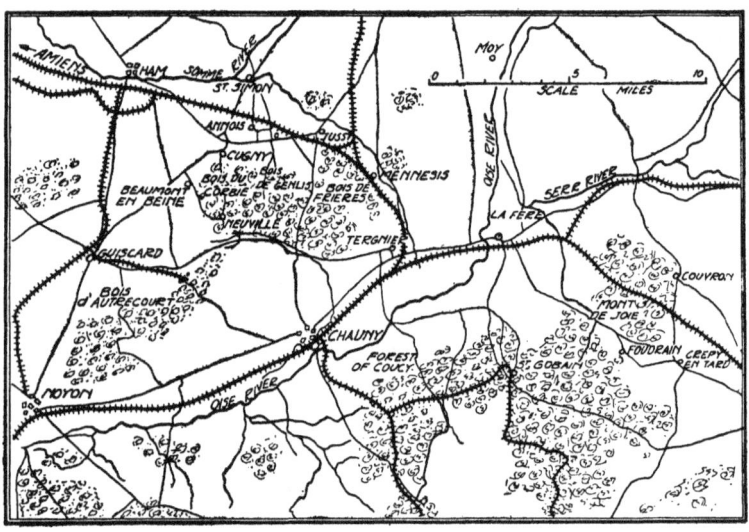

THE HAM-NOYON-CRÉPY REGION

maximum range of the 8.26-inch guns then firing on Paris. It was plain that the rebored guns could not be used at the present active Crépy position. The abandoned No. 3 position there was 73.9 miles from Paris, and the active No. 2 position 74.5 miles. The ballisticians had early reached the conclusion that the use of 8.26-inch guns at a range of 74.5 miles of their possible 79.5 miles resulted in a distressingly short life. So no position could be considered for the 70.8-mile guns other than one as close to Paris as would be reasonably consistent with a hoped-for immunity from counter-battery shelling. These considerations ruled out the Bois de Mennesis and the Bois de

THE BEAUMONT BATTERY

Frières. It probably would have to be the Bois de Corbie. Further study of that wood, and the necessary roadway construction to reach it revealed that there lay within that wood an unusual and unique opportunity for concealment, and the difficulties of road construction of the three miles of railway that would have to be laid from the main line west of Annois south could be materially reduced if desired by laying the track on the existing vehicle road. So the Bois de Corbie it would be.

April was well on before the demands on the engineers in assisting the armies within the now great salient were relaxed to the point where they could begin laying the railway south to the wood, consider the elaborate measures necessary to conceal the real position, and construct false positions so that attention would be directed there rather than to the gun itself. But by the end of April work was well in progress, and when the last shot had been fired from Crépy on May 1 and most of the personnel there released things went along more rapidly in the Corbie Wood east of the little village of Beaumont. The battery commander had been informed that the next offensive for which the gun would have to be ready would begin late in May. No date had yet been set. That offensive which had already been designated under the code name 'Blücher,' would be waged by the Army Group of the Crown Prince on the Chemin-des-Dames, and the objective was the Vesle from Soissons to Rheims, including those cities if possible.

Even if the next offensive were to be delayed to the very end of May, there would be none too much time to prepare the gun position and have the gun ready to fire on the first day of the offensive. A new problem had developed, or rather had been developing. When carriages were under consideration for the great guns over a year before, one had been designed for all-round traverse, so that the gun on it might be turned on any target within its range if desired. That one had finally found its way to Position No. 1, had operated in the opening of the bombardment, and within a week was out of it, being replaced by a new concrete foundation of elaborate construction. The other two carriages designed but a short time after No. 1 were less elaborate. They were almost entirely of structural steel and were made to be mounted on timber platforms or bases. In each case—that is, the carriage for all-round fire and the other carriage for a very limited field of fire—they were unwieldy, unsatisfactory things from two very vital emergency considerations. One of the emergencies had developed promptly. Within thirty-six hours of the firing of the first shot from No. 1, a succession of 12-inch shells had begun to drop about the supposedly well-concealed positions. The one that struck the tree and the other that later made a direct hit on Emplacement No. 1 proved conclusively that effective counter-battery shelling was a possibility, almost a certainty. This possibility had been anticipated months before the bombardment began. The other contingency, which certainly was not recognized yet as a probability but as one for which provision should nevertheless be made, was that of a hasty retreat. In the event of any such withdrawal as the one which the British Fifth Army had just been compelled to make, the clumsy, unwieldy carriages could not be got out, and probably the more than precious guns could not be removed. The latter was, of course, the more serious. The loss of a carriage was of little consequence.

In 1917, while design and construction work were under way for the huge railway-carriages for the 45-calibre 15-inch naval guns, the 'Long Maxes' that had been doing such effective work on Dunkirk from the tiny Belgian village Luegenboom, the question arose as to whether the long-range guns could be used on those carriages. Why not? The long-range guns were made from Long Maxes. The new gun was twice as long, twice as heavy, and it would not be wise to attempt to transport the gun on the carriage,

THE RAILWAY GUN-CARRIAGE

GANTRY CRANE USED IN INSTALLING THE STEEL CAISSON AND BASE FOR THE GUN-CARRIAGE

THE BEAUMONT BATTERY

but in an emergency that could be done. Here was an alluring possibility. Investigation showed that the carriage was capable of withstanding the reaction of firing, for the muzzle energy of the long gun with its light projectile was but little more than half that of the 15-inch gun with its heavy projectile. The carriage was strong enough to bear the dead load of the long gun on the emplacement, and in an emergency the gun could be left on the carriage and both be moved out of danger if great care were taken to strengthen the weaker bridges and roadways, and the getaway from the emplacement could be made within two hours, perhaps one.

Tests of every kind at the proving ground had shown all these possible; the carriage would answer well in all respects. The decision had therefore been made since the time of the installation of the carriages at Crépy that the gun or guns used at any new positions would be mounted on the 'Max' or 'Long Max' railway carriages. A few of these and the requisite elaborate bases were now available and would be used in succeeding offensives.

In their careful reconnaissance work over Corbie Wood in April the airmen had taken photographs which revealed that some unusually tall trees practically covered a hundred-yard section of a north and south road on which a railway line could easily be laid. And farther on, south, where the trees did not meet, the shadows were so deep as to conceal the usually very conspicuous white road. Here was a natural concealment that could not be bettered. Study of the terrain showed it excellent for a gun position, level, the earth hard, and the range exactly 68.4 miles. A position was selected a short distance north of the point where the road bent off to the east.

A railway line was laid from the main line south along the road from Saint-Simon to Cugny, and was completed early in May to the point of permitting the heavier equipment to be brought in. North of the wood a curve branched off the main line to the west, for a distance of about 150 yards, and an earth bumper was constructed at its end. This would serve for cars of supplies, locomotives standing by, and for any Headquarters trains that might come in on a visit. No attempt was made to conceal it. The sound-rangers would get the general location of the gun almost at once, and the enemy airmen must be permitted to find the less important parts of the installation. If an attempt were made to conceal everything the airmen might blunder on to the real position, as they probably had done at Crépy.

As the road entered the wood three hundred yards farther south, a second curve was run off toward the south-west for 130 yards into the wood. Ballast, ties, and rails were laid, but the switch was only such a resemblance of one as would be satisfactorily deceptive to airmen. No real switch was used. Cars could not be run on to this curve. The section of rail of this curve between the rails of the main track was a plank spiked to the ties. The rails of the curve were laid hastily and carelessly, no attempt being made to join their ends.

At the end of this curve a circular pit about twenty-five feet in diameter by three feet deep was dug and crudely camouflaged with branches. Crude shelters were constructed in the wood for purposes of deception. As a finishing touch to this false emplacement, strips of tarred canvas were laid on the branches covering the pit. It was hoped that these would show on air photographs as an apparent indication of the gun and carriage. Test photos made by the airmen showed the scheme of this whole false curve to be about as good as could be hoped for. The next problem was to conceal all of the remainder of the installation, the real position of the gun.

The line of the track led for about ninety yards directly south from the false switch of the second curve (B) and then south-east for about thirty yards to the road. From here it led straight south along the vehicle road for a quarter

CAMOUFLAGE POSITION B

THE PIT FOR THE STEEL BASE AT POSITION C

THE BEAUMONT BATTERY

of a mile into the densely shaded section. This track was laid on a wide bed of ballast, the eastern edge of which would serve for the 24-inch narrow-gauge ammunition supply track. At the end of the line some careful clearing had to be done to accommodate the complete installation. First a circular pit, thirty-three feet in diameter and six feet in depth, had to be dug to receive the steel base-section of the railway-carriage platform. In the centre of this pit another pit about thirteen feet in diameter by about two feet in depth was dug. The digging of this great pit and the disposing of the earth, all by hand, proved no small job. The bottom had to be cut carefully to a perfect level, and the sides to vertical walls. The hundreds of men from the engineers and artillery units working on the job had the stimulant of the ceaseless roar of countless guns all about the salient, which by this time reached down to and included Noyon and Lassigny, and to the west past Montdidier, Albert, and almost to Arras. There was no quiet in all that region. The British armies had been pushed back a maximum distance of thirty-seven miles from Saint-Quentin to Cantigny, the very point of the salient in the recently finished offensive, and had suffered terrible losses; widely advertised and most encouraging Army reports said that a hundred thousand men had been captured, thousands of guns, and mountains of supplies. But in spite of all this it had developed that the Allies had had or had found the necessary divisions to dam the break, and for weeks now the artillery duelling had been continuous and violent. The rumble of heavy and of the medium and lighter guns grew at times to the crescendo of drum-fire. Victory seemed nearer than ever before; two more offensives ought to break the Allies, but just now they were stinging back viciously, with heavy artillery all about the great salient. The music of that fire lent all the stimulus necessary to make every one engaged in the preparing of the new position for the great ' Jack's Bean-stalk ' work with vigour day and night.

It was necessary to proceed most cautiously and carefully on all work on the quarter-mile of track beyond curve B and on the emplacement itself. At any time French or British airmen might come over on reconnaissance and take back a chance picture that would reveal the whole installation. Men were forbidden to walk in the road during the day from curve B to the emplacement, and, as soon as the work of clearing out the necessary trees had been completed, camouflage netting with grass tied all over it was strung from the trees on one side to the other over the area marked for the pit. It was possible then to proceed with the work on the pit and tracks, which were somewhat in the open, without fear of premature detection.

All of this work of track-laying and excavating was completed by the middle of May. And well it was, for secret orders reached the battery commander at that time from General Headquarters that 'y' day of the offensive 'Blücher' was set for May 27; not two weeks off.

While the track was being laid and the pit excavated six heavy shelters were constructed in the wood on either side of the road. Five of them on the east side, two behind or north of the emplacement, two south, and the shelter for the Post Commander just within the wood some fifteen yards to the north, east of the pit. The other shelter (they were all of heavy wood beams, covered with earth) was built in the wood on the west side and about fifteen yards north of the centre of the pit.

Short sections of track were laid on either side of the pit for the gantry crane.

Eighteen I-beams were laid on ballast in ditches dug radially in the bottom of the pit from the outer edge to the edge of the deeper hole in the centre. A complete floor or platform of heavy sheets of steel three inches thick was laid on these beams. When joined these made a great disc of the outside diameter of the pit—that is, thirty-three feet with a thirteen-foot hole in the centre.

THE ROTATING STEEL BASE ON WHICH THE GUN-CARRIAGE RESTED

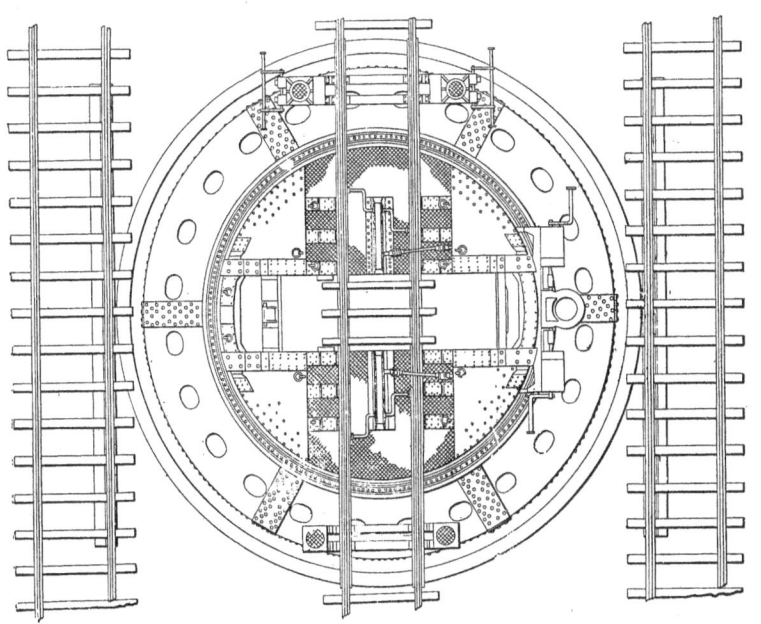

PLAN OF THE EMPLACEMENT

THE BEAUMONT BATTERY

The base-section of the railway-carriage platform was an annular ring of rectangular cross-section. The outside diameter was thirty-three feet, the inside about nineteen, and the height six. It had been made in six identical parts for convenience in handling. Each was of heavy sheet steel throughout. Each of these six sections was divided within into four sections by two vertical partition plates. In the top or floor of each section there were eight manholes, two for each of the four sections, through which men might pass to bolt the sections to each other. When the six base-sections had been bolted together and the whole levelled as well as could be, tons of sand and earth in bags were passed in through the manholes. This additional weight would make any appreciable shifting of the entire base quite unlikely.

Along the inner edge and on the top of each base-section a heavy steel plate, four inches thick by twenty-four wide, had been riveted and its top surface planed. The ends of these plates fitted to each other so perfectly as to form in effect one perfect ring about the inner edge of the base for the parts of the bearing and traversing mechanisms. The lower ball-bearing ring was fastened on top of this. Outside this bearing ring was fastened a circular gear, a part of the traversing mechanism.

The rotating section of the platform, which, like the base, was made almost entirely of plates, angles, channels, and I-beams, came to the field in four parts. One of the large sections contained most of the traversing, or turning, mechanism.

Ninety-six steel balls, eight inches in diameter, were placed on the grooved ball path fastened to the top of the base. The balls were placed within a bronze spacing ring, with holes through it at regular intervals to keep the balls at exact distances from each other. Four powerful hydraulic jacks, two low and two high ones, were bolted to two special cross-beams resting on the base. The low jacks were on the

THE PARIS GUN

far side and the high ones on the side on which the railway carriage would enter. They had a total lifting capacity of

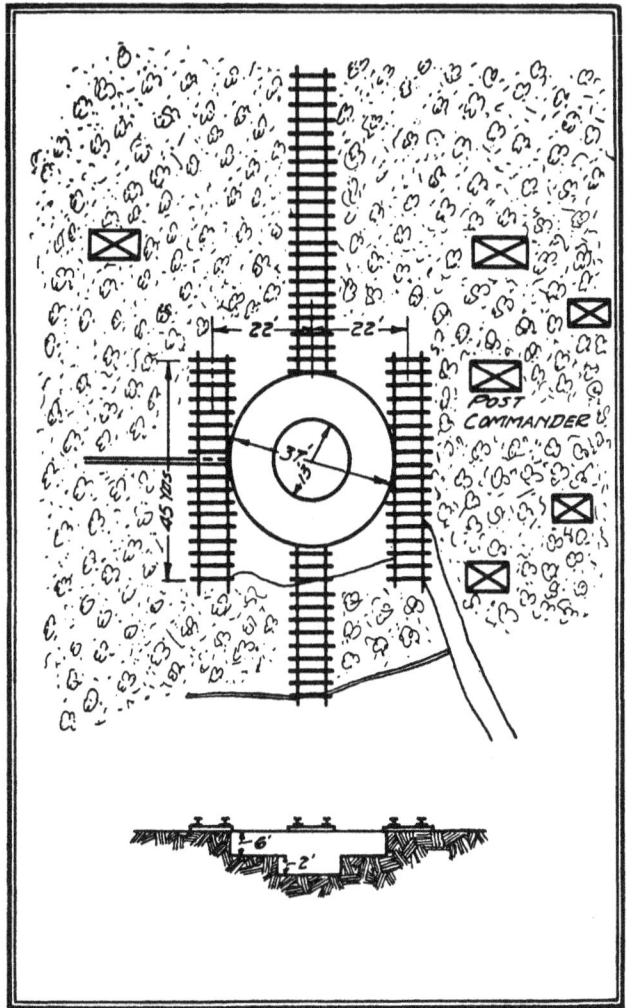

PLAN OF THE BEAUMONT GUN EMPLACEMENT

about 400 tons, more than sufficient to raise the whole carriage and gun too, if need be, off the trucks.

The great railway carriage, minus the gun, was already

THE BEAUMONT BATTERY

standing by on the approach track, imposing and awesome. From the hour when a puffing locomotive had pushed it down into the wood with that solid grinding sound of wheels on rails, unmistakably indicative of massive, heavy, solidly built engines of war or peace, it had not ceased to excite the admiration of every soldier, officer, or civilian engineer who passed and paused to study it. None of them had seen such a carriage before. It was 103.5 feet from front to rear buffers, the cushion or spring types of buffers common on European cars. It was supported on eighteen axles, thirty-six wheels. Seemingly there was more weight forward than back; there were two five-axle trucks forward and two four-axle trucks at the rear. These trucks were connected in pairs by what are known as span-bolsters, and the ends of the carriage body rested on pivots at the centre and top of these bolsters. The distance from centre to centre of these bolster pivots was sixty-nine feet; this, then, was the length of the carriage, though actually it was about five feet longer.

The carriage had no gun on it as it stood. The gun was on several other special flat cars to the rear. The height from the rails to the centre of the trunnion bearings in which the great sleeve or cradle that would contain the gun would rest was ten feet, and the weight of the carriage without the gun was 210 tons.

As soon as the platform was finished and everything declared ready the order was given to place the carriage. The locomotive that had brought the last equipment on to the approach track had remained; it would remain till the carriage was removed. Slowly the great carriage approached the emplacement, grinding heavily, solidly, as it crept along. The front trucks moved on to the rails bridging the space between the approach track and the racer. The great hollow base-section sang like a huge drum beaten softly. Then on to the racer, across it, and the carriage was astride its platform. It was necessary then to place it most perfectly, to set it in position to the millimetre, for when the carriage body had been raised by the four jacks there would be no possibility of shifting it even a hundredth of an inch to make it fit with the key-plates on the racer. So backward and forward it was adjusted until the mark provided on the carriage for just this purpose matched with the complementary mark on the racer.

Heavy steel beams were then lifted into place beside the carriage fore and aft at the jacks by the gantry crane, and worked across under the carriage body and on top of the jacks. These would provide more even bearing and minimize any tendency to twist the carriage body if any single jack should not function properly. Three men were ready at each of the high jack handles, and at the signal began to pump in unison. Each rear jack was connected by small pipes with the corresponding low forward jack, so they rose in unison. Slowly the carriage rose from its trucks, until in fifteen minutes it had been raised nearly an inch. This cleared it from the bolster pivots. The forward trucks were pulled out from under on to the forward central track by the gantry crane. The rear trucks were withdrawn by the locomotive, leaving the carriage suspended on the jacks and looking broadside like a huge bird with extended wings.

The racer, or rotating section of the base, was then turned a quarter turn by means of the rapid traversing mechanism, until the pads, or key-plates, on the racer were under the corresponding plates on the bottom of the side girders of the car body. The valves in the jacks were opened slightly, and the massive body slowly descended to fit perfectly in place with the bolt holes in the car body plates matching those on the racer. The carriage was in place, and in the short period of little more than an hour. While the men were busy bolting it fast the two slow-speed traversing gear-cases were lifted into place on either side of the carriage between the rails of the racer. Each of these had two-man hand-cranks, and they were connected with the traversing gearing under the rear of the carriage by shafts, with universal joints. This gearing was designed to permit eight men to rotate the great load of the racer, carriage, and gun with ease, and to set or point the gun in direction perfectly. The work of installing the gun was no mean job. It weighed 154 tons, and the cradle twenty-six tons more. A crane of unusual strength was required to handle such weights. The gun was lifted by special slings made of cables so placed that the gun balanced perfectly. After it had been transferred safely to the carriage with the cradle trunnions, huge steel pins, so to speak, on either side of the recoil sleeve, or cradle, resting in the bearings on the side girders of the car, the laborious job of adjusting the roller-bearing mechanisms under the trunnions began. Unless the utmost care were taken in adjusting these friction-reducing roller-bearings designed to carry the 180-ton dead load of the gun and cradle, it would be impossible for even eight men to elevate and depress the gun for firing and loading.

And then the job of aligning the gun. Nothing new in this at least. They had already done it five times at Crépy, and fortunate for them they had, for there was but little time to spare. They could have begun firing on the 25th if necessary. Orders had been received directing them to begin firing on the morning of the 27th. There was therefore a day in which the hard-worked battery personnel could rest and relax from the tension that had prevailed during the long siege of forced labour. The artillery activity that had been so intense all about them in the salient in previous weeks had been noticeably slackening. It was said that the forces holding the salient had been appreciably weakened to provide ample reserves to insure complete success on schedule time on the Chemin-des-Dames. Secret orders defined the Vesle river from Soissons to Rheims, with those two cities included, if possible, as the objectives. The most minute directions had been given for every detail. Colonel Bruckmüller, a past master at the art, had charge of all artillery preparations, and it would be nothing short of a miracle if those in the path of the cyclone were not utterly destroyed by the planned rain of destruction, gas and high explosive.

The ballistic officer and his assistant arrived on the 26th, Sunday, ready for another orgy of calculations. They knew quite well by this time what to expect of the 8.26-inch guns, but felt sure that they had new experiences in store for them with the combination of a rebored gun and a shorter range. They had to deal with a heavier and a slightly differently shaped shell. The larger size of the gun would make a difference too. They were delighted with the beautifully designed new installation that they found—what a contrast between this unit and the improvised ones on timber bases at Crépy!

There was no sleep for any member of the battery after 1 A.M., 'X' hour for the artillery, on the 27th. The bombardment was not confined to the sector to the east. It reached out and all about the salient, though of course it was not so violent there as in the east. To them as artillerymen it was music, and when it rose quickly, as it did to the volume of drum-fire, it was thrilling. Perhaps few, if any, could be accused of connecting the deafening noise with the terrible effects on men on the other side, the destruction of homes, the already forming lines of refugees that by morning would be choking the roads. Hardened as they were to all that war meant, they did not glory in that. They heard the heavy concussions, saw the great shells going over to bury themselves deep in the earth beside or in heavy, laboriously constructed shelters, and send them up in geysers of smoke, flame, timbers, and earth. They saw trenches blown in, roads torn up, railways cut, communications and war's trappings demolished, preparatory to the advance of their men, which, in spite of all that the artillery could and would do, would be none too easy; the advance of March had shown that.

Ganz geheim.　　　　　Nr.

Schußtafelauszug
für die
lange 23,2 cm Kanone in Schießgerüst
mit Sprenggranaten L. 4,1 m. Bdz. u. Jz.
(mit Haube).

Gewicht des Geschosses: 124 bis 126 kg
„ der Sprengladung: 8,7 kg (Fp. 1)
„ „ Ladung in der Hauptkartusche:
70 kg R. P. C 12 (1230 · 20 8).

Die Schußtafel ist aufgestellt für 761 mm Barometerstand. Unter Barometerstand ist derjenige am Geschützaufstellungsort und nicht der auf Meeresspiegel reduzierte zu verstehen.

Berlin, 1918.
Reichs-Marine-Amt.

FRONT PAGE OF FIRING-LIST FOR THE 9·13-INCH GUN IN THE BOIS DE CORBIE

THE BEAUMONT BATTERY

The first shell was loaded and the breech closed with almost the same suppressed excitement, ceremony, and meticulous attention to details that had marked the preparations for firing the first shell more than two months before with gun No. 1 at Crépy. The crew had not fired a shot for a month; a new and momentous offensive had begun five hours before. They had a new and beautifully designed complete installation, gun, carriage, and emplacement. Again they were to bring the enemy's greatest city under shell-fire, to contribute their share to the morale-breaking phase of the great history-making and war-ending campaigns of 1918. So no wonder the suppressed excitement, the ceremony.

At 7.27 the order to fire was given, and with that characteristic deep, full, and truly terrible roar the cannon which represented the height of development of man's most destructive engine of personal conflict, a thing that had originated seven centuries before as a device so crude as to be ludicrous even then, had sent the hundred and eighty-sixth shell off through space at the fabled speed of magic! The great mechanism functioned perfectly. The weight of nearly 400 tons resting on the ninety-six 8-inch steel balls was turned as accurately as the finest surveyor's transit; and almost as easily, so far as smoothness of action was concerned. No wonder they were all bursting with pride over their wonderful engine; which is precisely what it was, a 9,000,000-horse-power internal-combustion engine; the cylinder immensely long, the piston a high-explosive shell, and the fuel 432 pounds of smokeless powder. It would have taken the energy of two waterfalls, each larger than Niagara, to impart to the projectile in the time allowed, a fiftieth of a second, sufficient energy to send it the same distance. So far had man progressed in his understanding and employment of the resources of nature, inert materials lying about him, in six centuries.

Fifteen shells were sent forth on their mission by noon,

without a single hitch. The gun behaved beautifully. Measurements of the progress of erosion showed that the rate was far less than with the smaller guns; on March 23 the first gun had shown serious signs of wear, was one-third worn out, and was beginning to perform erratically by the fifteenth shell. On this morning the gauges for every shot showed normal or over-pressures. Some reductions could be made from the charges specified in the tables. The order to cease firing was given with the fifteenth shot at 11.25.

By noon information began to come in by 'phone and wireless of the situation to the east. Corps Staabs, or Winkler, of Boehn's Seventh Army, had descended like a cyclone on those troublesome French counter-batteries at Vailly, had captured them, and was already approaching the Aisne river. Joy was unbounded over the reports in the evening that the Aisne had been passed, and south of Vailly the Vesle, the objective itself, had also been reached and passed. Surely a clean break-through. Victory for Ludendorff, the master-mind behind the mighty offensive. And it was reported that Bruckmüller's artillery preparation had been faultless. The French and British divisions in the way had been smothered, drenched with gas, stunned or put out with high explosive. There had been little resistance to the waves of infantry that had gone over with the creeping barrages at four o'clock.

Firing began earlier on the 28th, the first shot at 5.36. A high pressure for this one. It probably fell entirely over the city. This was to the accompaniment of a hellish racket that had started to the west in the direction of Montdidier at 5.30, while the crew was loading the gun. There was considerable concern over that bombardment which in a few minutes had risen to the scale of drum-fire. No German offensive had been scheduled for this region; that is, no one had heard of any, and one invariably heard of such events long in advance, and within two days of ' y ' day every soldier knew of it. Obviously the enemy had started something.

Reduzierte Schußweitentafel für 50° Erhöhung bei 761 mm Barometerstand, Schußrichtung SW und 15° Pulvertemperatur.

Reduzierte Entfernung km.	Anfangs- geschwin- digkeit m	Zeiten veränder- bung	Fall- winkel	Flug- zeit	Endge- schwindig keit
114	1648	49	55°	182,6	764
112	1637	49	55°	180,5	757
110	1626	49	55°	179,4	749
108	1614	49	55°	178,2	740
106	1603	49	55°	176,5	731
104	1591	49	55°	175,3	722
102	1579	49	55°	174,0	713
100	1567	49	56°	172,5	705
98	1554	49	56°	171,4	699
96	1542	49	56°	170,2	694
94	1529	49	56°	169,0	688
92	1517	49	56°	167,8	683
90	1504	49	56°	166,5	677
88	1491	49	57°	165,3	671
86	1478	49	57°	163,8	665
84	1465	49	57°	162,4	658
82	1452	49	57°	160,8	650
80	1438	49	58°	159,2	640
78	1424	49	58°	157,7	630
76	1409	49	58°	154,8	620
74	1393	49	58°	152,4	610
72	1377	49	59°	149,9	600
70	1361	49	59°	147,4	590

THE BEAUMONT BATTERY

Four shots were fired by 9.12 ; the first and fourth showed almost the same high over-pressures. The second and third were more nearly normal. Those shells must have fallen in the city, but over the target. By this time it had been learned that the hour of heavy bombardment from 5.30 to 6.30 had been a prelude to the storming and taking of Cantigny by the Americans at the very point of the salient west of Montdidier. It had been done thoroughly, with real snap. The Americans now held all of the town, and were digging in several hundred yards east of it. Many were the predictions, with broad smiles and knowing grins, of what would happen to those Americans before the day was over. They would be driven out and back to where they had been so sharply that they would remember the lesson. The German Army was on the look-out for Americans ; the plan had been, opposite Toul, and was still, for any sectors where they were known to be to give them the roughest doses of war ; the old idea of *Schrecklichkeit,* the very idea of the big gun itself, to make war unbearably terrible for the new recruits to the Allied Army and to Allied civilians.

Three more shots were fired from 12.4 to 1.53, and the last three of the day from 5.7 to 5.53; ten for the day. The scheme developed at Crépy of firing in groups of three or four was used, both to save the gun and to hinder sound spotting.

Joy and hilarity were unbounded when it was learned in the evening that the Crown Prince's armies, those of Boehn and Mudra, had passed the Vesle river from Rheims to its junction with the Aisne and had the Aisne to the outskirts of Soissons. All of the objectives reached and passed with but little opposition on the second day. Other reports, not so cheering, had likewise come in saying that in spite of continuous and violent shelling and three determined counter-attacks since eight o'clock in the morning, the Americans still held Cantigny as they had dug in at seven o'clock. And the casualties in the assault waves of the counter-attacks had been appalling.

THE PARIS GUN

A momentous conference was in progress at Grand Headquarters. The Kaiser, the Crown Prince, Generals Hindenburg and Ludendorff were considering a question that they recognized to be of the utmost gravity. Combat orders from Ludendorff had set the Vesle as the objective of this offensive, 'Blücher.' It had been passed everywhere before evening, and though Soissons had not yet been taken, the centre of Boehn's army was just outside the city, and it would fall in the morning. Practically all divisions had reached and passed their objectives and were digging in. But there was no opposition, no organized resistance before them, practically from Soissons to Rheims. The populace of Germany was wild with joy over the unprecedented success. A break-through had been achieved; literally the first on the Western Front. Other attempts had been made on both sides to achieve such an end during the four years, but it had never materialized. Here it was, and it had been neither considered in the plans for the offensive nor expected. 'Blücher' had been planned merely as the second of a series of crushing blows to sap the strength of the Allies, drain their reserves, compel them to shift the weight of their resistance. Rupprecht's armies in Belgium were about ready to deliver a similar blow to the British armies there. Haig had been expecting it there for weeks; he had found every sign of it and had begged Foch for aid.

With the desperate need to keep up the morale of the German people to the end, which in spite of every favour of Fate would prove most costly, could the General Staff afford to neglect this opportunity to exploit an unlooked-for success to the limit, perhaps to a *débâcle* of the Allied armies? As a master strategist, Ludendorff saw clearly what could happen if the extent of the success apparently in sight should prove but a mirage. If they were to convert the limited offensive into a general engagement and get into one of those dangerous deep pockets, the corners of which could not be broken down—then Rupprecht's offen-

THE BEAUMONT BATTERY

sive would have to be delayed, and the next, and perhaps still another, offensive would have to be waged on the present scene of action, where such reserves as the Allies had would, of course, be concentrated; a process of fighting it out with the enemy where he knew one had to attack and where he would have the greatest strength. Ludendorff did not regard the seemingly possible gain as worth the risk. The other three did. So before midnight the order went as rapidly as possible to all division headquarters, and by 'phone, runners, flash-signals to companies everywhere: "The attack will be pressed!" No limit to objectives; the order to exploit successes to the limit, until stopped or told to stop. A momentous decision.

Two shells were off on Wednesday morning, the 29th, between six and seven—at 6.24 and 6.36. Then two more at 1.30 and 1.44; another at 4.17. The first four of these showed pressures that would drop the shells in the city about or somewhat over the target. The fifth showed quite an under-pressure, possibly short of the city. The remaining six projectiles were off at 6.31, 7.37, 7.51, 8.4, 8.15, and 8.21, and all, except the sixth shell at 6.31, must have burst in the suburbs over the city from the high pressures shown by gauges. The pressure for the 6.31 shell was normal, so it probably burst near the target.

As yet there was no counter activity. It had not been expected. But at Crépy so many unexpected things had happened during the first three days that one need not be surprised at anything. French 'planes had been over and about, but had been promptly driven off.

The battery had learned in the morning of the order and bulletin, signed by the Kaiser and Hindenburg, and sent out in the night, to the effect that the attack would be pressed. This could only mean that a break-through had been achieved in the two days, and, instead of stopping on the Vesle as had been planned, the armies, which probably found almost no resistance before them, were to hurry on as rapidly as possible. Once again the headlong rush of German divisions, operating under Hutier's plan with a perfect artillery preparation, had swept all resistance, obstacles, out of the way. This time more completely than in March. A great time for Germany and its armies; the mere word ' Blücher ' would have a thrilling significance in the future.

But the expected come-back had not materialized at Cantigny. Three more counter-offensives had been staged during the day with heavy artillery support. The area was completely shot up. But the Americans were still where they had dug in at 7.30 Tuesday morning. Their casualties must have mounted high by this time from artillery fire; but the German casualties had proved worse. One significant element had developed, the deadly American rifle fire at ranges of from three to five hundred yards. Whether they were seasoned soldiers or not, they were deadly with a rifle. This had not been expected. It was playing havoc with morale in German battalions sent over to rout the Americans out of their new trenches. Possibly it would be necessary to cease the counter-attacks and punish the invaders with artillery.

The failure to regain the lost ground at Cantigny meant nothing, however, in comparison with what the army reports, received late in the day, said had been gained in the east. The French line had broken down as far west as Noyon. Soissons had been taken. In the centre the army had advanced to within half a mile of Fère-en-Tardenois; had reached the Ourcq west of it. The lines were drawing closer to and about Rheims. The German armies were winning, were beating down, sweeping aside, all resistance. " What are the thoughts of the millions in Paris ? " asked members of the battery of each other. 'Planes dropping bombs on them at night, the great gun shelling them by day, the French front between Soissons and Rheims obviously broken, and the Germans again sweeping down on

THE BEAUMONT BATTERY

the Marne with every prospect of crumpling the French corner at Soissons and then sweeping westward toward the capital.

The battery commander decided during the evening of Wednesday, the 29th, to add all that he could to the accumulating weight of disaster which it was hoped would soon break the French will to resist. So Thursday's bombardment was scheduled to begin in the early morning hours. They had tried this on April 14. A shell bursting within the city in the quiet of the night could be heard a great distance and would awaken many people. They would be listening for more, and would have ample opportunity to think, with the pessimism and gloom characteristic of night, of the growing disaster only fifty miles east of them. The first shot was fired at 2.37. The pressure was low; perhaps because of a cold gun. The shell must have struck in the extreme north-east of the city. The second shot was fired at 3.3, and the third at 3.59. This one may have burst three or four miles short of the target. The firing was stopped then lest observers on the French line or airmen got the opportunity to locate the flashes. If two observers could see a flash simultaneously through transits or similar instruments from two widely separated points they would have the exact location of the gun. None doubted that to the west and south there were such observers, scores, hundreds of them, listening, watching for anything and everything of small or great significance. Every sound, every unusual event, even an ordinary event, is regarded suspiciously in war. While the great gun was firing there were French, English, and American soldiers in listening posts, the Germans on the other side, straining every sense to catch the unusual. Others equally vigilant were on all places of prominence watching for the tiniest light, flash-signals, the flash of cannon, signs of the passage of truck trains over back roads. They would not miss anything so vivid as the flash of the great gun. Seeing it once would serve them little. But a third or fourth time would enable them to get their instruments on it.

The fourth shot was fired at 7.1; another at 7.17, and two more at 8.31 and 8.55. The battery was silent then until evening, when six shells were fired in fairly rapid succession, at 6.42, 8, 8.17, 8.36, 8.56, and 9.2. The first of these showed a considerable under-pressure. The shell may have struck four or five miles short of the target. A cold gun again, and possibly the change of wind. What a joy it was to operate this larger calibre gun! It had fired forty-nine shots when the order was given to cease firing on the 30th, the fourth day, shortly after nine o'clock in the evening. But it was yet far from being worn out. The forty-ninth shot had shown a normal pressure, the shell must have fallen very close to the target. The forty-eighth had fallen over the target, the forty-seventh far over the city. In checking this performance with that of the gun which began to fire from Emplacement No. 2 at Crépy on Good Friday afternoon, March 29, and had to be removed on April 7 after firing forty-eight rounds, it was clear that the rebored gun, operating at the reduced range, was a far superior weapon. Comparing the last fifteen shots from that gun with the thirteen of the day from the larger gun, it was seen that but four of the fifteen shells from the Crépy gun had reached the target. The remaining eleven had fallen short. The average range of the fifteen had been 72.6 miles—2.3 miles short of the target.

Of the thirteen shells of this day, May 30, seven had developed such over-pressures that four of them must have fallen entirely over the city and the remaining three over the target and within the city; an eighth had shown a normal pressure. The average range of the thirteen for the day had been 68.1 miles, a fifth of a mile short. To this point then the new gun had proved distinctly superior. There had been, and still was, apprehension, however, for as experienced artillerists they knew that a gun finally

THE BEAUMONT BATTERY

reaches a point in wear or erosion when it begins to break down at an alarmingly rapid rate. Excessively high pressures with the consequent high temperatures cause the havoc. Howitzers with their low pressures have a long life. This gun with its unusual length to give the projectile the necessary extreme velocity was subjected to punishment not experienced by the ordinary gun. The shell remained in the gun for a longer time. The interior of the gun was subjected to extremely high temperatures longer. Thus the dense hot gases streaming up the bore of the gun from the powder-chamber, grinding almost as a blast of sand on metal, or a stream of water in a placer mine, found the surfaces nearer the powder-chamber a trifle softened from the longer period of exposure to extreme heat. Naturally the erosion at the rear then was excessive, and the rougher the surface became the more rapid the progress of erosion.

The last five shots of the day were fired to the accompaniment of the exhilarating news that the armies had made wonderful progress. They had reached the Marne. And the line directly south of the gun position had broken down to and beyond Noyon. Surely the Allied armies had broken down completely to permit so great a total advance in four days, and such an extreme advance in the centre for this day. Men of the battery could not get very detailed information, nothing to tell them exactly what the rapidly advancing armies were encountering; but surely the decision heralded by the order of the night of the 28th was now shown to be the result of an unexpected but virtual break-through. Such enthusiasm had not prevailed over the achievements of their comrades since the brilliant coups of Hindenburg at Tannenburg and of Mackenzen on his sweep through Roumania. Already there were suggestions that the brilliant gains of the past four days had put at the disposal of the battery a rather wide choice of new positions within less than 60 miles of Paris. If a reduction of range from 74.6 to 68.3 miles worked so greatly to the advantage of the gun as the performance to the end of this day had shown, would not a further reduction of ten, or perhaps fifteen, miles work even greater advantages? And the installation of one of the steel bases would be an easy matter now that they had had the opportunity to install one rather leisurely. The fact that there was no extra 232-mm., or 9.13-inch, gun available, in the event of the sudden complete wearing out of the one in use, added materially to the attractiveness of the newly won territory. But the main railway-junction point, Soissons, through which the railways of the area passed, would have to be strongly consolidated to justify taking so valuable a weapon through it and down toward the Marne. Desperate efforts were being made by the French to hold that Soissons Corner. Nothing more had been gained there during the day.

While Boehn's Seventh Army was striving mightily on Friday to push back the lines of French and British divisions all along the western wall of the great Marne pocket, and particularly in the region of Soissons, where such stubborn resistance had developed, the Paris Gun crew got off six rounds from 8.7 to 1.44, with such radically different results as to make them sit up and take notice. Every shot showed a marked under-pressure. The pressure for the first was so low that it must have fallen as much as seven, or possibly eight, miles short of the target. The highest pressure, that for the fifth shot at 1.37, could hardly have sent the shell within the city; a most disconcerting contrast with the highly commendable behaviour during the previous four days. Otherwise every mechanism of the gun, carriage, and base continued to function perfectly.

The long-expected counter-bombardment began during the day with some heavy shells dropping in and about the wood, but nowhere close to the gun position. Obviously the French gunners had only the sound-rangers' locations to guide them this time and they were working from a much greater distance. There was no cause for any such alarm

THE BEAUMONT BATTERY

as had been created by the shell which dropped in the meadow between gun positions 1 and 3 at 12.30, noon, on March 24.

The reports of the evening indicated that substantial gains had been made from Noyon south-east past Soissons to the Marne. The German Army was in possession of the north bank of the Marne from the Jaulgonne bend west to and including Château-Thierry. Heavy fighting was in progress all along the river. The passage of the river was being bitterly contested.

Saturday, June 1, and Monday, the 3rd, were for the Paris Gun but repetitions of Friday, May 31. Eight shots were fired on Saturday, none on Sunday, and six on Monday, fourteen in all. The pressures for every shot were low. This made a total of sixty-nine shots, more than had been fired from any previous gun. The gun showed pronounced wear, but not to the point yet to justify condemnation. And they were in no position to do so. There were no other 232-mm. guns available. This gun was not yet so badly worn as some of the 210-mm. guns at Crépy, certainly not so badly as the last one which had fired fifty-two rounds by May 1.

It appeared from the greater number of heavy shells that fell in and about Corbie Wood on Saturday that another heavy French gun had joined in the counter-bombardment. But there was still no serious cause for alarm. There was no indication that French airmen had secured any photographs. It was hoped that when they would secure such photographs they would be deceived by the trick of camouflage, that of providing the false emplacement and railway curve just at the edge of the wood.

The battery fired four shots on Tuesday, none on Wednesday nor Thursday, seven on Friday, and six on Saturday, June 8: a total of eighty-six. All four of Tuesday showed such pressures as to indicate that the shells had struck within the city, though short of the target. The most erratic

THE PARIS GUN

behaviour to date occurred when the first shot of Saturday showed the highest pressure recorded so far. That shell could easily have fallen four or five miles over the target. Shots 4, 5, and 6 showed such extremely low pressures as to leave the crew in doubt as to what to do. The sixth was the lowest so far; that shell could have fallen six or seven miles short of the target. The first at 11.27, four miles over, and the sixth at 8.4 P.M., seven under, an extreme variation for the day of eleven miles; a record.

The 5th was a beautifully clear day, and French airmen were over frequently. It seemed certain that they were securing numerous photographs of the region. The next day's counter-bombardment proved the supposition correct, and made it clear too that they had not discovered the real emplacement. The centre of the bombardment had shifted to the region of the camouflaged false emplacement. How annoyed the French artillerymen must have been to find that the mean point located by the sound-rangers and on which they had been firing was so far from the point revealed on the photograph! It was possible now that a chance shell might cut the railway line in the rear, but that was not serious. The entire battery personnel were so grateful for the freedom from the intolerable shelling from the 6-inch guns which they had had to suffer at Crépy, that this shelling seemed of little consequence.

Vicious fighting was in progress all about the great Marne salient without registry of real gains of territory from the night of May 31 through Saturday, June 8. Obviously the Allies had somehow established a line where they now stood which they meant to maintain, else they would have been pushed back in those eight days. The German casualties were beginning to mount fearfully; battalions on the line were being gassed and cut to pieces by the never-ceasing rain of high explosive and machine-gun fire, and exhausted in the continual necessity to meet counter-attacks and heavy combat patrols. While no formidable counter-attack had

POSITION NO. 2
Pit for timber base in the foreground. Timber loading platform at left with removable gang-plank.

TREE LADDER AT POSITION NO. 3 FOR PLACING AND REMOVING CAMOUFLAGE NETTING

RELATIVE SIZES OF THE SHELL AND POWDER CHARGE OF THE PARIS GUN

208

THE BEAUMONT BATTERY

been attempted, the Allied units from Noyon to the Marne and from there to Rheims were like angry hornets stinging viciously and without cease either by day or by night. German units were too exhausted by the first five days' hard driving to do more than stay where they were. Even so, the process of attrition was rapidly rendering some of them ineffective. They would have to be replaced, and quickly. A delicate situation was preparing; the situation that Ludendorff had foreseen on the evening of the 28th when the momentous question had come up for decision and the council had voted three to one to push on without limit to objectives. He saw clearly now on June 8 that the Allies had comprehended fully the possibilities to them of holding on to the Soissons, now the Villers-Cotterets, and the Rheims corners. It was clear that they had let the centre go, and had concentrated reserves on both sides at those corners, and had taken the few days between the 28th and the 31st to establish a line on the Marne to hold the advancing centre when it should arrive there. So an attempt was necessary at once to break down at least one of the corners before the Allies could consolidate or organize too solidly.

On Sunday morning, June 9, the Paris Gun battery were awakened early by the noise of a heavy bombardment all along the line south of them. It was the offensive ordered in Hutier's Eighteenth Army to break the French line and cut off one of those two intolerable corners. If even this could be done and the line straightened out, they would be some nine miles nearer Paris, perhaps drive the French Government into a panic, and they themselves would be free of the ever-present menace of a formidable counter-attack by Foch at Soissons. When the preliminary bombardment with all its usual embellishments switched to a barrage the line drove forward from Noyon west to Montdidier. They advanced during the day across the Lassigny hills to a depth of five miles against the fiercest resistance.

THE PARIS GUN

No such gains as on May 28, and what a vast difference in the type of resistance! Every hundred yards was gained by stubborn, costly, and discouraging fighting.

The next day the advancing front was narrowed by a half; this spear thrust itself forward about the same distance as the gain of the day before. On the 11th the left of Hutier's army drove forward for a gain of five miles in the centre on a front of eleven miles. The 12th and 13th saw each of these bulges in the line advanced a few miles further. But, beginning in the afternoon of the 10th, Hutier had had to contend with an unexpected flank attack of Mangin ("the Butcher") from the west, and on the 13th the battle, which was going badly, was called off. It was obvious that a heavy preparation was necessary to break down either of the corners. This engagement of Hutier's had helped but little.

The Paris Gun battery had fired twelve shots on Sunday, the 9th, from 7.52 A.M. to 5 P.M., five on Monday, and one on Tuesday, the last at 5.47 P.M. Only three of these eighteen showed pressures sufficient to send the shells into the city. This made a total of 104 shots from the larger gun, a vastly superior record to that of any previous gun.

Orders were received on Tuesday to cease firing and prepare to move battery.

VI

THE THIRD AND LAST GREAT OFFENSIVE

THE THIRD BOMBARDMENT

On July 15, or 18, as one prefers, disaster and doom for the German Armies were written by the Fates in their ledger of wars. Since only they knew of this when the second brilliantly successful offensive was ended on June 12, we have chosen to chronicle in greater detail than heretofore the shaping of the plans of the armies for the next move in their phase of the campaign, to show how in the month of delay, which had never been anticipated in the year's aggressive activities, the German nation, and particularly the armies, began to doubt themselves, and the reserves of the Allies were built up to the point of enabling them to grasp a fortuitous, psychological opportunity.

THE STATE OF AFFAIRS ON JUNE 12

THE German armies were in just that predicament, the possibility of which gave General Ludendorff so much concern at the famous conference on the evening of May 28 and caused him to cast his vote, " No," against a conversion of the limited objective offensive into a general one. Somehow the Allies had held the Soissons and Rheims corners against persistent, gruelling, and merciless hammering. Twice Ludendorff had found incredibly weak spots in the Allied line; on each occasion there had been promise of a break-through, of conversion of the trench warfare into warfare of movement; each time the Allies had found the reserves to dam the break. In each case they had lost heavily in men, supplies, and territory, but at the same time each operation had ended with the German Army no closer to their goal, victory, than by just those losses in men and supplies. From the beginning of the ' Blücher ' offensive on the Chemin-des-Dames on May 27 to the end of ' Hammer Blow ' from Soissons west to Montdidier on June 13 the Germans had captured 61,000 men, the equivalent of about six divisions, as they were reckoned in the French and German armies. In addition, more divisions had been accounted for in casualties. So the Allied reserve had been exhausted by probably eight divisions. Eight hundred guns had been captured. Fifteen hundred officers had been taken.

But at the same time the cost to the German Army had been terrific. Hindenburg and Ludendorff had told the Reichstag that the casualties might run to a million and a half for a decision during the year. The formidable casualty list for the two offensives gave promise of a fulfilment of that prediction. Each of the two offensives had cost in money the equivalent of a very respectable national debt. It was expected, of course, that the Allies would eventually pay that bill.

All plans for the immediate launching of the already prepared offensive by the Army Group Rupprecht in Belgium had to be abandoned. On the 13th the major flow of energy was from within the great salient out. The positions gained had not been consolidated; there had been no time for that. The Allied reserves had arrived, and the resistance had stiffened all about the great pocket to the point of requiring prohibitively costly effort on the part of those within to make any further progress. The Allies were just holding. The German divisions then on the front of the First and Seventh Armies were certainly weary of striving, of the gruelling days and nights of fighting through underbrush, through wheat fields, across ravines, brooks, creeks. The great war-machine was as formidable as ever; no one

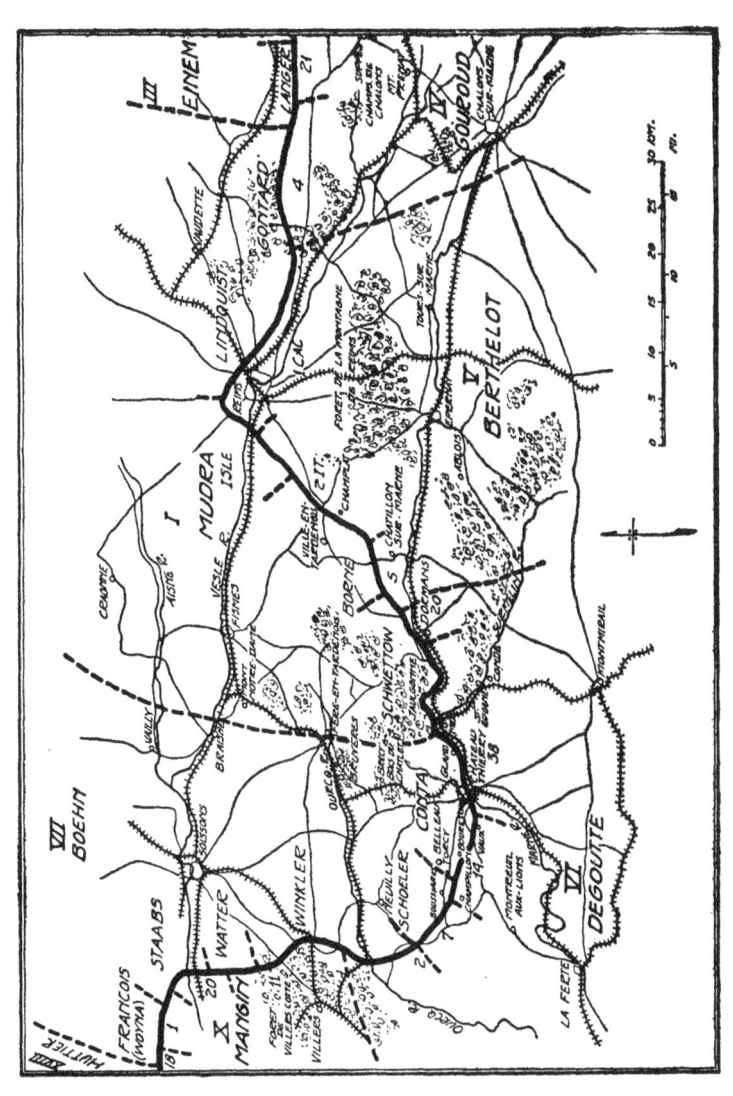

THE MARNE FRONT ON JUNE 12, 1918

doubted its ability to make further progress, to win to eventual victory; but it must be refuelled, re-energized, the wear and tear repaired.

There was a real question as to whether it would not be wise to start the offensive in Flanders at once, since the plans for it were practically complete in every detail. A goodly share of the Allied reserves had been drawn from all parts of the line down about the Soissons-Château-Thierry-Rheims salient. The holding of Verdun and Rheims was a point of honour with the French armies, as demonstrated by their resistance at those two points in 1916 and during the previous two weeks. So a lunge into the line at Ypres might find the same amazing weakness discovered on the front of the British Fifth Army in March and between Soissons and Rheims on May 27. There was not sufficiently definite knowledge of the Allied strength, however, to warrant ignoring entirely the serious possibilities of the Marne position. There were far too many men in that area to be supplied over the available railway lines. The only inlet was through Soissons, which was easily under the Allies' guns and was being shelled and bombed constantly. A goodly portion of the salient was not served by any railways at all. No doubt of it, the area had too many men in it to be provisioned; and the Allied strength about it had become such that the strength within could not be reduced with safety. The men in it had to stay there. There was no choice, therefore, but to prepare at once to widen the salient, and there was no time to lose. This extra offensive to relieve a predicament had not been counted on; the fighting season was passing rapidly; and by autumn the Americans could possibly arrive in such force as to make the outcome doubtful. There seemed no choice but to delay the Flanders offensive temporarily and to prepare to take Rheims at once.

On June 14 all divisions in the salient and some outside received an order looking toward the next move.

THE LAST GREAT OFFENSIVE

GENERAL HEADQUARTERS
June 14, 1918

TO ALL ARMY GROUPS

All army groups will restrict active operations to those absolutely necessary.

The artillery and the trench mortar activity along the heretofore attack-front Montdidier-Marne, and along the Chambrecy-Rheims front will be continued. *It is desirable that the Entente believe that we intend to continue our offensive operations toward Paris.*

Army Group Crown Prince. The Eighteenth and Seventh Armies will make all necessary preparations for an attack along the front from Moreuil to the Marne. These headquarters reserve the right to decide as to local operations.

The Seventh Army will especially support the front between the forest of Villers-Cotterets and the Marne. *Hill 204 west of Château-Thierry must be held by us.*

The Seventh Army will make all preparations under the code word 'Marne Defence.'

The First Army will make all preparations for an attack east of Rheims (in the Prosnes sector) under the code word 'Rheims.'

Both armies will submit to these headquarters attack plans for 'Marne Defence' and 'Rheims,' which will indicate the missions and compositions of units as well as necessary requirements in infantry and artillery, etc. *The attack will be about July 10.*

Army Group Crown Price Rupprecht will execute 'Hagen.' The start of the attack will be about July 20.

Preparations for the attack will be continued on the Wilhelm front and also on the left of the Second Army.

These headquarters reserve the right to designate the diversion attack 'Echenbrecher' from the front of the Seventeenth Army.

Army Groups Gallwitz and Prince Albrecht will execute their operations against the Americans as ordered heretofore.

LUDENDORFF
Chief of Staff of the Field Army

I*a*. No. 8685, *secret*

This order seemed to contemplate a general attack on a long front; from Moreuil, south-east of Amiens, to the Marne, thence to Rheims, and on east on the front of the First Army a sufficient distance to insure securing both banks of the Marne as far as Châlons. If the Eighteenth and Seventh Armies were successful the Soissons menace would be eliminated; and if the Seventh and First Armies succeeded the sorely needed additional railway facilities through Rheims would be theirs; and all of the river crossings from Château-Thierry to Châlons would be available for a possible thrust southward and then westward on Paris. Detailed study of the problems, however, the difficulties, troops, artillery, and supplies required, might limit the extent of the attack front.

Activities on the Marne Front, June 13–15

If the German Army had found the Allies surprisingly weak in the ' Blücher ' attack, they certainly did not find them passive after the line became stabilized. For reasons which were not fully comprehended, the Allies had at once assumed a sort of offensive; the kind that, if kept up long enough, may break the nerve and will-to-fight of the stronger of the opponents. They found the Americans at Château-Thierry, and soon discovered them all along the Marne river east to Mézy. Then they found them in line west of Château-Thierry up past Bouresches, Belleau, Torcy, and past Bussiares. This was disquieting. What about the submarines and their part of the campaign? Americans were not supposed to be in France in force yet, and certainly not sufficiently trained to be at these vital places in the line.

Orders had been issued that offensive operations should cease, and only those activities that were necessary continue. But this did not contemplate a retirement at any point, nor was there much, if any, expectation that divisions in the line that had not seen too severe service before June 5 would be relieved until the next offensive should start. This was a stable and hence ' tranquil ' sector. There was a grim humour to the term ' tranquil '; especially grim to the front-line troops. The front-line divisions found themselves

THE LAST GREAT OFFENSIVE

in a veritable hornets' nest. They were in sufficient force, had sufficient supports available, ample supplies to hold where they were, but the punishment that began at once was gruelling. Their own artillery was not able to silence the hostile batteries, nor, indeed, was it possible even for the air reconnaissance to find the hostile batteries. On the 13th the 11th Bavarian Division of Corps Staabs were so heavily shelled with gas that the men had to wear their masks for twelve hours. There was so much gas about in the rain-soaked fields and underbrush even after that long period that when the masks were removed more than five hundred men were reported ill of gas. Air observers reported great activity of the Allies in and about the Villers-Cotterets Wood, the eastern section of which was held by Corps Winkler.

At noon on the 14th the enemy began a heavy interdiction fire,[1] particularly on the front of the 11th Bavarian Division of Corps Staabs, west of Soissons. Gradually it extended along the entire front to the Marne, rising at times to the volume of drum-fire. Much gas was used. This lasted throughout the afternoon and night, and after a drum-fire of an hour and a half, lasting till 4.30 A.M., on the 15th, the French launched a combined tank and infantry attack on the 11th Division front of Corps Staabs. That front was pushed in half a mile, and it was only after the most vicious and bloody fighting and numerous counter-attacks that the attackers were stopped. Hill 162 was held, but other lost ground could not be recovered.

Plans

Von Mudra, Commander-in-Chief of the First Army, made his first report to Headquarters of Army Group Crown Prince on plans for the Rheims-Marne attack on

[1] Howitzer and heavy gun fire on all railways and highways leading to a front, for the purpose of interrupting all traffic, passage of troops, supplies, etc.

the 16th; this in response to the directions of General Ludendorff's order of the 14th. Summarized to its barest essentials, this advised and informed:

> Objective of attack to be made by First Army requires junction with Seventh Army between Épernay and Bouzy; Seventh Army

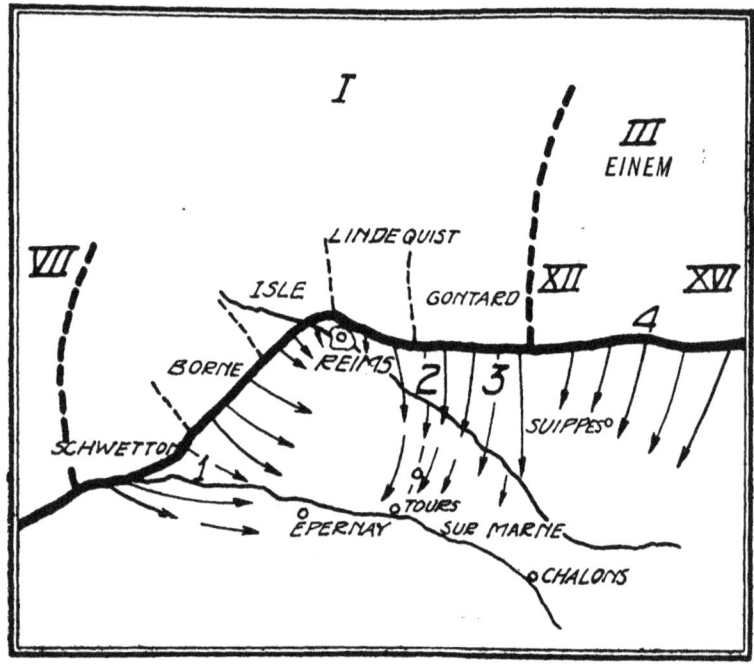

ATTACK DIRECTIONS PROPOSED BY THE FIRST ARMY

> must therefore direct centre of its attack toward the Marne. . . . Since in the 'Blücher' attack on May 27 the centre of the Seventh Army advanced 18 kilometres on the first day, and since terrain before us is easier than that of the Chemin-des-Dames, *we shall probably reach Marne on the first day.* . . . As before, the prerequisite for success is surprise of the enemy . . . Special measures of precaution must be taken to hide preparations since the enemy holds commanding hills and has good view of terrain of approach. . . . In addition to surprise we require extension of front for such a heavy attack to avoid hostile flank attacks. . . .

THE LAST GREAT OFFENSIVE

Assault troops must be formed into three groups; the centre composed of selected divisions will execute the attack with special force to the Marne and between the Marne and the Rheims mountains toward Épernay. . . . An advance on hills between Souain and Suippes and to the heights along the Suippes-Châlons road and north of Châlons is the best protective measure against danger from the east. . . . The hostile artillery, much reinforced in the past few days and echeloned in great depth, is about three hundred batteries strong. Besides first frontal resistance, we must expect main hostile counter-pressure to come from the east where the enemy can and will gather up local reserves and bring additional reserves from Verdun. Must also expect counter-attacks against the west wing, which will be the stronger, as the enemy's situation north of the Marne becomes more desperate. Centre Group will encounter hostile troops from camp at Mourmelon and from Châlons. . . . Corps Isle and Bourne about Rheims must be weakened in artillery in favour of the main attack front. . . . Comparing difficulties on this front with those on the Ailette on May 27, it seems that the time-table for this attack should be about the same as for the ' Blücher ' attack.

This report received an immediate reply from Ludendorff on the following day:

I approve the lateral extension of the attack and the estimate of the situation as to the enemy. . . . Hostile reinforcements are to be expected principally from Châlons. . . . Attack of Third Group should therefore be directed on that point. . . . The Left or Fourth Group should attack toward Mount Prenay and Suippes to meet hostile second-line reinforcements and reserves from the east. . . . Only weak resistance may be expected from Épernay. . . . The Second Group east of Rheims and astride the Marne canal should push forward to the Marne at Tours-sur-Marne *via* Ambonnay. . . . The First Group west of Rheims will cut off the enemy to the west. . . . Request you to insert especially strong group of artillery to neutralize hostile artillery on north-west edge of the Rheims hills. . . . On the 18th or 19th I shall be with the First Army to discuss location of battle zones and any necessary changes. Please have there the Chief of Staff of the Third Army and other officers familiar with the terrain.

THE PARIS GUN

On the same day, the 17th, Von Boehn, commanding the Seventh Army, forwarded his report on plans for their attack ' Marne Defence ' :

> The centre of the attack on Épernay must be carried across the river toward Ablois to sufficiently secure the southern flank. It appears necessary then to take the terrain west of Surmelin brook to the line Gland-Saint-Eugène in order to straighten out the deep

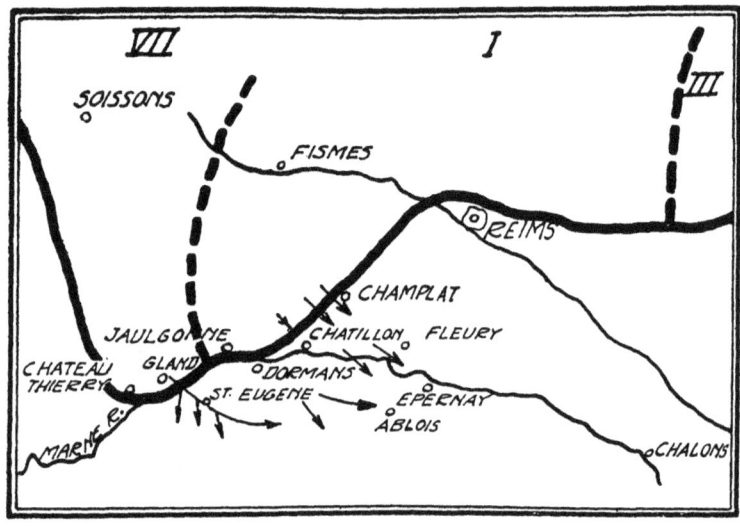

ATTACK DIRECTIONS SUGGESTED BY THE SEVENTH ARMY

> right flank. On the left the advance on Épernay is possible only if a simultaneous advance is made north of the Marne at least to the hills of Fleury la Rivière. Suggest the line Châtillon-Champlat as a base line for the attack north of the Marne. Regard it best not to take the line prior to the main attack in order not to attract attention of the enemy, who undoubtedly expects an attack here, and to avoid diminishing the factor of surprise. . . . If the surprise succeeds, *and this is the prerequisite for the attack*, then the centre of the Army will encounter relatively little resistance. On the other hand, we must count on stubborn defence north of the Marne. The enemy has already counted on an attack there and has prepared his defence. In the subsequent course of the

THE LAST GREAT OFFENSIVE

attack the enemy will probably exert strong pressure on the right flank in order to counteract success of the left wing in the progress east on both sides of the Marne.

Concerning plans for crossing the Marne, he said:

The Marne is about 250 feet broad and ten to twelve feet deep. The current averages one and one-half to two feet per second. Both banks are firm and from three to five feet high. There are routes of approach and departure. The hills close to the Marne valley are some five hundred feet high above the bottom of the valley. Their slopes are steep and mostly bare. The bringing up of crossing material and the approach of troops will therefore be subjected to hostile artillery fire and surprise will be hard to attain. The crossing will have to be made after the hostile batteries have been gassed. If the river obstacle has been overcome, then the railway embankment, which is admirably adapted for defence, will have to be assaulted. The infantry will take position in readiness for the assault on the south bank, under protection of our barrage, which concentrates approximately 500 yards south of the Marne. We must gain the foot of the hills on the south bank. There the attack will find many dead angles from where it can ascend the ridge under cover. *To take possession of the ridge will be the main object.*

In the matter of a time schedule:

It is advised that 'X' hour, when our artillery will open with surprise fire, be so determined that the start for the assault will be at the first signs of dawn. The heaviest artillery should open at 'X' plus ten minutes, and the strongest fire on hostile infantry should begin at 'X' plus fifty-five minutes. We should begin the construction of bridges at this same time. Two hours should be allowed to cross over the assaulting infantry. At 'X' plus sixty-five minutes a barrage should be concentrated 500 yards south of the Marne. Ten minutes later the infantry should have finished crossing and be in readiness for the assault. The barrage should advance for 200 minutes from 'X' plus 175 and at the rate of 20 yards per minute.

General Ludendorff appeared at First Army Headquarters on the 18th to discuss that Army's recommendation of an extension of the attack to the east and the location of battle zones. His decision was telephoned to Army Group Crown Prince that evening: "Based on to-day's discussion, attack Rheims will be enlarged to the east as far as the Wetterecke. For the attack 'Rheims' Army Crown Prince will take command of the First and Third Armies. . . ."

The general plans for the coming storm were thus virtually completed. In the four days since the 14th the idea of an offensive on the fronts of the Eighteenth, Seventh, and First Armies from Moreuil to the Marne, thence to Rheims and on east, had been modified to a plan for an attack, first by the left of the Seventh Army from the Marne to Rheims and by the First and Third Armies thence east, and in a subsequent offensive an attack by the Eighteenth Army and the right of the Seventh from the Somme to the Marne. Events would show if this were wise. It now remained to perfect details, find the reinforcements requested by the three armies that were to participate, and to proceed as rapidly as possible with the preparations. It seemed doubtful whether all that needed to be done could be completed by July 10, the tentative date set for the attack. The total attack involved a crossing of the Marne at the Jaulgonne Bend, west of Château-Thierry, by the Seventh Army, an advance to the heights south of the river, and then a movement east both north and south of the river to meet the First Army, which was to drive straight south to the Marne about Epernay and then west to cut off the French forces between Rheims and the Marne. The Third Army was simply to press forward to engage all forces in front of it that could otherwise become reserves for the French armies opposing the First Army. It would also prevent a repetition of the great 'sore thumb' Marne salient.

Had any of those so busily at work perfecting the plans for the great attack had the time to study the situation in a detached manner, several facts would have stood out prominently. First, the assumption of success; second, the

THE LAST GREAT OFFENSIVE

great necessity for secrecy; and, third, the enormous effort on the part of three armies, and the supplies of every description, already prepared and available, that would be required to accomplish the plans.

There was not the slightest thought but that the German armies would accomplish what they were planning to do. Why not? Had not the ' Michael ' and ' Blücher ' offensives proved the Allies incredibly weak and the German armies vastly superior in men and supplies? In the ' wearing out ' process which was the summer's plan the Allies in their desperation had used well-nigh all their available reserves to dam the two breaks. Soon they would have no more reserves except the raw Americans, and then would be the end.

The element of surprise was of the greatest importance; in fact, absolutely vital to the success of the headlong Hutier method of attack which they were employing. If the enemy could learn early enough of the time and place of the attack, those selected divisions in the centre, which would plunge forward recklessly with but little regard for their flanks, might find themselves in an area from which the enemy had withdrawn, and could be smothered, annihilated, by enemy artillery fire and planned flank attacks. As for the men and supplies that would be expended, that was but a part of the game; why speculate upon it, or upon the remote possibility of failure? But on the element of secrecy there was unquestioned need for the greatest care, and no opportunity was lost to emphasize this. Von Mudra sent out a special order on the subject on the 18th:

> The entire success of attack ' Rheims ' will depend principally on the degree of surprise caused the enemy. The first and principal duty during the period of preparations is secrecy. We must not only keep our plan hidden from the enemy, but we must avoid everything that might cause *our own troops* to get an inkling of what is intended. . . . Anyone disobeying orders on secrecy, no matter who, or what rank he holds, will be proceeded against with

THE PARIS GUN

the utmost severity. .... All occupied villages must be kept absolutely dark at night; no bivouac fires.

The Paris Gun

In the interval between the 11th and the 18th the crew of the Paris Gun at Beaumont had removed the gun from the carriage and sent it back to Essen for a second reboring. The removal of the gun was a tedious job. The subsequent removal of the railway carriage from the emplacement was but the work of a few hours; the reversal of the simple process by which it had been installed. Then began the work of dismantling the top or rotating section of the base into its four sections, the removal of the sandbags, and the taking apart and removing of the six base-sections and the placing of them on flat cars for transportation down into the great salient where a favourable position had been found which was only some fifty miles from Paris. By the 18th the position had been evacuated, and all of the material, with a new gun to follow later, was on the way south toward Soissons, the only port of entry into the triangle. There was a justifiable apprehension on the part of the crew for their beloved gun and its parts, for Soissons and the railway from there south had been under practically constant shell-fire since the line had become stabilized. But orders were orders, and soon the line would be pushed far to the east, south, and west of the new position.

Activity on the Marne Front, June 25–July 1

The weather began to clear on the 25th, and the entire front at once became active again. The hostile fire on various division fronts at times rose in volume to drum-fire. Much gas was used. Soissons received some eighty heavy shells during the day. 'Planes flew over constantly on the 25th, bombing villages and firing on batteries with machine-guns. The attack on the 87th Division was stopped, but

THE LAST GREAT OFFENSIVE

only with severe fighting. Corps Winkler was heavily shelled and bombed all that day and night.

Heavy artillery fire of every description continued on both sides on the 26th, 27th, and 28th, and Soissons was bombed. Two attacks were made by the enemy on the 80th Reserve Division on the 26th. The artillery fire against Corps Staabs continued throughout the 27th. It increased to great volume during the night and extended over on to Corps Watter. Following this preparation, the enemy attacked and pushed in the front of the 78th Reserve Division. Soissons was shelled on the 27th. The losses in the fighting with the Americans for the north corner of Belleau Wood, which was lost, were 450 men.

The enemy made alarming progress in the attack of the 27th, on the 34th and 14th Divisions of Corps Staabs. The attack which had been preceded by the strongest possible drum-fire was made with an unprecedented number of tanks and combat 'planes. The hills north and south of Cutry and the village of Hignières were taken. The battle declined in force by evening, with strong interdiction fire on rear roads continuing. It seemed imperative that the enemy be driven back by a vigorous counter-attack lest he use his newly won position as a jumping-off place in an attack on the vital railway centre, Soissons. Such a counter-attack would require several days' preparation. But a counter-attack could not be approved.

The 14th, 6th, 34th, 47th, and probably the 23rd Divisions were so completely battle-worn and used up that their immediate relief was imperative. They had been worn out by the ceaseless night and day hammering of enemy artillery, loss of sleep, and the endless limited attacks and perpetual necessity for being on guard against such attacks. Their losses in killed and wounded had materially reduced their strength. Von Boehn telephoned to the headquarters of the Crown Prince at 1.55 A.M. on the 28th:

You are informed, in view of to-day's battle and the consequent situation, that even if there be no counter-attack the artillery reinforcement must remain with Corps Watter and Staabs. The 14th Division must be replaced. It is impossible to withdraw any additional forces from the Marne Front, for 'Marne Defence.' It is not at all improbable that the battles at Soissons will be extended, which will interfere with the 'Marne Defence,' just as will also the epidemic of *grippe*.

The growing vigour of the attacks on the west side of the salient was becoming disquieting. General Ludendorff admitted his concern in a message to the Crown Prince on July 1:

I approve the July *defensive* fronts, the execution of the intended measures, and also the basic creation and location of the zones in rear, with the reservation that by the preparations for defence the idea that we will attack must not be crowded into the background. In case of hostile attacks on a large scale we shall have to reckon with numerous tank squadrons. Their defeat requires specially careful selection of the line of main resistance. Wherever possible, stream lines and similar obstacles should be selected.

Von Boehn admitted his anxiety in his telephone message of the same day to the Crown Prince:

It is recommended again, as already verbally and by telegraph, that the completely worn out 14th Division be replaced by a fresh position division, that sufficient replacements be assigned to the 34th, 47th Reserve, 45th Reserve, and 51st Reserve Divisions to bring their battalions up to 750 men effective strength. At the present time these divisions are too weak for fighting purposes. . . . *The Seventh Army believes the west front should be reinforced* for defence by fifty-four field batteries and eighteen heavy batteries.

It was accepted that there was no probability of the Soissons-Marne front ever becoming tranquil. Perhaps the limited attacks south of the Aisne need not be interpreted as a basis for or leading to a subsequent attack on a large scale, but rather as a continuous 'feeling out' of the inten-

THE LAST GREAT OFFENSIVE

tions of those within the salient and as a defensive measure to relieve the endangered forest terrain east of Villers-Cotterets. Prisoners brought in west of Soissons declared the object of the attack was mainly to better the position, as the old position in swampy terrain was untenable. The Lyons wireless message of 8 P.M., the 29th, emphasized the defensive object of the attack. In contrast thereto, however, was the statement of a prisoner, a sergeant of the French 153rd Division, who insisted that the attack was for the purpose of gaining a line of departure for a subsequent offensive on a large scale. This seemed reasonable, hence disquieting, though it was not apparent how the Allies could wage an offensive under the circumstances. It seemed certain that the enemy would continue the limited attacks in those places where he was compelled to keep strong artillery for his defence. This was especially true between the Oise and the Marne. It was apparent that, should the enemy gain much at Soissons, all the communications of the German Army within the Marne Salient would be endangered, and *this would at the same time relieve the enemy of his most pressing fear, a German advance on Paris.*

The increasing gravity of the situation necessitated extreme activities in securing information concerning the condition and intentions of the enemy. There was every evidence that he was making hasty, almost frantic efforts to protect himself against any further advance toward Paris; he was preparing for his possible retreat across the Marne, was preparing his second and third lines of defence south of the Marne. The air photographs taken on the 25th and 27th showed that he was throwing up trenches on the west front. He was active on the Paris protective position. The construction of lines in the rear, south of the Marne, was making rapid progress. Obstacles could be seen north of the Marne. And, most disquieting of all, he seemingly was preparing to strike on the western Marne-Soissons-Noyons front. He had the strength to strike at

THE PARIS GUN

but one point, where he was most strongly organized for defence.

Air reconnaissance on the morning of July 1 revealed five trains going north-east on the Paris-Crépy-en-Valois railway between 7 and 8 A.M. There were five to six trains under steam at each station. There was heavy traffic between the north and south railway stations in Paris; seven trains each way on the Esternay-Fère-Champenoise railway; eight trains on the side-tracks at Esternay; great motor traffic both ways on the Plessis-Belleville-Meaux roads and opposite Corps Watter and Staabs. A tent camp had appeared, and long columns of vehicles east of Jaux and south of Compiègne. Two new bridges had been thrown across the Marne south-west of Verneuil.

A New Army

Preparations were begun for the insertion or establishment of a Ninth Army to be between the Seventh and the Eighteenth. The new army would comprise the 7th Corps, the 39th Reserve Corps, and the 13th Württemberg Corps. The first general staff officers for that army reported at Seventh Army Headquarters to acquaint themselves with the situation.

The Paris Gun

Work on the position for the Paris Gun was well along by July 1. A spur had been run off to the south of the railway passing straight west from Fère-en-Tardenois toward Breny. An excellent position had been found along this line at the south end of the Valchrétien farm in the Bois de Bruyères, between Bruyères and Trugny. The railway carriage and the base had been brought in through Soissons, then east along the Vesle to Bazoches and south past Mont-Notre-Dame, where, ironically, the 305-mm. guns had been located which were ordered up to Vailly on

THE LAST GREAT OFFENSIVE

March 23 to begin shelling Position No. 1 at Crépy on the 24th. This railway led south to Fère-en-Tardenois, then west. The crew made rapid progress in constructing the emplacement, paying the most careful attention to its concealment. The location was quite favourable, and they had had the experience of installing it at Beaumont in May. There seemed no reason why they could not have everything ready by the 10th. At the village of Nanteuil-Notre-Dame, west of this position, a line branched off, leading south to Château-Thierry. On the west side of this railway and opposite Brecy was the Bois du Châtelet, into which another railway curve was run for a Max battery, a 15-inch naval gun on a railway carriage. The carriage and emplacements, or bases, for the long-range guns and the 15-inch Long Maxes were identical.

In the Allied Army

On the French side the situation was nothing short of desperate. The German attack of May 27 and advance from then till June 12 had been a distinct calamity. So badly had the Allies been caught, so completely had Ludendorff out-guessed Foch, that it was said that General Foch had offered his resignation to Clemenceau. If he did so, it had not been accepted.

Paris was the centre of gloom. It oozed gloom. The exodus of civilians, continuing throughout June, reached the million mark. From June 4, when the advance of the Germans in the Marne salient toward Paris had been stopped, there prevailed a fatalistic expectation that the next offensive could not be stopped, that the German column would make another headlong rush south through the line and then double west on Paris. The Est railway almost ceased to exist as a passenger carrier; the station was so deserted at times as to echo with the sound of a vacant building. Hotels in the vicinity had but few guests.

THE PARIS GUN

They had transported out of the city much of their valuable service property. If an advance began on Paris there would be no such thing as getting transportation for small property. The stocks in shops dwindled, theatres closed one by one, and the streets at night were the antithesis of cheer.

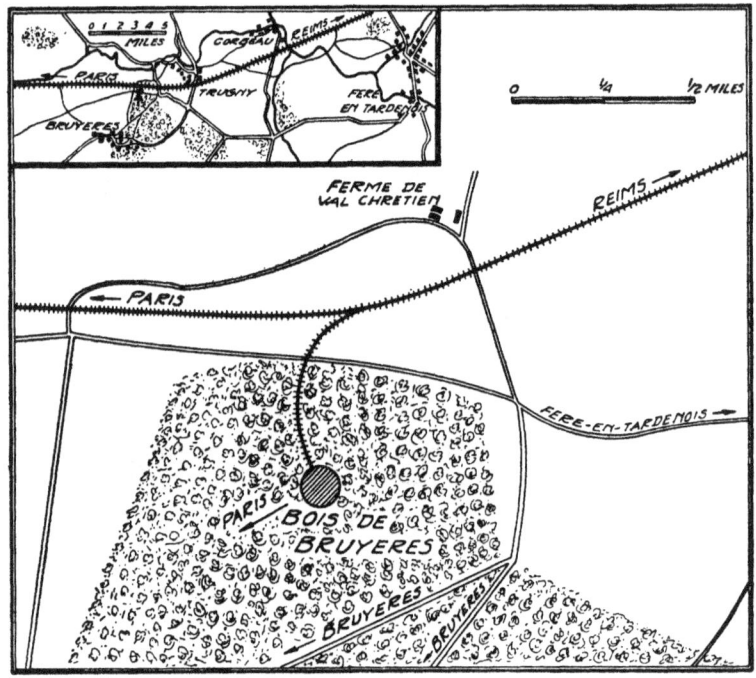

THE NEW POSITION OF THE PARIS GUN

Paris was in the 'zone of the advance,' under military rule.

North and east of Paris every sort of precaution barrier was being erected or dug to serve in an emergency. East along the Marne, south of the Marne at Château-Thierry, both north and south of the Marne past Épernay and Châlons and on east, 75-mm. and hand-rifle ammunition was being stored in canvas-covered piles along all north and south roads. These 'dumps' reached for miles south

THE LAST GREAT OFFENSIVE

of the Marne, and barbed-wire entanglements were being laid in all strategic positions where machine-guns might be placed in an emergency.

The various Allied Army staffs viewed the immediate future with the gravest concern. The British saw vigorous preparations opposite their Flanders front for an offensive that they expected on any day. The French armies with their American divisions all about the new Marne salient saw every evidence of a near renewal of hostilities there. General Pershing was vigorously insistent in his urging upon General Foch a near future Allied offensive to pinch off the salient. He felt that an offensive was the only salvation for the Allies. He had seen his troops tried, he had seen them take continuous punishment of the worst sort all through July, had seen them stop the prize shock troops of the Germans. He knew they were not yet as thoroughly seasoned as they should be, but that could not be helped. The Allies had on July 1 a strategic advantage that might not be theirs later. There had been no further attempt on the part of the German Army to advance. Until they did start such an advance the Allies were in a measure free to seize the offensive at some one point. General Pershing reported one million Americans in France on July 4. He was receiving men at the rate of 300,000 a month, twenty-five French, British, or German divisions, equivalent to twelve American. Thus he had in his million men, excluding all 'Service of Supply' forces, twenty-four American or forty-eight French combat divisions. He felt that his line divisions had demonstrated that they were first-class attack or shock troops. So he urged General Foch to prepare for an offensive that would be smashingly vigorous at some one point, and that would then gradually extend itself farther on the line. He would be receiving reserves faster than they could possibly be used up on even a continuous offensive, and the Germans could be prevented from launching any further offensives in 1918; their

THE PARIS GUN

reserves would gradually be drawn in, until, by the spring of 1919 at least, they would have none to draw upon. Gradually it came to be the feeling in the Allied Headquarters that though this might be a desperate chance, there was no other.

If through the expected stroke at Rheims and a later pincer attack west from that salient and south from the great Amiens salient the Germans were to get within 15-inch gun range of Paris, things would be more than serious for the French. This for two reasons. So many vital munitions manufacturing plants were located in and about Paris that its loss or even the near approach of the German Army to it would be a calamity to the French armies. Scarcely of lesser importance was the question of the psychological effect on the French nation, on their will-to-fight. There must be no repetition of the near *débâcle* of late 1916 and early 1917 when the defeatists almost had their way; when machine-guns had to be turned by Frenchmen on their comrades in mutinous battalions. Clemenceau and Pétain had had a close call in pulling the civilian population and the Army out of that and back to a fighting temper. The long-range-gun bombardment had for its sole purpose the breaking of this temper. It was not succeeding so well as the Germans had hoped. But if 15-inch guns could get at Paris as they had at Dunkirk, there was no question about the effect of such a bombardment. Without doubt, even in the existing desperate straits an offensive would be best—in fact, almost the only sensible defensive.

IN THE GERMAN ARMY

The limited attacks of the enemy continued with unabated vigour. In a sharp and decisive engagement on the morning of July 1 Americans had taken the village of Vaux in the creek valley between the continually contested Hill 204 which Ludendorff had ordered held at any cost,

THE LAST GREAT OFFENSIVE

and the Bois de la Moirette. Sixty machine-guns were lost, five hundred men were captured by the enemy, and three hundred more were killed. The enemy gained more ground on Hill 204. Corps Watter was shelled and attacked on July 2. The 42nd Division of that corps was pushed back. In the evening another attack was made on Corps Schoeler along the Vaux-Château-Thierry road. The Americans attempted to cross the river on the 10th Division front. Prisoners brought in on the 38th Division front denied attack intentions on a larger scale. On the front of the First Army it was observed that all call signals of all ground and wireless stations opposite their front had been changed since July 1. New ones heard and decoded indicated no material change in the hostile situation.

On July 4 definite information of the exact day of the new offensive was telephoned from General Headquarters to the Army Group Crown Prince and thence to the Seventh, First, and Third Armies: " General Headquarters has fixed July 15 as ' y ' day."

At 8 A.M., July 5, the newly organized Ninth Army took over Corps François, Staabs, and Watter. . . . The Seventh Army was thus either relieved or deprived, as one may wish, of the defence of their vital railway centre, Soissons. It now devolved on the new Ninth Army to maintain, protect, and keep clear that absolutely vital port of entry for the supply of the Seventh Army, entirely within the salient, and a portion of the First Army.

At 12.36, noon, on July 11 a most urgent message was telephoned from Army Group Headquarters to the Ninth and Seventh Armies; the improbable seemed impending:

> Deserters taken by Ninth and Seventh Armies speak of strong concentrations of troops in the woods of Villers-Cotterets and of an impending attack on a large scale. Early report desired as to your opinion of these statements and what measures you intend to take or which you recommend for defence. . . . This message to be handed to the Chief-of-Staff immediately.

THE PARIS GUN

The Paris Gun

By July 11 the work of installing the Paris Gun had been about completed; entirely completed, one might say. The great steel base was in, as at Beaumont, the railway carriage installed on it, the whole area carefully camouflaged, and the new gun, which had only recently been brought down, was on the carriage and the work of bracing it up about finished. An 11-inch gun on a railway carriage had also been installed near by, and a 15-inch gun on its railway carriage, identical with that of the long-range gun and on an identical base, had been installed in the Bois de Châtelet a few miles south-west of the Paris Gun position. Another Max railway battery had been installed at the village of Vaudêtre, where the famous old Roman road from Rheims to Trèves crossed the railway along the Suippes river. This gun was to shell Châlons during the offensive and prevent reinforcements from passing through by rail.

July 14

As fate persistently wills it, that final day before the dread day in war, the opening day of the offensive, arrived all too quickly for those, the horde of the army, for whom eternity might be just on the other side of to-morrow. But war was always a combination of chess and engineering on the one hand, and fate and human psychology on the other. The greater and lesser moves, of centre-lines of action, of detailed action, were discussed and arranged as dispassionately as if all of it concerned but the expenditure of energy and materials. That was chess. Then the materials were to be collected, their use planned; they were stored, men were trained to handle the equipment expertly; the necessary men to provide the energy were transported, placed in proper positions; and finally all that was finished. That was engineering. The remainder was all uncertainty, fate, and human psychology.

THE LAST GREAT OFFENSIVE

The pioneers had got all the required materials for the designated bridges, the boats, planking, timbers, ropes, chains, into the most advantageous places and under good concealment by '*y*' day minus one, the 14th. Batteries were in position, ammunition up as ordered both for the preparation and the advance. Regiments had been coming up by truck trains night after night to villages close to their appointed positions, and thence by night marches to within several hours' march of the line. Divisions on divisions were packed densely into that area that for some time had been spoken of as the 'sinister triangle.' The various headquarters were assured of the element of surprise; this in spite of the fact that one officer unfamiliar with the terrain had disobeyed orders while on reconnaissance, had taken maps with him, and he had disappeared. It was assumed he had been captured. It was hoped he had been able to destroy his tell-tale maps.

But the men—something had happened to them. Prior to the previous two offensives they had been full of enthusiasm, assurance, eagerness to go. Now they were moody, morose, nervous; the position divisions in the triangle had suffered such merciless punishment in the previous month that it was hard to believe that anything good or successful could come out of any venture in this region. Then, too, thousands upon thousands of men had been killed or badly wounded in the previous offensive; nearly 300,000 in the 'Michael' offensive, though they had been so spectacularly successful. Halves of regiments had disappeared, and replacements were but reminders of the tragedy. Other units had gone out of existence.

A staff officer of the Seventh Army entered in his diary on the 14th:

Jouaignes, July 14, 1918. Relatively tranquil day. Preparations for 'Road Construction'[1] are completed according to plan. The

---

[1] The code name for the combined 'Marne Defence' and 'Rheims' offensive.

picture we have gained of the enemy induces us to believe that our offensive intentions have been kept hidden from him; that we may expect to take him by surprise.

In the evening of the same day a grenadier of the 36th Division, which was then close down by the Marne, entered the shelter of his lieutenant and with great agitation asked if it were true that the Americans were in front of them and that the attack had been made known to them. His attitude represented that indefinable feeling so prevalent among the men that the attack would not succeed. So much for the contradictory versions as to the outcome of the offensive scheduled to begin shortly after midnight.

The Paris Gun

The ballistic commander of the Paris Gun who had the firing orders with him was late to his rendezvous. He reached Laon on his way south late on the evening of the 14th. His firing orders called for action the next day. He would have to remain there overnight. It was no longer under bombardment from artillery, for the enemy guns were too far away. But enemy air bombers were to be reckoned with, so no lights dared be shown about the railway station. Carrying his own luggage, since he could not find the car sent for him, he climbed the hill leading past the cathedral to the Quartermaster's department. For his night's lodging he was directed to the home of one of the more well-to-do citizens who had remained in the town.

Ready to Attack

The situations, missions, and experiences of almost any of the Seventh Army corps from Château-Thierry east along the Marne to Dormans and thence north-east toward Rheims were typical of those of the units on the Rheims attack front as a whole; with the exception, perhaps, of that

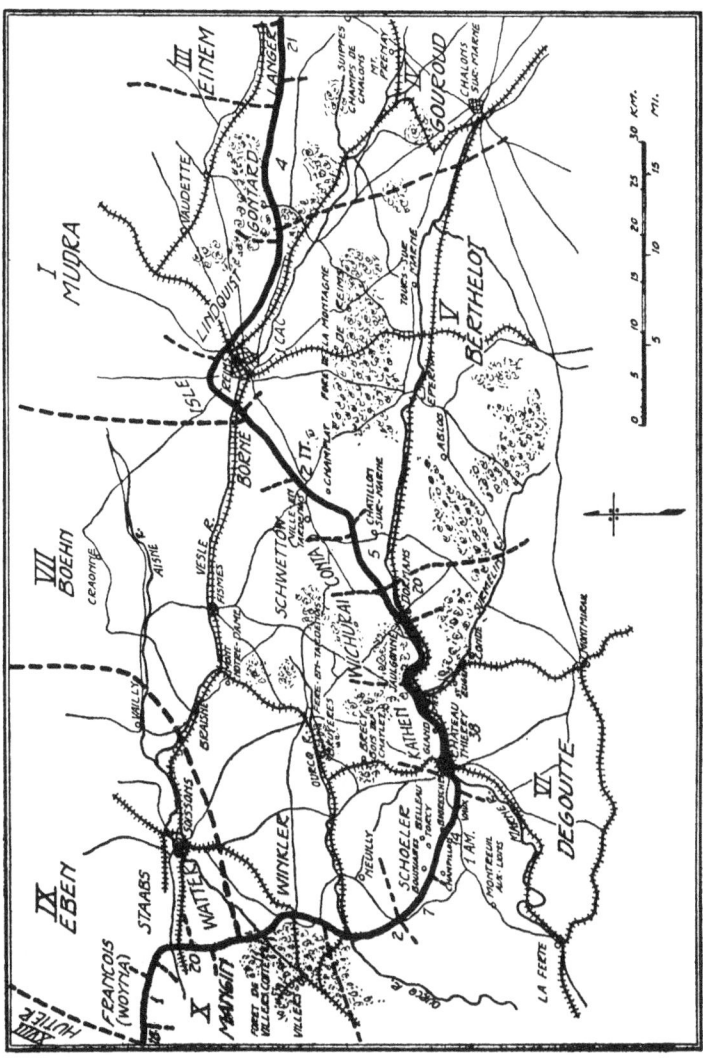

The Marne Salient and Attack Front on July 14, 1918

portion of the First Army front encircling Rheims. There would be little if any necessity for severe fighting there, no need for heavy artillery preparation. Rheims was not to be battered up any further. The encircling movements of the two armies were to pinch off that region. Starting at noon of 'y' day, however, Corps Isle was to lay a heavy interdiction fire on all roads leading from Rheims south. Real resistance was expected to the southward and then eastward progress of the right of the Third Army.

In the first week of July a general reorganization had been made in the army and corps boundaries from the Eighteenth Army west of Soissons to the Third Army east of Rheims. The newly organized Ninth Army had taken over the three former Seventh Army corps, François (Woyna), Staabs, and Watter, with an extension of these fronts, so that the already heavily burdened Seventh Army would be relieved of at least one of the troublesome problems, the holding of the Soissons Corner. The Seventh Army in turn took over the right of the front of the First Army up to the village of Gueux, west of Rheims, and about three miles south of the Vesle river. The new front of the Seventh Army was then divided into seven corps sections. Two of these were west of Château-Thierry; Corps Winkler on the right made contact with the Ninth Army, and Corps Schoeler filled in down to the Marne. Two new corps commands, Kathen and Wichura, took over with their five front-line divisions the river front from Château-Thierry east past Dormans to Verneuil. Corps command Conta filled in between Wichura and the two corps, Schwettow and Borne, transferred from the First Army.

In the attack plans issued on June 25 Corps Winkler and Schoeler, west of Château-Thierry, were instructed to cover the rear and flank of the Seventh Army by holding absolutely their existing positions. Corps Kathen, Wichura, and Conta were to drive south across the Marne and then

THE LAST GREAT OFFENSIVE

east. Corps Schwettow and Borne were to drive south-east to the Marne and then east on the north side of the river. The Seventh Army was in a real predicament with its right

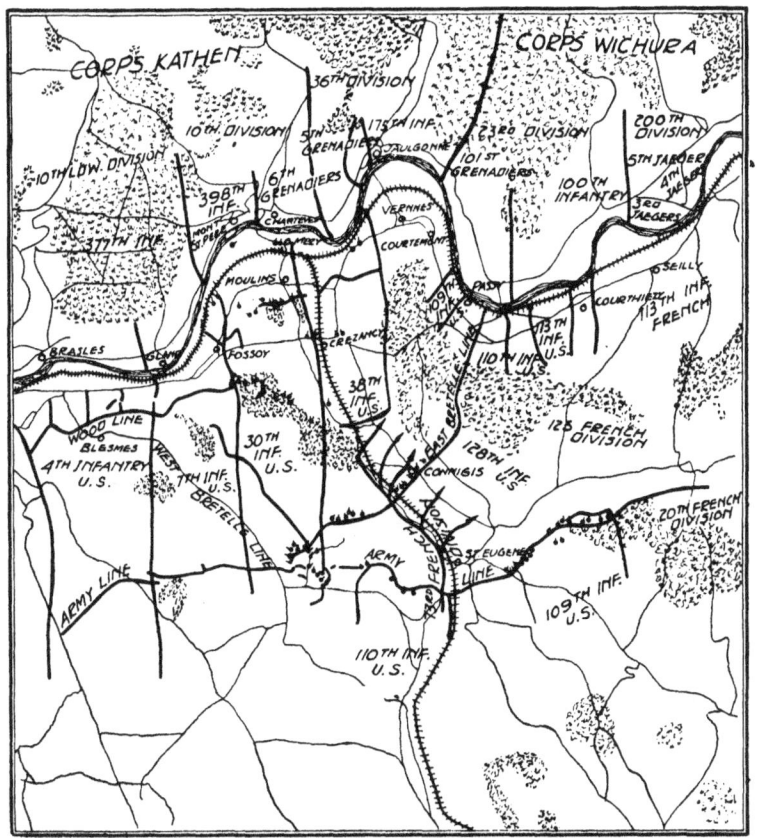

THE OPPOSING FORCES ON THE MARNE IN 1918

facing a hornets' nest toward the west, its centre facing south on the Marne, and its left facing east and organized for a formidable attack south and east.

The left of the 10th and the entire front of the 36th Infantry Divisions of Corps Kathen from Gland east to Jaulgonne on the Marne had particularly difficult missions.

THE PARIS GUN

They were to cross the river at four designated points between Gland and Mézy. Since all French bridges from Château-Thierry east to Châtillon had been blown up, the crossings would have to be by ferry or on temporary bridges, pontoon or timber, the boats, planks, and logs for which the pioneers had already assembled along the river. These units would run serious risk of being flanked on their right, for they constituted the extreme right of the attacking front. They were to advance on the general line from Gland to Saint-Eugène, but they had many things to do on the way. They had to make a thorough job of it and establish a new main zone of resistance, a new ' front line.'

The infantry in the region of the Jaulgonne Bend marched into its advance position after dark on the night of the 14th. They deployed in the middle of woods, six to eight hundred yards from the river, on the slopes of the hills which extended downward to the Marne. There was no protection for them, neither shelter nor trenches. Little flags, which could not be distinguished in the night, marked the line of departure.

The men could not remember a night so dark. In the woods one could not see one's hand before one's face. The men ran into trees, the ground was sloppy, the air was filled with gas, one heard the whistling of large shells sent over by the enemy. The infantry, which had had two hours to go a mile and a half, failed to arrive at their destination in that time. The efforts of the troops were enormous, and when they finally arrived at the proper place the reports received were far from comforting : losses during the march, great fatigue of the men, some losses of material. But everybody was finally at the place where he should be.

On this part of the Front the 5th Grenadiers were on the right of the 36th Division, and were to cross the river at two points near Jaulgonne, in *liaison* on the right with the 10th Division, their combat neighbour at Saint-Quentin and at the Chemin-des-Dames. The 175th Infantry was to be on the left. The infantry and machine-guns were to be crossed in boats or on rafts; the artillery and vehicles on bridges. Embarkation and debarkation drills for the river crossing had been carried out along the Vesle, at Fismes.

The 6th Grenadier Regiment had asked permission to move into the provisional point of assembly during the day of July 14, in order that it might reach the points of assembly indicated on the Marne before 1 A.M. The battalions arrived at the provisional points of assembly toward 9 P.M. on July 14, without losses by fire from the enemy artillery. They advanced from the provisional points to the indicated points of assembly on the Marne at midnight, and arrived there without any losses. All along the line similar last-minute preparations were successfully completed with more or less difficulty. There seems never any time to do things, great or small, deliberately, in war. Men in divisions which have been in back areas for rest for weeks or months are brought up in trucks at the last minute, arrive at the detraining point with perhaps the loss of a night's sleep, and then tramp weary miles in the dark to arrive at their appointed places hardly before 'X' hour.

The artillery preparation was to commence at 1.10 A.M. on July 16, and at 3.40 A.M. the artillery was to increase its range 200 yards. The infantry was then to begin crossing the river. At 4.50 A.M. the rolling barrage was to move forward and the infantry assault to commence.

July 15

The Offensive begins

Just before 1 A.M. a tremendous artillery fire began along the line. The enemy had begun a concentrated fire before the German schedule. Shells, small and large, fell all about; nothing escaped. At 1.10, exactly on schedule, the German artillery opened up. For ten minutes it increased in intensity, reached its maximum, and then began to diminish.

THE PARIS GUN

Apparently the enemy was gassing the German batteries. The intensity of the enemy fire continued. In a short time the carefully laid telephone lines to the front and rear were cut, destroyed. Runners and signal-lamps would have to be depended upon.

The infantry in the Jaulgonne Forest was lying down without shelter, where the underbrush was so thick that all movement was impossible, with only a very few trees to offer protection against bullets. The hostile artillery fire was tremendous. Not a point was spared. The effect of the continuous fire of the heavy batteries was frightful, and shattered the men's nerves. A clearing near by was rapidly being transformed into a field of shell-holes by a rain of shells from a light battery at intervals of five minutes. Big shrapnel shells came over like so many comets and dropped into a narrow valley to the right. It was crowded with men. They ran here and there, trying to find some place under cover. Some yelled, some, who had been hit, moaned and whimpered. Then the whistling sound and dull explosions of gas shells. Nothing could be seen through the masks; darkness was complete. Some wept, and some prayed for the coming of day. Finally, the company commanders, aware of the gravity of the situation, ordered the men forward. They advanced through valleys raked by fire. All of the roads in this region were in deep ravines between the steep hills; the only routes to the river. The engineers were a little farther on. There were but very few of them. The infantry themselves carried the boats for some two hundred yards, the distance to the river. Just then the enemy laid down a new artillery barrage. The men scattered; many were killed.

The accompanying artillery advanced (each regiment of infantry had one or two batteries). Some of the guns had been destroyed by direct hits, poles destroyed, wheels smashed. The artillery received orders to stop and seek positions in a zone not covered by hostile fire. A mountain

THE LAST GREAT OFFENSIVE

battery was already in action in rear of a crossing landing, in a narrow ravine where all lateral movements were impossible. Shells fell on the men. The horses were killed; the ammunition blew up.

Farther down at the river the engineers with a rifle battalion had worked better; two boats were ready, but there should have been six. The first boat, overloaded, started off; a machine-gun on the opposite side commenced to fire on them, but too high. Everybody crouched low. The farther bank was reached. The soldiers hoisted themselves up, but they met barbed wire which no field-glass had discovered. Behind it was a trench.

The regimental staff of the 6th Grenadiers left battle headquarters at 4.30 A.M. On its way to the Marne, it met several companies of the 5th Grenadiers at the south edge of the woods, north-east of Le Psaultier, who, in spite of repeated orders on the part of the regimental commander and the staff officers, could not be induced to go down to the Marne. They stated that several companies had already suffered direct hits of high-explosive shells and that it was impossible to cross the river.

A runner brought in the report that the 1st Battalion of the 6th Grenadiers had reached the railway embankment at 4.30 A.M. Immediately afterward an American prisoner, a first lieutenant, was brought in. His statements were forwarded to the division by carrier pigeons. " The attack was betrayed by a deserter a week ago; American counter-attack divisions are behind the front positions. Fifteen to twenty American regiments are between Château-Thierry and Mézy; next to them on the right the French."

The river crossing continued, but with great difficulty. The rolling barrage started exactly on time, but long before sufficient troops had crossed. The companies were given new objectives because nothing could be carried out as planned. The railway was crossed. The railway station at Varennes was captured after a short combat; the Moulins-

Varennes highway was crossed. The line had advanced already 1000 yards from the Marne, and commenced to ascend the steep slopes south of the river. On the right, through the morning mist, through the wheat, assaulting columns in brown, Americans were seen. The commanders of the 2nd and Rifle Battalions, seeing the danger, ordered everybody who could fire to turn to the right, facing the threat against the flank. The enemy advanced without a pause, stopping only when the machine-guns and desperate infantry fire had caused bloody losses in their ranks. The danger was momentarily averted, but only momentarily.

When the regimental staff of the 6th Grenadiers landed on the south bank of the Marne at about 5.10 A.M. it was still so dark and foggy that the foreground could not be surveyed. Heavy enemy machine-gun and infantry fire was heard at this time from the direction of Mézy and Moulins. The distant impression was that the German battalions were facing a greatly superior enemy. As it grew lighter enemy detachments were observed rushing down the heights east of Moulins in close, massed ranks, in the direction of the railway bridge over the Surmelin brook. Enemy effectives also came down from the heights south-west of Mézy in the direction of Mézy.

The rolling barrage went on steadily. But not a single shell fell on the hotly disputed railway embankment nor on the advancing enemy companies. The trench mortars could not be brought into action, as the regiment had only two pontoons fit for use, and no rowboat ferries had been arranged at any point. The German battalions were being thrust back from the railway embankment by greatly superior forces. The enemy immediately, everywhere, brought his machine-guns into position and fired over the railway embankment at the men north of it. The Americans soon gained the upper hand in fire by means of their numerical superiority in machine-guns and rifles and held down the battalions to such an extent that they could stand up-

THE LAST GREAT OFFENSIVE

right on the railway embankment and shoot down the men individually. In the meantime more and more Americans gathered under the railway bridge crossing the Surmelin brook, and brought machine-guns into position on the left flank, so that the 6th Grenadiers were encircled more and more. From the heights east of Moulins, too, heavy machine-gun fire constantly struck the Marne, the space between the Marne and the railway embankment, and the slopes north of the Marne. The ferry positions on the Marne were soon taken under such severe, raking machine-gun fire from the direction of the mouth of the Surmelin that a crossing now seemed scarcely possible.

The situation was so critical that the regimental commander sent the artillery *liaison* officer back with orders to point out the desperate plight of the regiment to the 1st Detachment of the 56th Field Artillery.

Everybody felt that the attack had failed. Apparently nothing remained except to hold the line reached, in the face of a very superior enemy. The railway embankment seemed to be the natural line of resistance. The advance elements retired by echelon. The menaced right flank was strongly reinforced, and *liaison* with neighbours on the left was assured by 11 A.M. Never had there seemed so many dead; never such a frightful sight. On the right the Americans, in close combat, had completely annihilated two German companies. Lying down in the wheat, they had allowed the troops to approach, and then annihilated them by fire at a range of thirty to fifty paces. The oft-heard statement among the troops before the attack, that "The Americans killed every one," became a cry of fear on July 15.

Since individual men of the 6th Grenadiers could be seen running back and crossing the Marne, the regimental commander transferred his battle headquarters to a height 300 yards north of the Marne in order to stop them by his personal influence. These headquarters were quickly under such heavy machine-gun fire that many were soon wounded.

All efforts to reorganize the retreating men into units on the northern bank proved impossible. Many were without arms, since they had swum across the Marne. The reforming units were in plain view of the southern bank of the Marne, and were under heavy machine-gun and artillery fire which killed many. The staff of the regiment therefore ordered a withdrawal to the woods. From the woods it could be observed still how every one in the valley was being shot down by the enemy. The ferry traffic had stopped completely, as the enemy kept the Marne under constant artillery fire. Individual men were seen swimming back through the Marne, some of them being caught in the enemy fire. The losses of the regiment were: 6 officers killed, 7 wounded, 8 missing; 32 men killed, 169 wounded, 622 missing. There was no choice but to assume that the greater part of the missing men were dead or wounded.

The Situation in General

The progress and success of the various divisions along the entire attack front of the Seventh, First, and Third Armies during the first six hours of the offensive after the 'jump off' at 4.50 was anything but satisfactory or promising. Penetration to the strongly defended French position succeeded only at isolated points. Corps Wichura, Conta, Schwettow, and Borne between the Marne and Rheims met with more promising success than those of the First and Third Armies east of Rheims. But even their success was gained at such cost and their difficulties mounted at such a rate as to forecast failure. The right of Corps Wichura reached the plateau north of Saint-Agnan south of the Marne by noon. The 1st Guard Division on its left had had bloody fighting at Champaille, and was pushing forward toward Comblizy. The right of Corps Conta

THE LAST GREAT OFFENSIVE

reached the line Patis-de-Troissy, Bois du Crochet, west of Mareuil le Port, south of the Marne. The 2nd Guard Division on its left reached and captured the hill west of Châtillon and the central portion of the wood at Rarrey.

The right of Corps Schwettow gained possession of the north of the strongly defended Bois de Rarrey, and was

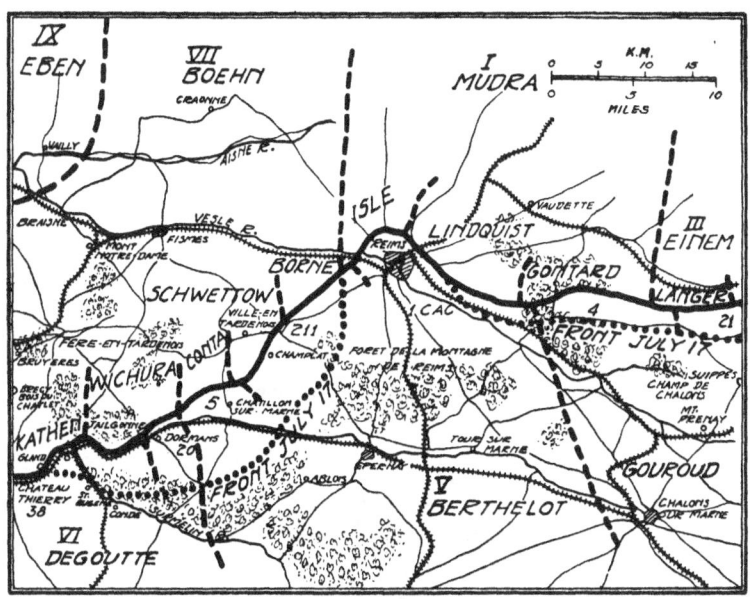

GERMAN GAINS IN THE OFFENSIVE OF JULY 15, 1918

advancing against the Bois de Rodemat. Its left reached Paradis and the Ardré valley and Espilly. Corps Borne, which faced the 2nd Italian Corps, pushed them back to Saint-Euphaise. But before noon the divisions had reached and were held up before a strongly organized and defended second position. There seemed no possibility of a rapid penetration of this line. The opponent could no longer be run over. He could only be pushed back by stubborn fighting from hill to hill, and from wood to wood. The army still held to the view, however, that after this second position, a strategic defence organized in great depth, had been taken the attack would move along more easily and rapidly.

Despite later development to the contrary, the chances of success had appeared more favourable at the start along the front of the First and Third Armies. The assault troops, following closely on the rolling barrage, penetrated into the hostile lines, and overran the sacrifice machine-gun groups. Then they encountered a deep curtain barrage which was murderously destructive and indicated that the enemy had withdrawn his troops. As the sadly cut up companies emerged from this barrage they at once encountered the enemy second position, actually his first position now, where the centres of resistance were so numerous and so heavily and thoroughly organized that they were brought to an abrupt halt. It was plain that the enemy had been waiting for the attack. That he knew of it was proved by his preliminary bombardment of the German troops in their advance positions at midnight. Reconnaissance from the air revealed that he had organized very deeply with his infantry and artillery, had created a deep foreground held only by scattered sacrifice groups with machine-guns, and that he had placed his main line of resistance along the Roman road. Prisoners confirmed this.

The accompanying batteries and other artillery and ammunition columns that followed as rapidly as possible on the first penetration of the infantry were caught under an intense artillery fire as they were crossing the enemy's advance terrain, which their own artillery had blasted up thoroughly between 1 A.M. and the beginning of the rolling barrage at 4.50. They were so cut to pieces, horses killed, carriages and wheels shattered, wagons overturned, men wounded, that they were unable to give their infantry the assistance which was absolutely essential for any progress against the determined and strong resistance they had encountered. The enemy artillery had suffered but little from the German gas-fire, because of the strong wind, and

THE LAST GREAT OFFENSIVE

operated in full force not only against the artillery and supply columns trying to cross the advance terrain, but on the waves of infantry as well, particularly as they began to approach the advance French forces and their positions could be accurately reported. It was apparent that no further advance could be made on that front without most intense artillery preparation, for which a new artillery concentration requiring a whole day would be necessary. And since the element of surprise was gone, it seemed that there was little chance of success under any circumstances, and the prospects for heavy losses were almost certain.

The conduct of the Allies was an excellent example of the 'giving way' tactics that the German Army had been more or less directed to pursue since the battle of the Somme. Decisive, apt leadership can readily evade a superior hostile attack by this mobile defence. Foch and his aids had somehow secured sufficient information to enable them to decide when and where to fall back. In creating the deep foreground they had, of course, abandoned some terrain. But the fire of the German batteries fell harmlessly on abandoned trenches. Subsequently the attackers were caught under a well-directed gas, high explosive, and shrapnel fire as they were crossing this abandoned terrain, and their accompanying artillery destroyed. All of this before the real defence positions, entirely unharmed and manned by troops who had suffered no artillery fire, had been encountered. Those who thought they had the element of surprise on their side were the surprised ones, and the really effective artillery preparation had been visited on them by an enemy who had had a whole morning to organize and watch them labouring across gas-soaked and shell-torn fields.

The progress of Corps Wichura and Conta south of the Marne was regarded at Army Group Headquarters as a fair success. The attack would be continued there as well as north of the river where the reaching of the ridge between

THE PARIS GUN

Coulommes and Sermiers might cause the enemy to evacuate the Rheims Basin. To accomplish this it would be necessary to take the hill west of Fleury. It was clear that the object of the operation, however, to cut off the enemy in the Rheims valley through a junction of the Seventh and First Armies in the vicinity east of Épernay, could not be attained. Orders were therefore issued at noon cancelling the previous missions and directing new ones. The First and Third Armies were to continue their pressure, even at the heavy cost they were then suffering, against the enemy second position to prevent him from noticing that the attack had failed, and sending his reserves against the Seventh Army. The Seventh Army was ordered to continue the attack in full force.

The Paris Gun

Early on the morning of the 15th, after a night that was far from restful, what with the late arrival, the difficulty in finding headquarters, the explosion of a few bombs about midnight, and the beginning of the Allied artillery fire at one o'clock and the German fire at 1.10, the ballistic commander of the Paris Gun found his motor-car and started south. The way into the triangle led over the Chemin-des-Dames, the scene of the beginning of the wonderful offensive of May 27. This had been the most hotly contested battle-field for nearly four years. Everything was grey and dreary, oh, so dreary! As far as the eye could reach there were shell-holes upon shell-holes. Every sign of civilization had vanished. And the smells at times! Hardly had one side had time to bury their dead, in shallow trenches at best, before the other dug them up with high-explosive shells. Few remains found in that region would ever be identified.

But once that dread region of buzzards, ruin, and dead was passed, one could scarcely persuade himself that only

THE LAST GREAT OFFENSIVE

recently the most formidable of offensives had passed over. Down through Vailly and Braisne to Jouaignes into the lovely valley of the Aisne, in full summer array and showing scarcely a trace of war. The wheat, full of the blood-red poppies, was not yet cut. It billowed in the gentle breeze as a sea of yellow. All this time the furious firing of artillery to the south, east, and west was growing louder. And an idle thought of the ballistic commander, journeying south unmolested through this beautiful country: that in Paris they were expecting another bombardment; the bursting of a shell at some spot awaited merely his arrival at his destination. He had the firing order, and firing would begin at once on his arrival.

The road finally led to Fère-en-Tardenois. It was under enemy shell-fire; wagons were going at a gallop, figures moving stealthily. Then in twenty minutes, by the Fère-Coincy highway, branching off soon to the north-west toward Trugny, he reached the Valchrétien farmhouse, his headquarters. It was stone-paved, the yards dirty, and alive with vermin and flies.

The Paris Gun, carefully camouflaged from air observation, was ready for action in the Bruyères Wood near by. After a brief inspection had been made of the position, which had been excellently constructed, firing began at once. The first shot was fired at 1.54. Almost at once, and by mere chance, enemy 'planes were overhead, and continued all about for several hours. Firing was therefore ordered to be stopped until they should be safe from detection by airmen.

Shortly after the first shot had been fired disquieting information began to come in concerning the progress of the offensive. It was not going well. Something unforeseen had happened at the very beginning. The enemy had begun a bombardment ten minutes (some reports had it an hour) before the German artillery began on its schedule. And so furious, thorough, and effective had it been that one could conclude that it had been carefully planned, with ample knowledge of the coming storm. Little, if anything, was happening according to schedule across the river. Some units had not been able to cross, others that had got across had had to retire. Some units that had crossed had been annihilated. The centre and left wing of the Seventh Army had made most progress, almost due east between Rheims and Épernay, but had been almost stopped by noon. The First Army, east of Rheims, had hardly started. It appeared as though the offensive would have to be stopped at once to avert a calamity, if it could be averted even so.

The enemy 'planes disappeared at about five o'clock, and nine more shots were fired from 5.23 to 8.41. All of these were from Series 2 of the 232-mm. shells. They were the first ten of the series. There was considerable speculation as to the probable life of the gun in this new position. The range here was 56.6 miles. It had been 68.9 miles at Beaumont. The maximum powder-pressure was but 42,000 pounds as against 58,000 pounds for the 68.9-mile range. It ought to prove possible to fire at least 200 rounds on Paris from one gun at this position before it would have to be rebored. There would be no need to change positions again during the summer. This range of 56.6 miles was ideal.

The Offensive fails

The reports that came in during the evening were more disquieting than those of the day. There was no doubt but that the enemy had had fairly complete information in advance, long in advance, and had prepared a trap. The momentum of the initial rush of the offensive was spent. Units were either stopped, half or completely annihilated, or were retiring. The detailed report was that the 10th Division of Group Kathen, especially, had suffered from a heavy raking artillery and machine-gun fire from the west, and was able only to gain the hill south of Mézy and

THE LAST GREAT OFFENSIVE

Fossoy; Crezancy, which was captured temporarily, was lost again.

During the course of the afternoon Group Kathen carried the attack of the 36th Division to the ridge of Courtemont-Saint-Agnan; it reached the Surmelin brook by evening. The 10th Division, however, was held up by heavy artillery fire that raked it on the front and right, and it was ordered to withdraw across the river during the night. The divisions of Group Wichura penetrated, in a hard fight, into the deeply formed battle zone of the hostile second position, which was fortified with many machine-guns. The 23rd and 200th Divisions reached the depression of Saint-Agnan, and the 1st Guard Division reached the line, close to the Milon farm hill west of Comblizy. There it came to a halt in the face of continually increasing hostile artillery and machine-gun fire.

At Group Conta the numerous and dense clumps of woods enabled the enemy to form nests of resistance strongly supported by machine-guns and single field-pieces. These were finally taken after stubborn fights. The 31st Division captured the Bois de Nesles, the Bois du Crochet, and in the evening the Bois de Chataignier also; the 113th Division captured Cerseuil, Leuvrigny, Reuil, and the Bois du Missy; the 2nd Guard Division reached the line Châtillon, Montigny, Binson-Orquigny, and Villers-sous-Châtillon. Group Schwettow also encountered in the woods many ably defended hostile nests of resistance. In the course of the afternoon the 195th Division pushed into the Bois de Rodemat, the 22nd Division reached the woods west of Belval, and the 123rd Division captured Marfaux. With the assault troops of the 86th Division Group Borne broke the resistance of the Italians, but on its left encountered strong French resistance.

At midnight on the 15th Ludendorff telephoned an order to the Headquarters of the Crown Prince changing the extent of the 'Rheims' attack:

THE PARIS GUN

The Seventh and First Armies will continue the attack on the 16th and the Third Army as well, but only on its right. The Army Group will place the centre of gravity of the advance of the Seventh Army along the north of the Marne in order to force the enemy to evacuate the Rheims Arc. Since troops will continue to be sent to Army Group Rupprecht (for the attack against the English on the 20th), the attack of the Third Army will be narrowed. The principal effort in the attack east of Rheims will be made by the First Army. It will be necessary to gain ground toward Mourmelon-le-Petit and Mourmelon-le-Grand in order to carry out the original intention of the operation [the taking of Rheims and the Rheims Basin].

General von Boehn of the Seventh Army ordered the withdrawal of the 10th Division of Corps Kathen during the night. The encounters of the 398th and 47th Infantry and the 6th Grenadiers with the Americans during the morning had been so disastrous as to leave them in no position to hold what they had gained south of the river.

In the West

A report from Corps Schoeler and Winkler west of Château-Thierry on the events of the day contained a disquieting sentence: " The enemy has started a strong aerial blockade on the west front."

The Paris Gun

Any sort of rest during the night for the Paris Gun battery was out of the question. The anti-aircraft guns roared the whole night long. Swarms of enemy 'planes hummed overhead, and bombs tore through the air, and their crashing explosions were heard in every direction. The fearful glare of artillery firing all about the horizon, its ceaseless roll and rumble, and the shells bursting in all directions were not conducive to rest. On the morning of the 16th there was no change. Enemy 'planes were over

THE LAST GREAT OFFENSIVE

in squadrons of twenty and twenty-four. Only a few German 'planes were out to meet them. The rattle of the machine-guns in the air went on ceaselessly. There could be no such thing as continuous firing. The air was fairly clear of aeroplanes at 10.20, and a shot was fired at 10.27. Another was fired at 12.32. 'Planes were all about again for several hours, apparently hunting the gun. A third shot was fired at 4.52 and another, the last for the day, at 5.17. Shells 1 to 14 of Series 2 had been fired in exact order. Everything had worked perfectly. If only the affairs of the front-line troops had gone as smoothly!

The Second Day

It was necessary to assume the defensive everywhere south of the Marne on the second day. There was no more crossing of troops. Further and desperate attempts were made by the Seventh, First, and Third Armies to so relieve the situation north of the Marne that further attention could then be given the predicament on the other bank. In the First Army, Corps Lindequist, Gontard, and Langer attacked at 11 A.M. after heavy artillery preparation. The attack gained but little ground, however, because of the well-organized enemy barrage. During all the afternoon the enemy kept up a heavy fire on the front positions and the terrain of the rear. The casualties were frightful because of the dense packing of the assault divisions so close to the Front. By noon the First Army had taken a total of 3400 prisoners.

At noon on the 16th Von Einem, commanding the Third Army, telephoned to the Headquarters of the Crown Prince that all captured officers stated the enemy had prepared the terrain in front of his second position as the foreground zone and the second position as the main line of resistance. His artillery was formed in great depth. His main forces were behind the third position. Only single batteries were in front of the second position. The great depth was taken only in the last few days. The remarkably small amount of traffic to the rear on the enemy's roads on the 15th showed that he had withdrawn his advance troops on the 14th or before, and had brought up his reserves before the offensive started.

At Army Group Headquarters the battles of the 16th only confirmed the view gained from those of the 15th. It became clear that the attack south of the Marne could make no material progress. The attacks of the 16th had gained ground on a large scale only on the Seventh Army front north of the Marne. On the fronts of the First and Third Armies the enemy had prepared his positions so thoroughly that any progress without the most minute preparations was hopeless. This was not so true on the Seventh Army front north of the Marne. South of the Marne the terrain, the natural protection, was all in favour of the enemy. The enemy refrained from any formidable attacks on the forces south of the Marne on the 16th, but those on that side of the river knew that such an attack was merely a matter of hours.

At 12.20 noon on the 17th Ludendorff sent out a significant order. It was telephoned through the headquarters of the Crown Prince to the First and Seventh Armies. The first sentence: "The enemy will be driven out of the Rheims Arc" showed his recognition of the desperate need for the railway connexions through Rheims, and the moral necessity for gaining something of practical value from a costly and disastrous attack. He had walked into a trap, a nasty one. He had sent forward more than a score of divisions merely to be cut up and gassed. Those divisions had to capture more or retire badly beaten. The legend of uncanny success that had come to be associated with his name was in serious danger. The capture of something of obvious practical value might save the day.

The second sentence of the order: " Main pressure will

THE LAST GREAT OFFENSIVE

be exerted along the boundary between the Seventh and First Armies " showed how drastically he was reducing the initial objectives to be gained. Originally they were to take the Marne from Château-Thierry to Châlons. Now they were merely to drive east below Rheims and cut it off. Of course the enemy might retire to the Marne after he had lost the city which he had been holding so stubbornly.

The third sentence: " Preparations are to be hastened, especially the shifting of the artillery and the bringing up of ammunition so that the attack can be executed without fail on the 21st " showed his acceptance of the fact that his armies were now definitely stopped. Von Mudra of the First Army had telephoned at noon on the 15th that his army could make no further progress east of Rheims without another artillery preparation. But the Seventh Army was then still slowly forging eastward between the Marne and Rheims, and continued to do so on the 16th, though more and more slowly and at greater and greater cost. Four days at the most was allowed for the bringing up and placing of the artillery and ammunition. The attack ' Hagen ' by Army Group Rupprecht had been set for the 20th. It had been expected that all of the Marne objectives would have been gained before that date.

The remainder of the order dealt with details:

> The Seventh and the First Armies will employ their long-range gun batteries as much as possible for the support of the attack. The attack will be made simultaneously on all fronts. The Army Group will designate the hour. Plans for attack to be submitted to Army Group Headquarters by 9 A.M., July 18; these plans will indicate what mutual support is demanded from the Seventh and First Armies.

In mid-afternoon Von Boehn of the Seventh Army telephoned to Army Group Headquarters that strong French counter-attacks had begun against the divisions south of the Marne. After strong artillery preparation, Corps Wichura and Kathen had been attacked. The full force of

THE PARIS GUN

the attack was mainly on the Corps Wichura front. It was assuming the shape of a battle on an extensive scale. . . . From an infantry point of view the engagement with the infantry forces then available opposed to fresh, numerically equal hostile forces promised no success. The reports received concerning the condition of the infantry were alarming, as not only the infantry in the first line, but also the reserves, had suffered much by artillery fire and aerial bombardment. The Seventh Army had no interest in holding the south bank of the river, so far as its own situation was concerned. It was necessary, therefore, to decide what should be done in consideration of the *entire* situation. If the decision should be to evacuate the south bank, then the Seventh Army Headquarters would appreciate early orders so that preparations might be commenced without delay (this night), as the retreat would be most difficult.

So constantly were the enemy 'planes over during the 17th and in such numbers that no firing was done from the Paris Gun.

The Tide turns

The aerial blockade started by the enemy on the 15th on the western front of the Marne salient continued throughout the 16th and 17th. He began a heavy interdiction fire on that front in the evening of the 17th. Shortly after midnight of the 17th two enemy deserters were brought in on the front of the Ninth Army. They stated that a heavy attack was to be made on that front between 5 and 6 A.M. The 11th Bavarian Division at once began annihilation fire in the front of its sector. At 4.30 A.M. the noise of enemy motors was plainly heard on the front of Corps Winkler. Apparently he was bringing tanks into position. Front-line observers were seeing things or had jumpy nerves. They kept calling with their red flares for artillery barrages all up and down the line.

The interdiction fire continued to increase in intensity.

THE PARIS GUN

THE LAST GREAT OFFENSIVE

Heavier guns began to fire on the roads farther back of the German lines. At 5.45 the enemy artillery fire suddenly increased to the volume of drum-fire on the entire front of Corps Staabs and Watter of the Ninth Army and Winkler and Schoeler of the Seventh. Simultaneously the enemy divisions, mostly Americans, swarmed forward, preceded by a great number of tanks. The Seventh Army was in a desperate plight. It was virtually facing south and east. It had been trying to cross the Marne and make a junction with the First Army at Épernay. Now, almost without warning, it was attacked in the rear. The attack promised to be a formidable one. By seven o'clock more than three hundred tanks had been counted on the entire front. Eighty were counted on the front of Corps Winkler alone. The enemy had already penetrated the lines to considerable depth. He had reached the main line of resistance of the 10th Bavarian Division of Corps Winkler, and the 40th Division on the north was being heavily gassed. The 45th Reserve Division was just then entering the battle to assist the 10th Bavarian. The 10th Division, which had turned over its sector along the Marne at 9 A.M. on the 17th to the 10th Landwehr and had become an Army reserve, was at once ordered to be ready for action. This in spite of the fact that some of its regiments had been reduced to less than half-strength, the 6th Grenadiers to a quarter, in the fighting of the 16th and 17th.

Before noon Von Boehn was instructed from the headquarters of the Crown Prince to withdraw to the north bank of the Marne the troops then south of the river as soon as the situation would permit. The artillery, less accompanying artillery, and all troops not required for a defensive battle on the 19th would be withdrawn during the night. Withdrawal positions would be prepared on the north bank for artillery and infantry, and especially machine-guns. The entire south front would be made ready by dawn of the 19th for defence, and the heavier fighting would be confined to the selected line of resistance. Attacks would be made to deceive the enemy and to improve the positions.

During the night of July 19–20, up to 10 P.M., July 19, the entire front would stand unchanged. Commencing at that hour, the battle reserves would fall back. . . . At 11 P.M. the front line would fall back through the covering positions to the Marne, and occupy the railway embankment. Prior to this time the south exits of villages on the river would be fortified. At 3 A.M. the detachments in readiness would fall back across the Marne and proceed immediately north. The railway embankment would be held until every unit had passed. Some of the railway embankment sectors would have to be held as bridge heads until the night of July 20–21.

Strong battle patrols, equipped with light and heavy machine-guns and led by officers, would remain in all covering positions on roads leading from the south to the Marne until after 5 A.M. These patrols with the assistance of the artillery on the north bank would offer tenacious resistance to any pursuing enemy. The machine-guns would be used to the last possible moment; their loss by capture was of secondary importance.

Since the progress of the retirement ordered for the night of July 18–19 might be delayed by unforeseen difficulties, it might be necessary to prolong the situation ordered for the 19th. In such event the movements prescribed for the night of July 19–20 would be delayed until the night of July 20–21. All orders would be issued with such contingency in view.

The reports on the situation in the west which reached the Paris Gun Headquarters during the 18th were more than disquieting. It appeared by evening that the enemy, who had already reached Chaudun on the Soissons-Paris highway, might cut the Soissons railway connexions. It was doubtful whether the gun could be got out of the triangle. The routine report of the 18th, which was entered

THE LAST GREAT OFFENSIVE

in the Seventh Army " Record of Daily Progress and Events " summed up the situation completely:

JOUAIGNES
July 18, 1918

... The enemy started a carefully planned and prepared double offensive with enormous fighting means against the salient Ambleny-Château-Thierry-Venteuil-Rheims. The weaker attack struck the east front of the Seventh Army and was in general defeated; *the main attack, however, almost completely shattered the divisions of Ninth Army along a broad front between the Aisne and the Clignon brook,* as these divisions had been badly shaken by the previous continual limited attack. (See July 13.)

The enemy was in a certain sense fortunate in attaining a practical surprise. ... According to statements of different prisoners, the attack was a surprise to the troops. The attack orders were issued at 1 A.M., July 18. During the early morning hours of July 18 two deserters arrived in the vicinity of Cutry who stated that between 5 and 6 A.M. a French attack on a large scale would be started against the German front between the Aisne and Marne. Noise of motors reported from the same direction during the night seemed to indicate that tanks were going into position of readiness. These were the only signs which indicated that an attack on a large scale was imminent. The attack was started at 5.38 A.M. it is said, without artillery preparation, the attack starting simultaneously with the rolling barrage. The attack has been pressed throughout the day with such vigour that some of our divisions are completely used up. The Ninth Army reports that the 241st and 11th Bavarian Divisions have hardly any fighting units left. ...

It now appears that we did not appreciate fully the number of his troops. ... We expected that our successful advance on Rheims would compel French General Headquarters immediately to throw the forces it had intended for the west front of the Seventh Army and the south part of the Ninth Army against the arc, Épernay-Rheims-Châlons, to prevent annihilation there. This calculation was based, first, on the assumption that our offensive would overrun a weak and surprised army without interruption, or, in other words, that a catastrophe would develop in the Rheims

THE PARIS GUN

Arc, into which the available hostile reserves would be drawn. This first assumption was based on a second, which assumed that the number of divisions opposed to the Army Group German Crown Prince was so low that a simultaneous concentration in the Villers-Cotterets woods and a strong occupation of the Rheims front was out of the question. . . .

Both assumptions were wrong. The opponent had early information of the preparations for the attack against Rheims and Châlons, and had been able to arrange his defence. He adopted our system of defence with a deep foreground in front of a rear zone strongly supported by artillery and infantry. . . .

Finally, we had underestimated the offensive value of tanks. The November battles of 1917, at Cambrai, ought to have furnished us some indications as to what success might be attained by the surprise use in mass of tanks in an attack. We now know that our enemies grasped that fact, improved their tanks technically, and augmented their numbers. We, on our part, paid little attention to this auxiliary arm and did not believe that the enemy had done so.

During the offensive of March and of May 1918 tanks appeared but infrequently; as they are principally an offensive arm, they could find little employment at that time, as our opponent in those days was strictly on the defensive. Our placing no very high value on tanks as an auxiliary arm seemed justified. But July 18, for the first time, taught us differently. Armoured tanks, employed in mass heretofore unknown and technically highly developed, preceded the infantry, at their lumbering gait, in long, connected lines. Our defence had not been prepared for this mass employment on a broad front, and we could work only through gaps; our infantry felt helpless opposite the fire-disgorging, rapidly moving machines and lost their nerve. . . .

Thus the enemy was enabled on the first day, and on a broad front, to gain ground and capture supplies, but he did not understand how to take advantage thereof on the same day. When our defence coming from the rear became effective, and his tanks commenced to suffer, the hostile advance the very next day commenced to halt, and his objective, which without doubt was to cut off the German forces between the Aisne and the Marne, could not, on the 18th, be accomplished. But nevertheless the effort to recover ourselves and support the front between the Aisne and

THE LAST GREAT OFFENSIVE

Marne cost us so heavily that the Army Group German Crown Prince was forced to give up all intentions of continuing our offensive for some time to come. Here, we at once see an undoubtedly great strategic success for Marshal Foch.

THE GREAT RETREAT BEGINS

The situation south of the Marne was becoming more desperate. The troops were attacked on the 17th, but not so heavily. Their orders were to hold where they were. On the 18th the enemy made a series of attacks in rapid succession against the 113th and the 10th Reserve divisions. He employed tanks and flame-throwers. He was held off again, but with heavy losses. Several units received the orders to retire to the north bank of the river on the night of the 18th–19th. The bridge had already been constructed, and they passed over without much loss.

The afternoon of the 18th was not sufficient to notify all of the units south of the Marne of the decision to retire. The members of corps and division staffs had had no rest for days, and the system of communications was in a condition of chaos. But during the day of the 19th the general order for the retirement reached even the more isolated companies. Until 10 P.M. the front on the south bank would remain unchanged, and the main line of resistance would be held even in case of a battle on a large scale. Beginning at 10.10 P.M., the Falkenstein group would evacuate the support position. At 4 A.M. the railway embankment would be abandoned. . . . If the enemy should not press too closely, a ferry would remain near Soilly until 7 A.M., in order to allow stragglers to cross. There would furthermore be several temporary rafts permitting individuals to cross. All German or hostile material which could not be taken away would be rendered useless. Care would be taken that all maps or orders were either taken away or destroyed.

THE PARIS GUN

It became clear on the 19th that the newly begun attack on the west was not one of the endless limited attacks with which that front had been favoured for a month and a half. It was a formidable general attack, and apparently was to continue. It seemed incredible that the enemy could wage any formidable offensive on the west after concentrating so heavily as to stop the tremendous force of the offensive on the south. But somehow he had accumulated the reserves to begin such an attack; probably those reserves were American. There were no longer any mistaken impressions of the fighting qualities of those Americans. Their skill with the rifle and machine-gun, their *naïve* confidence in themselves, their reckless courage, made them first-class shock troops. It was ominous that such troops were the reserves obviously depended upon by the enemy.

It was clear that the Paris Gun, the crew of which had begun the third bombardment with such assurance four days before, would have to be got out at once if at all. It was dismounted with feverish speed, a crew left behind to get out the base if possible, and was started at once for Soissons. Fortunately the line over which it had been brought in was well within the triangle that was now truly 'sinister.' This line led east past Fère-en-Tardenois, north toward Fismes, and then west to Soissons. The enemy was making every attempt to render the railways in Soissons impassable. Men repaired the roadway and shell-broken track under constant shell-fire. But the carriage, gun, and even the base were got through. It was nothing short of a miracle that it was accomplished. The Paris Gun battery proceeded at once to its former position at Beaumont.

Meanwhile hell had broken loose for those divisions so densely packed in the great Marne salient: ("Noon Reports, Seventh Army," July 20, 1918) "New heavy battles are now raging along the entire west front. . . ."

VII

THE GREAT RETREAT

THE FOURTH BOMBARDMENT

FROM early June, when the Germans had got themselves into a situation that for them was intolerable, and the Allies found they could hold the Soissons Corner, General Foch had wanted to strike at and south of Soissons where the great salient invited attack. The only inlet to the railway system over which the Germans had to transport their supplies was through Soissons, easily within heavy-gun range. General Pershing saw the invitation and twice urged General Foch to permit an American attack there. Mangin, who was holding the Soissons Corner with the Tenth French Army, also urged an attack.

By the middle of July the German intentions were clear, and Foch had accumulated a free reserve of nearly 200,000 Americans. He decided to attack at Soissons, provided Gouraud's Fourth Army could hold the Germans from advancing east of Rheims to the Marne for a junction with Boehn's Seventh German Army, which he knew would cross the river and advance east on Épernay. Gouraud held.

The right of the Tenth French Army of Mangin, stretching from Fontenoy on the Aisne south to the Ourcq, was to make the main attack. The left of De Goutte's Sixth French Army reached from the Ourcq to the Marne. Half of Mangin's line troops and a third of De Goutte's were Americans. The 20th Army Corps, made up of Moroccans, the Foreign Legion, and the American 1st and 2nd Divisions, were to form the spearhead of the attack in the Tenth Army.

THE PARIS GUN

The day and night of the 17th were rainy. The American 1st Division managed to get its batteries in place during the night of the 17th–18th only by making forced marches. The 2nd Division had got into its jumping-off positions with great difficulty. While a part was in position shortly before the attack, other units arrived by forced marches only a few minutes before 'H' hour; still others, arriving even on the double time, were too late and continued on double time until they caught up with the advancing line.

It was known that the Germans were strongly organized for defence in this vital region, so the attack would have to be entirely by surprise if an effective advance were to be attained. There would therefore be no artillery preparation prior to 'H' hour, 4.35 A.M. of the 18th. Shortly before 'H' hour a German front-line observer fired a red rocket, calling for a defensive barrage. It came down promptly and on the massed Americans in their jumping-off places, as had a similar barrage fallen on the masses of Germans along the Marne three days before. But in a few minutes the barrage ceased. The rocket had been fired by an observer who had jumpy nerves. He did not know what was before him, nor what the barrage he had called for had done.

At exactly 4.35 the Allied guns opened up with the rolling barrage, and the 20th Corps moved forward. The 28th American Infantry struggled through the heavily fortified Missy-aux-Bois ravine leading into the valley of the Aisne. The 26th did likewise. These two had been called upon for a similar task at Cantigny.

The 18th Infantry on the right of the 1st Division advanced against heavy machine-gun and artillery fire from Chaudun and took it. On the fourth day the remnants of the 26th and 28th Infantry regiments took Bercy-le-Sec and the hill on which it was situated. This hill commanded the Soissons-Château-Thierry highway and the heights of Buzancy beyond. The 1st Division was thus facing

THE GREAT RETREAT

north-east, astride the Soissons-Château-Thierry highway, held the commanding hills on both sides, and endangered all of the German line to the south. The Germans had thrown in a total of seven of their precious reserve divisions here to hold the spearhead from a further advance than the six miles it had made in the four days. A further loss would spell catastrophe for the scores of divisions to the south and east.

The high bluff on the northern bank of the Marne from Château-Thierry east to Dormans is the crest of the Étrepilly plateau, which drops off gently toward the north to the Ourcq river. The western edge of this plateau runs in an irregular line from Château-Thierry north-west to Neuilly. So long as the Germans held the southern and western crests of this plateau the troops to the north and east were safe, barring the threat at Soissons, and might retire on the highways and the railway from Château-Thierry to Fère-en-Tardenois, if necessary, in comparative safety. But if they lost the crest of the plateau at any place between Château-Thierry and Neuilly they lost the Château-Thierry-Soissons highway, and Château-Thierry itself. So they had to hold this plateau at any cost. The possession of the steep and high southern and western bluffs was greatly in their favour.

It was the business of the 2nd and 7th French and the 1st American Corps of De Goutte's Sixth French Army to take the crest of the plateau north of Château-Thierry. The 1st American Corps under General Liggett held the line from the right of the French 7th at Bussiares east past Vaux. Belleau Wood, at the base of the plateau and on the left of the 1st Corps, was a strategic jumping-off place, the spearhead of the attack of that portion of the Sixth Army. It was imperative that the Germans stop any advance in the west so long as any of their divisions were south of the Marne. The progress made by the Allies on the 18th and 19th was therefore chiefly from Belleau Wood north to and past Soissons. The progress of the Tenth Army toward Buzancy and Bercy-le-Sec by the evening of the 18th was such as to endanger the entire railway supply system of the whole great salient and the scores of divisions packed so densely in it and flung across the Marne. So despite the fact that the Allies had made but little progress from the Ourcq to the Marne, General Boehn, commanding the Seventh Army, issued orders late that night to Corps Kathen, Wichura, and Conta to withdraw to the north bank of the Marne the ten divisions which had crossed at such terrible cost on the 15th and up to the 17th. The withdrawal was ordered for the following night, July 19–20. It was successfully accomplished.

American and French divisions which had participated in the determined stand of Gouraud's Fourth Army east of Rheims were quickly shifted around to the west to help the American 1st Corps break the resistance on the plateau. The Germans abandoned the crest of the plateau from Belleau around to Mézy on the 21st, and the Allied divisions crossed the Marne at Château-Thierry that day, ascended the steep bluffs, and made rapid progress until the evening of the 22nd.

The Germans had established the Ourcq, the high ground north of which offered advantages somewhat similar to those of the plateau crest on the Marne, as their next stand. The going of the Allies was rough and costly from the 22nd to August 1, when the line of the Ourcq was finally broken. During all of this time every movement of the Allied divisions was in full view of the Germans, and they suffered fearful casualties. No doubt the Germans wondered in a sort of growing despair where the Allies had acquired the strength, the reserves, to wage this costly, relentless counter-attack, offensive really as it had now become. Had they been deceived, had they walked into a trap on the Marne? And to make it worse all of this

THE GREAT RETREAT

warfare was in the open, and American divisions were to be found everywhere. The Americans were proving formidable in open warfare. Their deadly accuracy with the hand-rifle combined with their recklessness and individual resourcefulness drove the German soldiers into something of a panic.

The village of Trugny, on the Ourcq west of Fère-en-Tardenois, changed hands twice on the 26th. There was a deep general advance to the east the next day, and on the 28th Trugny was taken for good. On this day an Intelligence officer from French General Headquarters, who was following the Allied line closely to gather all captured documents, found a pit in the Bois de Bruyères to the south-west of Trugny that was identical with the one in the Bois de Châtelet north of Château-Thierry from which the Germans had been unable to remove the steel emplacement. Beside the pit he found the remains of fourteen crates in which the fourteen shells which had been fired into Paris on the 15th and 16th had been shipped to the field. There had been no time to burn them. The crates bore marks corresponding to those on certain fragments of shells which had burst in Paris on those two days. The crate was identified in which the third shell, stamped 3:, which burst in Paris at 5.26 P.M., July 15, had been enclosed. Crates for the shells 5, 6, 7, 9, 11, and 14, which had been identified in Paris, were also found.

On August 2 the line of the Ourcq was broken, and in three days the Germans made a hasty retreat to the Aisne; so hasty indeed that the Allies could barely keep up with them. On the 4th there was some nasty fighting west of Fismes, where the American 4th and 32nd Divisions attempted to break their centre and cross the river. General Foch called a halt here, however; the Germans had been amply punished, and the Allies had lost more heavily in men in winning. The German Army, badly shaken, with many precious reserve divisions used up, was back on its

THE PARIS GUN

May 27 objective, the Vesle. It looked as though it had lost the initiative as well as the preponderance of power. It might have retained both had it stopped on the Vesle on the night of May 28, and had Rupprecht at once begun the offensive for which he was fully prepared in Flanders.

THE PARIS GUN

The installation of the Paris Gun on its old position was by coincidence completed on the day that the great Allied counter-drive had run its course. It began firing in its fourth bombardment on the 5th at 9.52 in the morning. How different from the Marne position! Almost perfect concealment, no trouble with 'planes about everywhere dropping bombs as down there; no artillery all about shelling every railway and highway day and night. Seventeen shots were fired during the day, eleven from 9.52 to 2.22, and six more from 5.9 to 7.37. Everything worked perfectly; the gun was still almost new, having fired only a few test shots and the fourteen at Paris on July 15 and 16. Series 2 shells were still being used.

Eighteen shots were fired on the 6th. Paris was to pay for the reverses suffered by the German armies in the south. Firing began at 8.47 and continued till 6.57 P.M.

On the 7th twelve shots were fired; the first at 12.27, noon, and the last at 5.43. This made a total of sixty-one from the gun, including the fourteen fired on July 15 and 16 down on the Marne.

THE 'BLACK DAY' FOR THE GERMAN ARMY

On August 8 the British Army launched an attack in the west on the Amiens front, where its Fifth Army had been almost annihilated between March 23 and April 1. The tactics of July 18 were repeated. The artillery preparation was of such short duration that the unprecedented concentration of 435 tanks broke through the line and opened

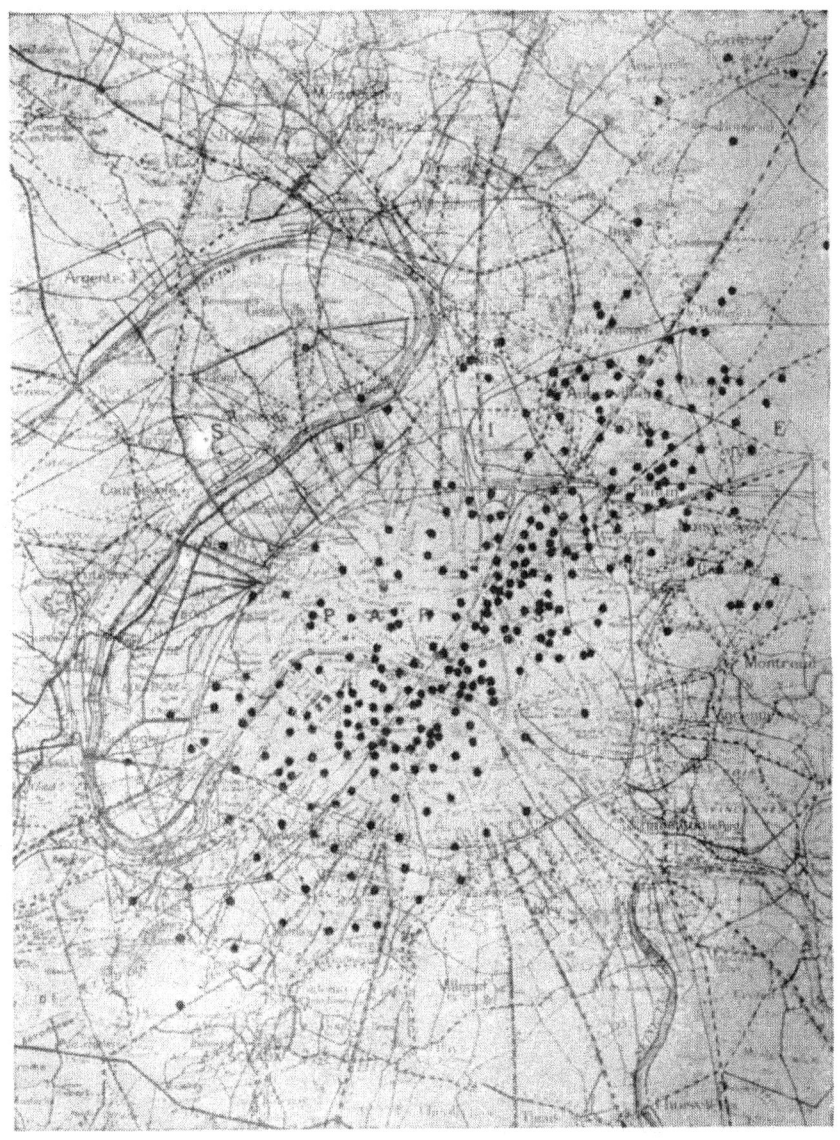

GENERAL DISTRIBUTION OF THE SHELLS (367) OF THE FOUR BOMBARDMENTS
Some circles represent two or three shells.

THE GREAT RETREAT

out gaps through which regiments of cavalry plunged before any warning could be given. Regimental, even Division Headquarters staffs, were surprised at their breakfasts and were captured. Such was the morale in the German Army that whole divisions in line refused to fight.

Five shots were fired from the Paris Gun; the first was fired at 12.37 and the last at 4.22.

The situation looked no better for the Germans on the 9th. If anything, it was worse. The British armies with their French and American units were still advancing, and it looked as though the entire gain of March as well as that of June would be lost. By evening the situation was such as to compel the immediate evacuation of the Beaumont Paris Gun position. Twelve shots had been fired on Paris, between 9.13 and 2 P.M. Even if the enemy did not reach the gun position, they were already within heavy field-gun range of it and they knew exactly where it was. The work of removing the gun and carriage was rushed with all possible speed. The predicament of the enemy railway batteries at Vailly on May 27 was recalled. It would be terrible to have got through Soissons under such great difficulties and then get caught here under a smother of artillery fire. The gun, carriage, and base were all removed by the 12th. The bombardment of Paris, for the time at least, was over.

There was no point in emplacing the gun at Crépy again. That position could be used only for the 8.26-inch guns with their eighty-mile range. There was but one such gun available. It was not worth while to emplace the carriage there for the fifty shots of that gun. All of the remaining guns, six, had been rebored to 9.14 inches, their ranges reduced to 70.8 miles, and two of them had been used. Until the German Army should advance to some place within such a distance of Paris that the gun could be emplaced not more than sixty-eight miles away no more firing could be done. It was just possible, said some of the officers, who were most depressed over the turn of affairs, that the famous bombardment was finished.

The Great Retreat which began on July 19, but which had not yet been recognized as such, continued. The British and French armies regained all of their losses of March, April, May, and June. American reserves continued to arrive at the rate of twenty-five divisions (of European size) a month, and a newly organized American Army pinched off the great Saint-Mihiel salient in two days, on September 12 and 13.

The last air raid of the morale-breaking campaign on Paris occurred on the night of September 15–16, when fifty 'planes crossed the lines and the few which succeeded in getting through the barrage dropped twenty-two bombs. A million people had been driven from the city, but the campaign had failed.

Beginning on September 26, the American Army attacked through the Argonne forest west of the Meuse river in the attempt to break down at the hinge the great gate of the German Army which a frantic field staff was attempting to swing back about Metz on to a shorter, more easily supplied and defended line from Metz, north to Holland. While the American Army, at terrible cost, consumed the remaining reserve divisions of the German Army in the Argonne, the French and British armies hammered them ceaselessly from there to the Belgian coast. On November 1 the German line was broken. Their reserves were gone. The 'wearing out' process which they had started with such spectacular success in March had been turned about. Two of the three millions of Americans which Foch had begged for in June were already in France.

Between October 27 and November 11 four of the American long-range 14-inch railway-guns, located at Charny and Thierville, a few miles north and east of Verdun, continuously shelled the vital Sedan-Metz railway line. They kept the railway broken at Montmédy and

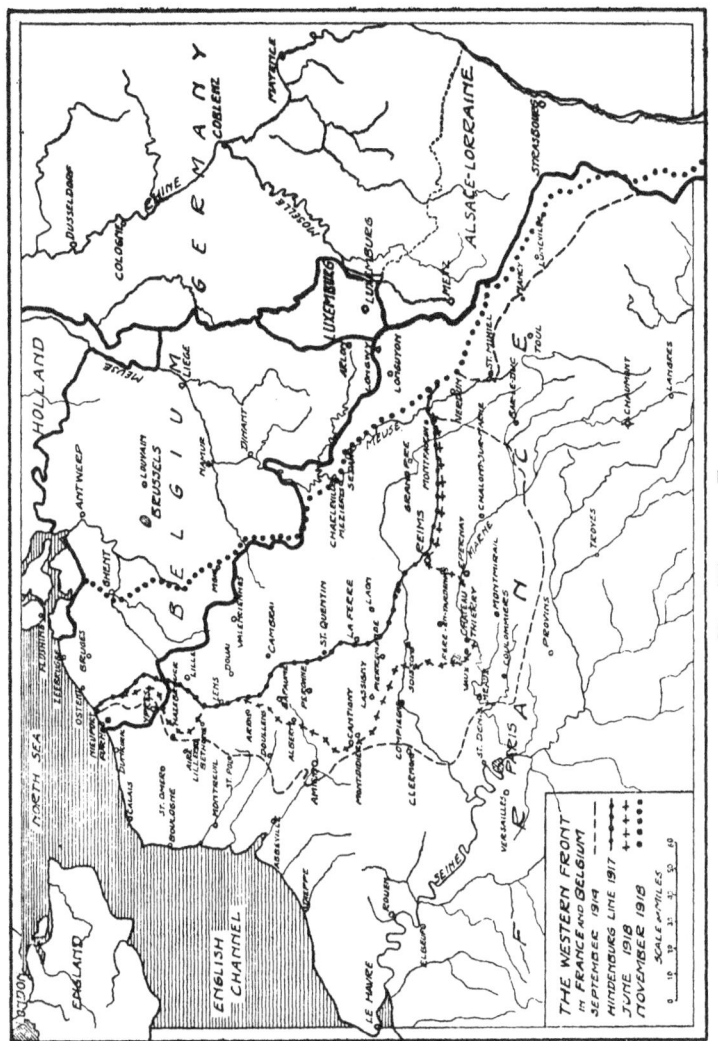

THE WESTERN FRONT

THE PARIS GUN

Longuyon most of that time. They also shelled the railway line south from Montmédy at Louppy and Remoiville and the vital main highways crossing at Mangiennes. French guns kept the Longuyon-Conflans-Metz line broken north of Gondrecourt. As a consequence of this the American Army found in every small town along the railway scores of guns of every calibre which the German Army had been trying to get out but could not. A battery of the famous 42-cm. guns was found at Spincourt and another at Rouvrois. The breaks at Montmédy, Longuyon, and Gondrecourt prevented any railway traffic. And one of the German emissaries is reported to have said when signing the Armistice Agreement in the car of Marshal Foch at Compiègne early in the morning of November 11 that " We do not regard ourselves defeated, but since our main railway line has been broken almost continuously by long-range shell-fire for nearly two weeks, nearly half a million of our men are starving, having had nothing to eat for the past four days; we must therefore cease."

How clearly the truth of a philosophy of Marshal Foch had been demonstrated by the events of the summer and autumn! He had been persistent in saying to his students while he was an instructor and later the Director of the École de Guerre: " Gentlemen, a defeat is a situation in which one of the opponents acknowledges himself beaten." Paris had been whipped, but refused to admit it. Perhaps the Allied armies were defeated in June, but they refused to accept it. And events of the years since the Armistice only prove how wise the Germans have been in refusing ever to admit defeat.

BIBLIOGRAPHY

Newspapers and Periodicals

German

A.
1. *Artilleristische Monatshefte*, January and February 1926.
2. *Berliner Lokalanzeiger*, March 1918.
3. *Berliner Tageblatt*, March 24 and April 1, 1918, and June 11, 1920.
4. *Deutscher Ingenieurverein*.
5. *Hamburger Correspondenz*, April 13, 1922.
6. *Münchener Neueste Nachrichten*, March 29, 1920.
7. *Schweizerische Zeitschrift für Artillerie und Genie*, No. 9, September 1919.
8. *Westdeutsche Rundschau*, 1921.

French

B.
1. *L'Action française*, April 17, 19, and 26, 1923.
2. *Armée, marine, colonies*, March 13, 1927.
3. *L'Avenir économique*, February 28, 1919.
4. *Bulletin de renseignement de l'artillerie*, Nos. 7 and 11, April, May, and September 1918.
5. *Les Documents politiques*, June 1925.
6. *L'Écho de Paris*, March 25 onward, 1918.
7. *Excelsior*, May 1, 1918, January 9, 1919, and April 18, 19, 20, and 23, 1923.
8. *Gazette des Ardennes*, March 23, 1918.
9. *Génie civil*, April 20, 1918.
10. *Havas Public Report*, March 23, 24, 25, 1918.
11. *L'Illustration*, March 30, April 6, and June 1, 1918, January 4 and 5, 1919, June 5 and July 10, 1920, and May 5, 1923.
12. *L'Intransigeant* (Paris), March 23, 1921.
13. *Le Journal*, March 24 onward, 1918.
14. *Le Matin*, March 24 onward and August 10, 1918, and April 18, 20, and 24, 1923.
15. *Le Pays de France*, No. 222, January 16, 1919.
16. *Le Petit Parisien*, March 24, 1918.

THE PARIS GUN

17. *Revue de l'artillerie*, November 1926.
18. *Le Temps*, March 25 onward, 1918.

English and American
C.
1. *Army Ordnance.*
2. *Hearst's International*, December 1921.
3. *Journal, Royal Artillery* (British), July 1918.
4. *Journal, U.S. Artillery*, September 1919.
5. *The Evening News* (London), May 1, 1926.
6. *The Times* (London), March 25 onward, 1918, and November 30, 1921.
7. *New York Times*, March 24 onward, 1918, and May 20, 1923.
8. *Science Service*, August 4, 1926.
9. *Scientific American*, March 1923.
10. *The Stars and Stripes.*
11. *Whitehall Gazette*, February 1923.

Others
D.
1. *Corriere della Sera*, March 24, 1918.
2. *Revue militaire Suisse*, August 1925.

BOOKS AND OTHER SOURCES OF INFORMATION
E.
1. *Album de la Guerre*, published by *L'Illustration*.
2. *Analyses of Shell Fragments*, by Citroën and Hatfield.
3. *Les Archives photographiques d'art et d'histoire.* Rue de Valois, Paris. Photos of destruction.
4. *La Croix de Guerre.* Bibliothèque et Musée de la Guerre.
5. Direction de l'Aéronautique, Ministry of Armament, France. Air photos of positions.
6. Files of the Inspecteur Général de l'Artillerie, French Army, Paris.
7. Office National des Recherches Scientifiques et Industrielles et des Inventions, Paris. Photos of destruction.
8. *Paris bombardée by Zeppelins, Gothas, and Berthas*, by Maurice Theiry.
9. *Renseignements généraux sur le camouflage dans l'armée allemande*, by Lieutenant-Colonel de Fossa. November 10, 1918.
10. Section Technique d'Artillerie, Paris. Analyses of shell fragments.
11. Archives, German War Department, Berlin.
12. *Auf See unbesiegt*, story by Commander Walter Kinsel.
13. "Ballistics of High-pressure Guns," *Schuss und Waffe.*
14. *Der Grosse Krieg in Feld und Heimat*, by Colonel Max Bauer.
15. *The A.E.F.*, by General Liggett.

BIBLIOGRAPHY

16. Files of the Technical Staff, Ordnance Department, Washington, D.C.
17. Files of the United States Signal Corps.
18. *The German Offensive of July 15, 1918.* General Service Schools, Fort Leavenworth, Kansas.
19. "General Pershing's Final Report," *Current History*, January and February 1920.
20. "Histories of American Divisions," *The Stars and Stripes.*
21. *History of the World War*, by F. H. Simonds.
22. *The Turn of the Tide*, by J. C. Wise.
23. Official pictures of the World War.
24. Private correspondence with French and German officers.
25. Personal observations on the scene of action in 1918.
26. Documents, etc., in possession of the writer, the source of which cannot be revealed.
27. Other sources which it seems better not to list.

www.ingramcontent.com/pod-product-compliance
Lightning Source LLC
Chambersburg PA
CBHW031134160426
43193CB00008B/132